SYSTEMS DEVELOPMENT CASE STUDIES

SYSTEMS DEVELOPMENT CASE STUDIES

M. Gordon Hunter

St. Francis Xavier University

Irwin
McGraw-Hill

Boston, Massachusetts   Burr Ridge, Illinois   Dubuque, Iowa
Madison, Wisconsin   New York, New York   San Francisco, California   St. Louis, Missouri

Irwin/McGraw-Hill

A Division of The **McGraw·Hill** Companies

SYSTEMS DEVELOPMENT CASE STUDIES

Copyright © 1998 by The McGraw-Hill Companies, Inc. All rights reserved. Printed in the United States of America. Except as permitted under the United States Copyright Act of 1976, no part of this publication may be reproduced or distributed in any form or by any means, or stored in a database or retrieval system, without the prior written permission of the publisher.

This book is printed on acid-free paper.

1 2 3 4 5 6 7 8 9 0 DOC/DOC 9 0 9 8 7

ISBN 0–256–27056–2

Vice president and editorial director: *Michael W. Junior*
Senior sponsoring editor: *Rick Williamson*
Editorial coordinator: *Carrie Berkshire*
Marketing manager: *Jim Rogers*
Project manager: *Christina Thornton-Villagomez*
Production supervisor: *Scott Hamilton*
Senior designer: *Kiera Cunningham*
Compositor: *Shepherd, Inc.*
Typeface: *10/12 New Century SchoolBook*
Printer: *R. R. Donnelley & Sons Company*

Library of Congress Cataloging-in-Publication Data

Hunter, M. Gordon.
    Systems development case studies/M. Gordon Hunter.
      p. cm.
    ISBN 0–256–27056–2
    Includes bibliographical references.
    1. System design—Case studies. I. Title.
QA76.9.S88H86 1998
004.2–dc21   97–17864

http://www.mhhe.com

To my sons, Robb and Jeff,
and
to my wife and best friend, Shirley

Introduction

An information system is an integrated arrangement of personnel with hardware and software to support the daily operations of a business. The information system should address the information needs of decision makers as they carry out their managerial responsibilities.

The management process consists of planning, organizing, staffing, directing, and controlling. All of these processes require decisions to be made. The quality of a manager's decision making often depends on the quality of the available information. Thus the goal of the systems analyst is to supply an information system that will provide the required quality of information relative to the decision being made within the specific management process.

This casebook is meant to be used in conjunction with a textbook. The casebook is organized by systems development life cycle (SDLC) stages. The sequence of the stages and the description of the activities included in each stage have been left as generic as possible. This should support the use of the casebook with a wide variety of textbooks. The SDLC stages that served to direct the organization of this casebook follow:

1. **Initial Investigation**   The initial investigation stage is conducted in order to gather information about the problem or opportunity and to decide if the current situation warrants the development of a solution that would require the development of an information system.
2. **Requirements Analysis**   Using various fact-finding techniques, information is gathered about what the new information system should do. A requirement represents a feature that must be included in the new information system.
3. **System Specification and Design**   In the specification component of this stage a statement is developed to describe what the new information system will do. The design component describes how the new information system will operate.
4. **Construction**   The construction stage deals with the actual building of the new information system and ensures that the system performs as required.

5. **Installation**   In this stage the new information system is transferred into a working environment.
6. **Operation Maintenance**   This stage relates to that period of time when the information system is considered to be in production. The user is responsible for the daily operation of the system. Any changes to the system during this time will be conducted as maintenance.
7. **Review**   In this stage evaluations are conducted of the information system and the project that produced the system. Recommendations are usually produced regarding improving the information system and/or the method of conducting the project.

The casebook contains 27 cases. Each stage has more than one case, thus offering variability of subject matter. This variability allows the instructor to more appropriately tailor the use of the cases in the course to the students and the specific delivery method (i.e., lecture, student submission, class discussion, or group presentation). Each case contains a series of questions based on the facts of the case and the teaching objectives of each case author. Assignment questions are included in the casebook and are directed toward the development of a document by students for submission to the instructor. Discussion questions are included in the instructor's manual and are designed to guide in-class discussion of the case. The instructor's manual contains teaching notes and answer guides to the questions. Also, for the assistance of the instructor, Appendix A of the instructors' manual contains a brief article that suggests an interesting case analysis method.

M. Gordon Hunter

Acknowledgments

I am indebted to many individuals who contributed to the development of this casebook.

Without the work of the case authors this book would not have been possible. I thank each one of you for your quality contribution. The case authors are:

Yolande E. Chan, Queen's University

Ron Craig, Wilfrid Laurier University

David Erbach, University of Winnipeg

Gordon C. Everest, University of Minnesota

Len Fertuck, University of Toronto

Barry A. Frew, Navy Postgraduate School, Monterey, CA

Rick Gibson, American University

Susan Page Hocevar, Navy Postgraduate School, Monterey, CA

Sherry L. Jack, Calgary, Alberta

Bruce Johnson, Xavier University, Cincinnati, OH

Nancy J. Johnson, Metropolitan State University

Ernest A. Kallman, Bentley College

William K. McHenry, Georgetown University

Kathy Moffitt, California State University, Fresno

Doug Morgan, CFO, Duncan Enterprises

Karen S. Nantz, Eastern Illinois University

R. Ryan Nelson, University of Virginia

Laurie Schatzberg, University of New Mexico

Susan F. Schwab, Bentley College

Richard J. Simm, Deloitte and Touche

Bruce White, Dakota State University

Ellen Whitener, University of Virginia

Matt Zamary, American University

I would also like to thank the reviewers for their valuable comments, which certainly improved this book.

Carol Clark
Middle Tennessee State University

Jane M. Carey
Arizona State University West

Charles M. Lutz
Utah State University

Vincent Yen
Wright State University

Roberta M. Roth
The University of Northern Iowa

Robert L. Ashenhurst
The University of Chicago

Ronald Kizior
Loyola University of Chicago

Milton Jenkins
University of Baltimore

Finally, the staff at Irwin/McGraw-Hill provided its usual impeccable assistance in taking the manuscript and transforming it into a high-quality book.

I would especially like to thank Rick Williamson and Carrie Berkshire for their help and guidance throughout this project.

Contents

Chapter 1

Initial Investigation

This chapter presents the activities related to the first stage of the systems development life cycle (SDLC).

REASONS FOR INITIATING INFORMATION SYSTEMS DEVELOPMENT PROJECTS

Information systems development projects may be initiated for a number of reasons, which may be categorized as either problems or opportunities.

Identifying Problems

1. **User Complaints:** Users of information systems may communicate their displeasure with the functionality of their information systems directly to the systems analyst.
2. **Top Management Concerns:** Users may communicate their dissatisfaction to their senior management who, in turn, may pass the concern to the senior management or the systems analyst.
3. **Scouting:** Systems analysts, through their involvement with users may encourage the user to initiate a project request in order to officially commence work on an information system that may resolve a business problem.
4. **User Surveys:** Information systems departments may distribute questionnaires among users in order to determine if any general or specific problems can be identified within the user community.
5. **Audits:** Internal audit departments or external auditors may identify a situation with an information system that should be rectified.
6. **Analyzing Performance Trends:** Early detection of information performance problems may be identified by continually monitoring the performance of the information system. Typical problems are identified by an increase in the relative effort required of the user to operate the information system effectively. Potential problems may be identified

through symptoms, such as a bottleneck in processing transactions or a decrease in throughput.

Identifying Opportunities

Information systems development projects may be initiated because of an opportunity to apply a new idea or technology.

Idea.
1. **Integration of Business Areas:** Separate areas of the organization may be coordinated because of a revised approach to conducting business.
2. **Strategic Advantage:** The application of a new or revised information system may provide the organization with an advantage over its competitors.
3. **New Regulation:** A new requirement may be imposed upon an organization by the implementation of a new law or the adoption of a new accounting practice.

Technology.   These days technology is changing rapidly. New technology permits greater processing speed, faster information retrieval, reduced cost per item of data, and improved security. All of these advantages may lead to the initiation of an information systems development project.

THE PROJECT REQUEST

The project request, submitted by the user or the systems analyst to the steering committee (see below), is a critical element in launching the information development project. The request is a formal way of stating the problem or opportunity to be addressed.

INITIAL INVESTIGATION

The initial investigation is conducted in order to gather more information about the problem or opportunity and to decide if the current situation warrants a solution that would require the development of an information system. The two major areas for investigation are the environment and the direct problem.

The Environment.   There are a number of aspects that will affect whether and how the project will be conducted.

1. **Information System Policy Alternatives:** The systems analyst must be aware of policies such as centralization versus decentralization, charge back, vendor selection, outsourcing, and information systems development standards. All of these policies may indirectly affect a project.
2. **The Steering Committee:** This ongoing committee consists of top management who make business-type decisions about which information systems development projects to initiate and whether or not a project should proceed from one stage to another. Also this committee may give direction to the project team.
3. **The Project Team:** This ad hoc team will consist of representatives from the user area, systems analyst(s), and any necessary technical resources that may be required as the information systems project proceeds through the SDLC stages.

Investigation of the Problem. When conducting investigations into this initial problem, systems analysts must be aware that they are outsiders and may be treated with distrust. It is important to be able to deal with people and to develop trust and commitment to the task at this early stage of interaction with the user.

The systems analyst may conduct a direct investigation through interviews, questionnaires, or observation. A thorough knowledge of these fact-finding techniques will help the systems analyst obtain a detailed understanding of the problem situation.

The systems analyst may also carry out indirect investigation. The systems analyst may refer to existing documentation such as procedural flowcharts in order to trace information flows. Also records may be reviewed to determine what data are captured and used throughout the information system.

The information gathered in this initial investigation will be used now to determine the likelihood that solving the problem will be beneficial to the organization. Project feasibility will be tested in four ways.

Operational feasibility investigates whether there will be sufficient support for the project from management and users.

Technical feasibility determines if the necessary technology exists and is capable of providing adequate service.

Economic feasibility represents a general determination of whether the resulting benefits will exceed the anticipated costs of the solution.

Schedule feasibility determines if the resulting solution can be implemented within a time frame that will prove beneficial to the organization.

An initial investigation report is prepared at the end of this stage to document the specific problem and what has been determined through the initial investigation. This report represents closure to a reported problem

and allows management, through the steering committee, to make a decision about the allocation of scarce resources to the resolution of a business
problem.

The result of this initial investigation will be a recommendation to either
take no action, resolve the problem through personnel changes (either reas-
signment or training), or continue with a subsequent stage of the SDLC.

THE CASES

Genesis Process at Duncan Enterprises

Kathy Moffitt and Doug Morgan

The primary goal of this case is to demonstrate the power of end user teams
when they are properly formulated, trained, and supported. In the case, a
radical approach is taken to resolve the rather negative situation that exists
between end users and the information systems department. The approach
contributes to the successful implementation of a new integrated information system. The primary benefit of this case is the demonstration of the
importance of the behavioral issues that make for successful information
systems development and implementation.

The Southwest University for Pursuing Exceptional Rigor (SUPER) School of Management Undergraduate Advising Center

Laurie Schatzberg

A new director of a university undergraduate advising center has just been
appointed. The Undergraduate Advising Center exchanges information
with a variety of constituencies, both on the SUPER campus (e.g., students,
faculty, and administration) and off-campus (e.g., other academic institutions, current high school students, and potential transfer students). The
case requires that students analyze the current organization and systems,
propose alternatives for managing the advising center, and design and prototype parts of the chosen alternative.

The Ashworth Group

David Erbach

This case is based on an organization known as The Ashworth Group, a
regional stock brokerage company founded almost 100 years ago by two
wealthy entrepreneurs who foresaw that the economic development of western Canada would need a mechanism of capital formation. The thrust of the

case relates to the development of the annual information systems plan. The major points made concern addressing current technology and attempting to respond to dissatisfied end users.

The Application of Groupware at Coast Guard Headquarters

Rick Gibson

This case presents a situation involving the Coast Guard and the necessity to decide about the adoption of groupware to support group activities and improve the Coast Guard's level of readiness.

GENESIS PROCESS AT DUNCAN ENTERPRISES

Kathy Moffitt and Doug Morgan

One morning in February 1996 Doug Morgan, CFO of Duncan Enterprises, sat in his office and stared at the thick fog just outside his window. Morgan was pondering the accomplishments of the last 5 years and contemplating the key issues and directions for the future. A lot had changed since Morgan joined the company in late 1990 as its CFO and to whom information systems reports.

Duncan Enterprises is the world's leading manufacturer of hobby ceramic supplies, including molds, kilns, and a complete line of fired and nonfired paints and glazes. The company operates from a single location on 38 acres in Fresno, California, and distributes its ceramic products worldwide through a network of approximately 200 distribu-

tors, which in turn distribute through a network of approximately 50,000 dealers.

In 1989 Duncan Enterprises diversified into the "crafts" industry. While the manufacturing process is similar to that of the ceramics industry, the markets are significantly different. The existing information systems were incapable of responding to the demands of the new market. Distribution for crafts products is typically through large retail craft or discount store outlets. The effect of this different distribution was the need for different pricing structures, shipping and invoicing routines, and the demand for use of EDI and bar code applications. The corporate culture, along with the information systems, struggled to satisfy a new and very demanding customer.

The Need for Change

Morgan was brought into the company because of the talents he had in addressing consolidated financial issues. Although relatively unsophisticated in information systems issues, he quickly became aware that

This case was prepared by Kathy Moffitt, California State University, Fresno, and Doug Morgan, CFO, Duncan Enterprises, as the basis for class presentation and discussion rather than to illustrate either effective or ineffective handling of an administrative situation.

there were problems demanding attention. What he found was not unusual for organizations dealing with outdated legacy systems, rapid industry and competitive environment changes, frustrated end users, and an information systems staff that was extremely overburdened.

The continuous fire fighting required of the programming staff created a significant backlog of new system requirements and modifications. The size of the invisible backlog was enormous, as end users had given up all hope of getting anything out of the IS department. End users began developing their own applications and alternative procedures, both manual and automated. Some of these processes were valuable and endured the reengineering process that was, by chance, about to commence. End user conflict and demands were so extensive that in an attempt to satisfy users, many program "fixes" were achieved by changing the database information so that the users got the numbers they expected. Additionally, in an effort to expedite program modifications, many changes were being performed directly on production files without the benefit of a test environment. This created a vicious cycle in which programs became so complex after multiple undocumented and/or untested modifications, that people just started fixing the data. It is no wonder no one trusted the output of the information systems.

The outcome of the prior year's failed efforts to make an old system address new needs was evident—some screen refresh rates exceeded 15 minutes and the LAN (installed in 1988) had over 85 workstations of various models of IBM clones and was experiencing four to eight hours of downtime per week. As the problems and frustrations increased, teamwork by those impacted by the IS systems began to give way to increased accusations and responsibility avoidance. The end users wanted IS to "fix

their problems." When IS personnel attempted to create a team to address the issues, many end users said they did not have time to attend meetings. They would, however, send a memo setting forth the things they absolutely had to have because "that is how we do it now"—and could we please have it in the next 60 days.

The information systems present in the late 1980s included order entry, MRP II, and a nonintegrated internally developed financial package running on an IBM 4381-13. These programs had been extensively modified over a period of years to address the needs of various departments. The subsequent changes frequently caused problems for other departments. The outcome was a continuous mode of maintenance and "fire fighting." This resulted in the significant backlog of unmet user requests and finally in end users developing their own applications and alterative procedures, all without an overall view of the direction of Duncan Enterprises.

The first thing Morgan did was quite unusual and absolutely dumbfounded the IS staff. He told them to go home; they were not being fired, he just wanted them to go home, get some sleep, and let the system run itself. They did not want to go home; they were needed. What they did not realize was that Morgan was trying to find out just how "needed" they were. How long would the system function without them? It took just over a day before the entire system crashed to its knees. The programmers and a systems analyst were brought in to get the system back up. With a longevity of about 10 hours, the system was definitely broken!

Morgan recognized that the situation needed to be addressed immediately and fully understood that an implemented solution would be some time off. He needed to move quickly but effectively because the crafts market was rapidly changing and the customer loyalty present in the ceramics market would not be present due to different distribution outlets and channels. He understood the consequences of falling too far behind. But where to start . . . end user departments were not cooperating and no one was happy with the support received from information systems. Information systems felt overwhelmed by the enormous job of just trying to meet existing needs and had no time to even think of tomorrow let alone the future direction of information systems in the firm, whatever that was. There had been no planning but even if there had been, the daily burden would have prevented addressing it. A "time out" was needed but there was no time for a "time out."

Morgan took a "time out" and brought in Pat Garrett from Ernst & Young. Pat's job was to educate Doug in the area of information systems. There were two directions Duncan Enterprises could go: a new system to do old stuff or a new system to do the whole show. Information systems were both the problem and the solution but an information system solution without accompanying change in organizational culture was ultimately doomed to failure. This had been proven by so many organizations that jumped on the reengineering bandwagon only to find themselves facing the same old problems a few years later. What was needed was a change in organizational culture that was fully supported by information systems.

Formation of the Genesis Team

Realizing the "chicken-and-egg" nature of the problem, Morgan set out to create an opportunity out of the extensive conflict among and between end users, divisions, and IS. His goal was to effect wide-ranging culture change that would establish cross-divisional teamwork, revise decades of auto-

mated and manual procedures, and lay a foundation system that supported the strategic plan of the company. A team of seven end users, representing each of the significant areas in the company, was formed. Members were chosen based on knowledge of their chosen areas and were generally senior managers. Team members along with title and area represented are presented in Table 1–1.

The team, which became known as the Genesis Team, had a charter to

1. Critically evaluate how all systems (manual and automated) were used to accomplish the objectives of the business plan and consider alternative approaches that would be more appropriate given the current and expected business environment.
2. Evaluate commercially available software system(s) that would allow the company to decrease cycle time, reduce non-value-added activities, and improve the ability to provide customer service.

TABLE 1–1 Genesis Team Members with Title, and Area Represented in Parentheses

---

Mike Roley, Cost Accounting Manager, Project Leader

Monica Au, Material Control Manager (Manufacturing & Warehousing)

Ann Alvarez, Distributor & Consumer Services Manager (Sales & Marketing)

Ron Dodds, Corporate Controller (Finance)

Tom Bassett, Quality Control Manager (Research & Development)

Bruce Hammel,* Information Systems Manager (Information Systems)

Cindy Cameron, Human Resource Associate (Personnel)

*Hammel joined the company halfway through implementation; has AS/400 background.

---

3. Determine appropriate hardware configurations to support the selected systems.
4. Acquire and implement the selected system(s).

The Genesis Team was provided with the following resources:

1. The strategic objectives of the company.
2. The new vision for the development and use of information and information technology within the company—the IS Architecture, as it has come to be known.
3. Approval of additional staffing requests such that each member of the team could allocate 50 to 75 percent of their time to the project for a period of 15 months.
4. A budget of $4,000,000 for the acquisition of all hardware, software, and consulting services necessary to implement the system(s) and train personnel.
5. Inclusion of the "system overhaul" as a strategic objective of the company.

The following constraints were included in the team's charter:

1. The system would be acquired, as opposed to developed internally, if at all possible. Duncan Enterprises would rethink how it did business and would fit the software; the software does not have to fit us.
2. The system, when implemented, would require minimal maintenance with respect to upgrades. Accordingly, a goal of zero modifications would be established. (The objective was to reduce the complexity of the multitude of Duncan processes that had evolved over time, and essentially force the end users to reestablish the company operating procedures to be in line with the design of selected software.)
3. The team would be required to follow a problem/opportunity resolution and team interaction process structure, which became known as the Genesis Team Process (see Figure 1–1). This process was derived from the Growth Management Process created by Bob

FIGURE 1–1   Genesis Team Process

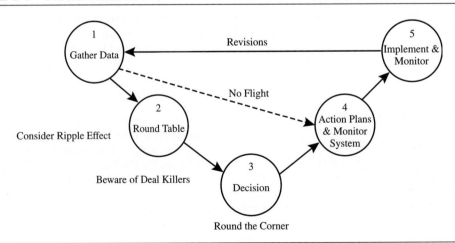

Eskridge, a strategy consultant to Duncan Enterprises. So long as the "process" was followed the team would be empowered to make all decisions and take whatever actions they considered appropriate to achieve their charter.

4. The team would be required to complete two weeks of facilitated team building during which they would be educated on the "process" through hands-on practice in solving a variety of small existing problems within the company.

5. Participation on the team was voluntary. However, should a member decline to be involved, and a replacement member not volunteer, that functional area was forever prohibited from commenting on the inadequacies of any system the remaining team selected. Executive management agreed to enforce this provision.

Team members were told to expect that at least 50 percent of their time would be devoted to the Genesis Project. To help create commitment, staff were hired behind them to take over the job duties that had to be "abandoned." Initially several members were reluctant to be on the team because they "knew nothing about computers and did not like them because they did not work." This actually worked to the advantage of the team when they found out they did not have to be computer jocks; they just needed to understand the business.

The departmental and personal conflicts that had developed over the several months prior to Morgan's arrival were well represented on the team. Several members simply did not like each other. The ground rules (Table 1–2) and team-building exercises were designed to address this. Members

went through two weeks, four hours per day, of team-building exercises. The exercises were designed to overcome animosities, concentrate on problem solving, help surface the decision styles of the various members, educate the team, and teach interviewing strategies. Morgan made it clear that they would live or die as a group; all of them would get the kudos or all would go up in flames.

Initially, the team was introduced to representatives of Ernst & Young for guidance on the process. The team had the choice of continuing with Ernst & Young or selecting a different consultant for each phase of the project: needs assessment and team formation, request for proposal, and implementation. Morgan's experience had shown that the best way to keep consultants on their toes was to make them compete for each phase of a project. As it turns out, Ernst & Young was used throughout all three phases. They had such a significant presence during implementation, that approximately a third of Duncan's regular employees thought the Ernst & Young staff were actually Duncan employees. The close interaction between Duncan and Ernst & Young employees helped keep the knowledge gained from the process inside the company. Morgan notes, "I didn't want all the acquired knowledge to get up and leave as soon as the project was over. This is a main reason we didn't outsource the process but instead brought consultants inside to work directly with us."

Implementation of the Genesis Process

The Genesis Team Process is depicted in Figure 1–1 and the ground rules are described in Table 1–2. The team's performance with respect to the "process" was monitored for several months. Coaching was provided during that period until the process became

---

TABLE 1–2   Genesis Team Process Ground Rules

---

1. Recognize that increased planning shortens the total time line only if participants understand their contributions to the goal.
2. Concept is based upon mutual interaction of "qualified participants" to achieve early recognition of relevant facts. If process is followed, a correctly formed "team" will achieve the *best* result possible.
3. Each team participant must look at his/her involvement as an integral part of the *everyday* job, not an add-on function.
4. To help achieve "mutual interaction" the actual interface of the team should use the following guidelines:
   a. Recognize that *every* aspect of the discussion may have an impact on *any* participant. Accordingly, every member must participate in every discussion. Note taking should be avoided . . . rely on the notes of the group as taken by the scribe.
   b. Each participant must have the authority to make decisions relevant to the charge of the team.
   c. Each participant must be involved for the team to gain from that individual's knowledge. A member not contributing should be replaced.
   d. Each participant should avoid those actions ("deal killers") which inhibit or direct the discussion solely to achieve a result. A strong participant can direct the thought process of others (i.e., the natural tendency to look for an "agenda"), which limits the strength of the team to the strength of that strong participant.
   e. Each member should be aware of the tendency toward "flight," especially in strong participants. The team can only "turn the corner" when each participant understands *how* the solution is appropriate. This does not imply 100 percent agreement.
   f. Each participant should constantly be aware of the effect on others (direct *and indirect*) of actions contemplated by the team. This is known as the *ripple effect.*
   g. The team should meet frequently and have definite and short agendas.
   h. Assigned tasks should be very specific as to who, what, and when . . . and the when should be very short. Recognize that tasks are not usually worked on until right before they are due. Long intervals between due dates slow down other participants and lead both to a loss of momentum and to the feeling that the team is an "add-on" function.
5. The team should have a facilitator who is charged with the following:
   a. Keeping the process moving forward at all times.
   b. Keeping all participants involved, and replacing those participants who prove detrimental to the team.
   c. Helping others to understand where the team is in the Genesis Team Process cycle.
   d. Know the difference between participant agreement and participant commitment. Achieve commitment before moving on.
   e. Keep it visual.
6. Use the Genesis Team Process to guide the discussion and decision process. Recognize that the process is useful not only in team settings, but in any instance where an action, selected from alternatives, is required.

R. L. Nolan, "Managing the Crisis in Data Processing," *Harvard Business Review* 57 (March–April 1979), pp. 115–126.

natural to the team. A Request for Proposal (RFP) was prepared and responses weighted against predetermined criteria. Ultimately the team selected a fully integrated package known as BPCS and an IBM AS/400 model D50 computer.

Tom Bassett, an original member of the Genesis Process Team, now heads up the team. In reflecting back on the original team, he notes:

> The team-building exercises were difficult, but in retrospect, critical. We could not have functioned as a team without them. The team was in charge, not individuals. The transition from giving orders to working as a group was difficult for many. At the same time, it was hard to learn to speak up and not be afraid to say what needed to be said. We had an agreement that no one could present "deal killers." If they did, we wadded up paper and threw it at them. It sounds silly, but it really broke down the walls that had built up and let us focus on Duncan Enterprises rather than our own little pieces of the pie. We allowed "storming" among team members but then it had to be put aside so the team could move forward. This helped air many things and kept the process rolling.

The rule that a member could be terminated helped get early buy-in, and the attention and allocation of hours that were needed. If a member's membership was terminated, the member's division lost all rights, first, to have a say in the system and, second, to gripe about the finished product.

Basset recalls, "We process flowcharted everything. 'What?' and 'Why?' were asked for each process. This broke the mold of doing everything just because we had always done it. It was a real eye opener. Some processes survived, some were canned and some were modified. This was critical to accomplishing our goal. Without it, nothing of substance would have changed."

Morgan, while keeping his distance so the team process could function as designed, remembers the crossroads day.

> We had completed the RFP and were preparing for the software show-and-tell at IBM headquarters in Fresno. The Genesis Team asked that executive staff not attend. The team felt they knew more than anyone else and could handle it. After deliberating, executive staff agreed not to attend the show-and-tell meeting. I could drop by to observe the process but would not stay long enough to obtain specific product knowledge. Up to this point, the team was moving at a pace of about 6 on a scale of 1 to 10. After this, they were moving at a pace of 10. It was like an on/off switch every day. They knew they were in charge and executive staff would not second-guess them. Their commitment level doubled overnight.

Basset quipped, "So did our anxiety level!"

The software show-and-tell was another interesting day, remembers Morgan.

> About halfway through the program, during a break, a vendor representative approached me and said he liked to meet the person who makes the decisions. I asked him what he thought of them. At first the rep had a quizzical expression on his face. He split as soon as he realized I was not making the decisions; the team was.
>
> The team process was truly evident. Two people on the team had strong finance backgrounds and yet when it came to selecting a software product, they voted with the team. They cast their votes for the product that did not have everything they wanted in a finance product, but was clearly better overall.

As mentioned earlier, one constraint given to the Genesis Team was that the system, when implemented, would require minimal maintenance with respect to upgrades. The goal of zero modifications was closely adhered to. The team understood the need to and reason for reducing the complexity of the multitude of isolated Duncan processes that had evolved over time. They also believed Morgan who said there should be "blood all over" any modifications that won the team's approval. Requests for modification had to be thoroughly justified. If the team thought it had a better way of doing something than did the biggest manufacturer of batch-related MRP systems, and could prove it, the modification was approved. This forced the team to identify not only how and why they were different, but most importantly, if they needed to be different. Only five modifications were made. The most significant modification was to order entry templates to facilitate the large number of order lines associated with a typical order.

System implementation was delayed approximately one month due to training. Morgan recalls, "We had to force the team to start addressing training. They did not understand how critical the timing of training could be. They found that people simply did not learn as quickly as they expected them to." Training was a major issue in making the new system work. Employees were trained prior to installation through a "Jeopardy-type" game. Since this time training has become a main focus at Duncan.

The implementation time line was developed to get the new system up and running before the busy season hit. This was just met. A potentially harmful situation developed immediately upon installation of the system. Trial runs showed that the AS/400 D50 would take 26 hours to process a day's work during the peak of busy season. The Genesis Team had selected an AS/400 model D50 even though the analysis of capacity needs indicated that a model D45 would be sufficient. They understood how system use grows and chose the D50 to build in room for growth. The decision was quickly made that an E60 was needed. IBM said it would take at least three weeks to switch out the system. This would put Duncan right in the middle of their busy season and thus increase risk tremendously. Garret stepped in and the E60 was in place within just a few days.

The Outcome

The result was successful phased implementation of a new integrated information system commencing in November 1991 and concluding in June 1992. The system is meeting the challenges of a rapidly changing industry. The Genesis Process has been adopted for all Duncan teams and is now known as the Duncan Process.

Training has taken on a quality assurance mode. Training is designed to provide enough background that employees will understand the upstream and downstream effects of their work. The trainer is responsible for everything the trainee does so there is considerable vested interest in making sure employees are properly and sufficiently trained. The hiring culture has even changed as a result of the focus on training. The first two to four weeks for new hires is spent in training. They aren't able to do their real job for almost a month. Training covers system security as well as the typical how to's. Employees lose their accounts if they break security and must go back through training. A second security breach could result in permanent loss of system access.

The hard work and grueling hours put in by the team and others did not go unnoticed. Some people were putting in 90+ hour weeks toward the end. The rewards basically amounted to time off and cash. They were told to "Go Party!" The party rules were that you had to go at least 150 miles away, could not spend any of your own money, and had to take your significant other. Significant others had, after all, suffered through this too. The $75,000 celebration took some on cruises, others to England and Hawaii.

The Current Situation

The Genesis Team is still hard at work guiding information systems direction at Duncan Enterprises. Most of the original team members have moved on. Their replacements are frequently the very people who were hired to take over aspects of their jobs when they originally came onto the team. Bassett notes, "From a succession planning point of view, this has been quite successful. New members have to be educated into the team process. Members have to be at a certain level, or the team just can't function." Team members are still devoting 10 to 15 percent of their time to guiding information systems. When asked why they still have the team, Morgan states, "We would derail without it. It is simply crucial to keep it going. The success is seen best in what hasn't happened. Other than for planned maintenance, we have not been down once in the last year. Our approach to preemptive and coordinated maintenance works."

With the problems of the past addressed, it was time to address the problems and opportunities of the future. The year 2000 is quickly descending upon Duncan. Software and operating system upgrades are needed to address the year 2000 problem. An operating system upgrade is needed to support the new software version that has a GUI interface. Morgan reflects, "We are running on Version 2.1 while the vendor is on Version 6. Software houses are simply releasing too frequently poorly tested systems. Our analy-

ses showed that we did not need the new features so we stayed with the old. The jump to a GUI interface will be a big one."

Capacity planning is surfacing as an issue. The team is currently studying what needs to be on-line versus what can be archived. Users never seem to be able to have too many years of back data but the amount, age, and type of historical data usage has never been assessed.

Some claim the Internet is fast becoming the medium of choice for organizations to address customer support and marketing. Should and how can Duncan Enterprises effectively make use of this new tool? Morgan was pleased that Greg Joseph, vice president—marketing & sales, has recently been turned on to the possibilities of the Internet and is secretly enjoying watching a full-blown stage of contagion. It brought back fond memories of the MIS class he took in his MBA program and the article read on Nolan's stages of growth model.[1] He is carefully watching for just the right time to provide a little control and guidance to ensure that Internet application and Duncan Enterprises strategy will be going in the same direction. A recent issue of *Business Week* (February 26, 1996) had a cover article on the power and use of intranets. Can these be appropriately and effectively used at Duncan Enterprises?

Reflecting Back on What Was Learned

A great deal has been learned over the last few years. Morgan emphasizes what he considers the highlights. First, nothing beats good planning. If you implement something poorly or put the wrong system in place, the

---

[1] R. L. Nolan (1979). "Managing the crisis in data processing." *Harvard Business Review* 57 (March–April): 115–126.

error will replicate itself at the speed of light! Second, nothing beats solid up-front training. A perfectly good system can fail due to lack of, or poorly timed, training. If you train too early, users forget what they learned; if you train too late, they have already experienced frustration with the system and have developed a negative attitude that will be hard to change. Third, empower users through real participation and team work. For empowerment to really work, the company has to practice what it preaches and not just pay lip service. Fourth, have a highly qualified consultant feed you information during vendor negotiations. You will save thousands of dollars for every penny spent. Last, know that there will be little time for rest. The rate of technological change is so rapid, you will be kept busy just assessing what is happening and determining if it is appropriate and effective for your organization.

THE SOUTHWEST UNIVERSITY FOR PURSUING EXCEPTIONAL RIGOR (SUPER) SCHOOL OF MANAGEMENT UNDERGRADUATE ADVISING CENTER

Laurie Schatzberg

Background

The mission of Southwest University for Pursuing Exceptional Rigor (SUPER) is to serve the educational needs of the citizens of the State of New Mexico. Toward that end,

---

This case was prepared by Laurie Schatzberg, University of New Mexico, as the basis for class presentation and discussion rather than to illustrate either effective or ineffective handling of an administrative situation.

Assignment Questions

1. Is it appropriate and/or advisable for a non-information systems-trained manager to direct the information systems function?
2. As much as we would like to build systems and have them last forever, retirement of legacy systems is a reality that must be faced and carefully planned for. Discuss why it is important to plan for the replacement of legacy systems and discuss the changes in how Duncan Enterprises approaches replacement/upgrade of legacy systems before and after Morgan's arrival.
3. Discuss the importance of the resources provided to the Genesis Team. In addition to these, what intangible resources were provided to the team?

SUPER (1) develops and offers comprehensive educational programs at the associate, baccalaureate, masters, and doctoral levels in a wide range of academic and professional fields; (2) conducts research and engages in other scholarly and creative work activities to support the educational programs and to create, interpret, apply, and accumulate knowledge; and (3) contributes to the quality of life in New Mexico by providing selected services to the public that are part of, contribute to, or originate from the university's teaching and scholarly activities. Institutional values include excellence, integrity, academic freedom, caring, industry, and diversity. Fifty thousand (50,000) students attend SUPER, an urban university in a region in which rich cultures have developed in concert for centuries. SUPER is situated on the banks of the Rio Grande in Albuquerque, a city which is both the demographic and geographic center of the state.

Undergraduate academic advising is partly decentralized at SUPER. For the first 2 years, most students are advised by University College advisers, who help students plan their college programs and keep students apprised of their progress toward meeting preadmission requirements to SUPER's several academic and professional schools (Architecture & Planning, Arts & Sciences, Education, Engineering, Fine Arts, Law, Management, Medicine, Nursing, and Pharmacy). When a student is admitted to the school of his/her choice, the student's advising record is transferred to that school, which then assumes responsibility for advising.

SUPER School of Management (SSM)

There are about 1,500 undergraduates and 800 MBA students enrolled in the SUPER School of Management (SSM), which is fully accredited by the American Assembly of Collegiate Schools of Business (AACSB). SSM is an upper-division school within SUPER, meaning that undergraduate students complete their first 2 years of courses before they are admitted to SSM. This case is focused on undergraduate advising, and all future reference to "student" will refer to "undergraduate student." Since students complete their first 2 years at a variety of institutions, the SSM Advising Center admission process must address a host of institutional and student needs.

Students may complete the required preadmission course work at SUPER, at other schools in New Mexico (contractual agreements guide intrastate transfer of credits), or at other schools worldwide. The minimum admission requirements are listed below. However, fulfillment of these minimum requirements does not guarantee admission to the SUPER School of Management.

SSM Minimum Admission Requirements

1. Minimum scholarship index of 2.5.
2. Competence in written communication evidenced by a C+ or better in SUPER's English 102, or achieving a score of 32 on the English portion of the ACT, or a score of 600 or higher on the verbal SAT.
3. Minimum grade of C+ in each of the specific requirements (see Appendix I) included in the preadmission course work.
4. Completion of 62 semester-hours of preadmission work (see Appendix I).

All SSM students complete an upper-division management core of courses (see Appendix II) before pursuing a concentration. Students may choose zero, one, or two concentrations to focus more sharply on their studies: accounting, finance, international management, management information systems, management of technology, marketing, organizational behavior/human resources, operations management, or strategy. Requirements for each concentration are given in Appendix III.

SSM Undergraduate Advising Center—Under New Management

The SSM Undergraduate Advising Center has begun a new era. The program manager has left the organization after being selected for a terrific job elsewhere at SUPER. That this manager was offered such a good position also suggests that, despite its problems, the Advising Center maintains a solid reputation. Thus, while there are clear areas for improvement, the center is highly valued.

The SSM deans recently filled the program manager position with Rosalinda Goldstein, a dynamic change agent. Rosalinda earned a BBA from the University of Pennsylvania and an MBA with a concentration in marketing from SSM, and has 10 years' experience in career counseling at a small private school in upstate New York. Ms. Goldstein was eager to move back to Albuquerque for this position.

Ms. Goldstein is determined to preserve the strengths of the Advising Center while moving quickly to improve customer service. She expects to implement powerful computer-assisted services to enable the staff to become more productive and offer higher-quality services to (potential and current) students, alumni, faculty, and administration. Ms. Goldstein is keenly aware of the need to please customers with proactive measures and is also intrigued by much of what she reads in the popular press about customer-oriented systems.

Ms. Goldstein has met her staff members and, in general, is favorably impressed with their motivation to help students and their general willingness to change their operations; they seem to understand that such change will require their learning new skills and, perhaps, new ways of working with customers. She has also taken a software and hardware inventory (see Appendix IV). She is sure that some efficiencies can be gained from a serious analysis and redesign of work flows—even if no computer-assisted functions are added. However, she is willing to invest in software, hardware, and training to bring the Advising Center to a new level of professionalism and campus leadership.

After a series of meetings with some current SSM students and alumni, a few lower-division students, her staff, interested faculty, and the dean, Ms. Goldstein's initial conclusion is that the most important priorities for Advising Center improvements are to (1) enable students to have on-line read and update access to their respective advising records; (2) train the staff with more in-depth advising knowledge about specific concentrations; (3) use and encourage e-mail communications; (4) replace the paper transfer of advising files with electronic transfer; and (5) develop prerequisite verification and notification procedures to accompany the class registration procedures. To accomplish these priorities, Ms. Goldstein understands that she must enlist the cooperation and support of her colleagues at University College, other SUPER schools, and other educational institutions.

SSM Undergraduate Advising Center—Many Views

After meeting with representatives of each of the Advising Center constituencies, Ms. Goldstein compiled her assessment of their concerns and priorities for working with the Advising Center. These notes will also provide background for the consultants she hires to lead their systems development initiatives.

Advisers' View

The SSM Undergraduate Advising Center provides several services to students, and as the SSM has grown in enrollment, advisers find themselves stretched to their limits. For that reason, they are eager to modernize their operation. Jerry Wolf, Florence Lee, and John Zinn are the full-time advisers. Jerry has a cautious attitude toward using computers. He has used e-mail and some basic PC tools, but is somewhat anxious about his work becoming dependent upon good computing skills. Florence, on the other hand, is eager to become more computer-capable and welcomes the thought of using new computer-based tools on her job. She expects to use new skills to become more competitive in the job market. John Zinn loves working with computers, and would enjoy helping to develop new applications for the Advising Center, although he lacks any formal training in systems development. He is an SSM grad who went on to earn a degree in career counseling.

Al Newman is the receptionist/scheduler. He maintains a calendar for scheduling all appointments for students to see their counselors. Students come into the office personally to set up appointments. Most appointments are for 15 minutes. Al is quite capable, but is discouraged from providing specific information to students on the phone or when they drop by. He is somewhat frustrated by this limited role, since he is kept well informed of requirements. On occasion, he answers students' questions anyway. Joan David is the work-study student this year. She runs errands, does filing, and often serves as a campus courier between the Advising Center and the registrar or University College. She is a music major and is quite personable, often chatting with students as they wait for their appointments. She is also quite bright and will "unofficially" inform students on the ins and outs of the SSM. Students have come to trust her insights, and see her as an excellent ambassador for the school.

There are two types of counseling responsibilities: direct student advising and related support functions. The Advising Center staff is proud of its ability to meet with each student during the semester but is frustrated by the many hours spent in repetitive types of activities. And, while staff members understand the need for much of

the data they generate, they feel overwhelmed by the volume of manual lists and reports they must create. They are certain that accuracy is not high, since they often find errors in their own work when they revisit student files.

The reporting and data analyses are done with very rudimentary tools (calculator and word processor) and result in a significant amount of redundancy, inconsistency, and inaccuracy. The advising discussions with students are generic. Since most of the discussion time is devoted to the selection of courses toward students' majors and tracking progress toward graduation, there is little opportunity for systematic personalized advising. Advisers' major tools for helping students select courses are the SUPER catalog that includes both SUPER and SSM BBA requirements, and their own memories. There has been no attempt to automate routine functions.

Student Advising. Rosalinda, Jerry, Florence, and John divide up the counseling load alphabetically: Rosalinda advises students whose surname begins with the letters A–D; Jerry advises students with surnames E–K; Florence advises students with surnames beginning L–R; and John advises students with surnames beginning with S–Z. Advising consists of (1) a scheduled meeting with each assigned student each semester to review and update the advisement summary (see Appendix V); (2) occasional meetings to discuss problems that arise during the course of a semester; and (3) graduation checks to verify that students who expect to graduate in a given semester are actually eligible to do so (see Appendix VI).

Support Functions. Related support functions include (1) manually updating the SSM advisement summary (Appendix V) and grade point averages (GPA) for current SSM students when grades are posted by the SUPER registrar [Note: SSM maintains not only the students' overall GPA, but also the GPA earned for all management and economics courses; at the end of each semester, the former is copied from registrar information, while that latter is computed with a calculator after official grades have been received from the registrar]; (2) evaluating and making decisions regarding admission applications; (3) coordinating and cooperating with SUPER University College and the other SUPER schools; (4) developing a variety of reports concerning the demographics of applicants, current students, and graduates; and (5) conducting appropriate SUPER, community, and statewide outreach activities to stimulate and maintain awareness and interest in SSM undergraduate programs.

Students' View

Students view the SSM Advising Center as the place to go for help in developing their plans of study and for information they might need on an ad hoc basis. To meet with an adviser requires an appointment and appointments are usually available within 48 hours of a request. For quick questions, students often get answers from Al or from Joan. While students know that only SSM advisers are *authorized* to advise them, they also know that Al and Joan have a reputation for being accurate and for knowing what the limits of their knowledge are. E-mail is not formally encouraged as a means of communication, but students do occasionally use e-mail to try to get quick "official" answers from advisers. Response time and thoroughness in e-mail queries is inconsistent.

Students like being assigned a specific adviser and generally feel that they are given clear instructions and choices. Since there are so many courses, possible concentrations, and combinations, advisers often are not able to answer detailed questions about courses that might relate to specific student interests. For answers to such questions, students are referred to a faculty member in the subject area, often needing another appointment.

Students view the "work" conducted during an advising session with mixed feelings, especially since they need appointments to have these meetings. The initial part of such a meeting is spent with the adviser checking off boxes or filling in spaces on a form based on a student's intentions or completed work. Then the adviser summarizes "what's left" and answers remaining questions. Students often say that they could do much of this without the adviser. Moreover, they might be considering several options that they'd like to evaluate on a "what if" basis. Given the nature of the work as currently designed, students are somewhat reluctant (and implicitly discouraged) from asking advisers to work out alternative plans for them. Further, students leave each session with their own notes and "to do" lists, as the Advising Center has no standard form for them to monitor their own progress and plans between advising sessions.

SSM Administration's View

The SSM deans call upon the Advising Center to provide a host of data and reports intended for the accrediting body (AACSB), SUPER administration, potential students (in high schools and in lower-division courses), and the legislature. Semiannual reports are tedious to compile since the data is not in an electronic form. Examples of reports generated include: enrollment by concentration, gender, and ethnicity; and admission and graduation statistics by concentration, gender, and ethnicity. Ad hoc reporting is rarely possible and spontaneous queries are unanswerable because of the manual data management process.

Recently, there is an interest to determine course-load patterns, time-from-admission-to-graduation trends, concentration-changing patterns, incoming computer skills and resources, and success rates as a function of students' lower-division preparation. None of these analyses is practical to consider at this time, and yet the insights that these types of queries could bring would be invaluable for positioning SSM resources to best match student needs. While the deans cannot anticipate all their reporting needs, they feel quite certain that if good data were available it would help them. Furthermore, they are beginning to recognize that the lack of such good data is a clear hindrance to the SSM progress. It is a new awareness, since they had previously felt that investing in systems to support a "support" function should not be a high priority.

SSM Faculty's View
The faculty of SSM functions as "shadow" advisers and, as a whole, invests a large amount of time meeting with individual students to refine their study plans. Such individualized tailoring has not been a formal or explicit function of the Advising Center, but seems absolutely necessary to enable students to get just the right courses to support their individual talents, interests, and career plans. Most faculty members feel that some level of advising is appropriate, but that their time should be reserved for truly unique situations beyond what the Advising Center staff can handle. Given the resource mix of the Advising Center, then, the faculty believe that the threshold for "ask a professor" is currently too low. That is, they would support automation to do the routine tasks, and training the Advising Center staff to conduct more appropriate advising sessions. Faculty advising would then be limited to those situations that require faculty insights.

SSM faculty members would also like to see additional services. They specifically want some type of course preregistration logic developed such that only students who have met all the prerequisites for a given course would be able to register for that course. Currently, prerequisites are checked (or not) manually and the issue is largely left to professors' announcing at the beginning of each semester that students who have not satisfied prerequisites will not get credit for the course *if they are caught.* This service might be a candidate for implementation either by the SSM Advising Center or universitywide by the registrar.

University College View
The staff of the University College is reasonably satisfied with interactions with the SSM Advising Center. Using campus mail, University College sends student files to the SSM Advising Center twice a semester on behalf of the students who have declared that they will apply for admission to the SUPER School of Management. The paper files contain student demographic information and a listing of all courses taken or transferred toward the degree. The listing includes the semester and year in which the courses were taken as well as the grades earned.

As a courtesy, the SSM Advising Center informs University College of the disposition of each student whose file they have received. There are several possible outcomes: (1) student never actually applied, (2) student applied and was admitted, (3) student applied and was not admitted [reason will be stated], (4) student applied and was given a probationary admittance [conditions will be stated], or (5) other [specifics will be stated]. Since the requirements for admission to SSM are well documented, most students who apply meet the minimum qualifications and, if space permits, they are admitted. See Appendix VII, Admission Tracking Card.

Potential Customers' View

Lower-division college students and high school students considering a business education are all potential customers. These potential customers are not well served by outreach activities, since the Advising Center staff is largely involved in daily student advising meetings. Many potential customers are not even aware of the opportunities available through SSM, and make their education and career choices without seriously considering a management education at SUPER School of Management. Potential students who do seek to learn more about business education possibilities are often unable to schedule appointments with an adviser (since advisers give priority to current students). Clearly, goodwill is lost in this process, as are some good students. There is no way to determine the exact cost of these failings.

SSM Undergraduate Advising Center— The New Beginning

Ms. Goldstein wants to hire a small team of systems developers to guide the process of change. She is interested in working with a team of excellent systems analysts and communicators who can demonstrate early on that they understand the environment, the issues, and the constraints under which the Advising Center must flourish. She expects a thorough, though rapid, analysis and design cycle and an implementation plan.

Teams who complete the milestones that accompany this case will develop and use a combination of skills: technical systems analysis, information modeling (using DFDs, ERDs, and a dialogue chart), business communication, and group project management. The result will be a comprehensive project repository, a functioning prototype of the new Advising Center system; and, for the users, system documentation and help files, and documentation for any new procedures, and training, implementation, and maintenance recommendations.

SSM Preadmission Requirements

This course work constitutes the first 62 semester-hours of the 128-semester-hour BBA degree.

General Education
Electives

Humanities:	English (excluding English 101 and 102); Communication and Journalism 1301; Modern and Classical Languages; Philosophy; Fine Arts (including Art History, Art Studio, Music, Theater, Dance, Film/TV); Religious Studies	9
Social Sciences:	Anthropology, History, Political Science, Geography	9
	Laboratory Science: Biology, Chemistry, Earth and Planetary Sciences, Physics (including Astronomy)	4

These courses are prerequisites to all 300 and 400 level courses. These prerequisites cannot be taken on a credit/no credit basis.

English 102 or the equivalent
Math 121 and 180 or the equivalent
Economics 200 and 201
Behavioral Sciences—either Psychology 105 and a 200 or higher-level psychology course or Sociology
    101 and a 200 level or higher course
Mgt 290 and 291 Statistics and Lab
Computer Science 150 or the equivalent
Mgt 202 Principles of Financial Accounting

Electives	9
Total	$\overline{62}$

Suggested Scheduling of Preadmission Course Work

		Credits
First Year—First Semester		16
Math 121 College Algebra	3	
Laboratory Science	4	
Humanities elective	3	
Social Sciences elective	3	
Elective (can include English 101)	3	
First Year—Second Semester		15
Math 180 Elem of Calculus I	3	
Econ 200 Princ & Problems	3	
Soc 101 or Psych 105	3	
Engl 102 Comp II: Analys & Arg	3	
Humanities Elective	3	
Second Year—First Semester		15
CS 150 Comp for Bus Students	3	
Econ 201 Principles of Economics	3	
Soc or Psych (200 level or above)	3	
Humanities Elective	3	
Elective	3	
Second Year—Second Semester		16
Mgt 290 Stat Methodology	3	
Mgt 291 Business Stat Lab	1	
Mgt 202 Intro to Accounting	3	
Social Sciences Electives	6	
Elective	3	

Students desiring to enter the SUPER School of Management (SSM) should obtain advisement from the BBA Advisement Center at SSM. Suggested programs for the junior and senior years are available for each concentration. There are no minors available in the BBA degree.

APPENDIX II   SUPER School of Management

SSM Management Core Requirements

All students complete a group of professional management courses. Students must maintain a "C" or higher in all core classes.

Mgt 300 Operations Management	3
Mgt 301 Management Information Systems	3
Mgt 303 Accounting for Management Control	3
Mgt 306 Organization Behavior	3
Mgt 307 Organization Innovation	3
Mgt 308 Ethical, Political, Social Environment of Business	3
Mgt 309 Law and Society or Mgt 310 Legal Environment of Management	3
Mgt 322 Marketing Management	3
Mgt 326 Financial Management	3
Mgt 328 International Management	3
Mgt 498 Senior Seminar	3
Econ 300 Microeconomic Theory	3
Total SSM core	36

APPENDIX III   SUPER School of Management

SSM Concentration Requirements

Management Concentrations and Other Electives—30 Hours

Students must complete requirements for a management concentration with additional free electives such that completed concentration and free electives total 30 hours. At least 12 hours must be in management courses. No more than 9 units of free electives or 6 units of internship may be used in meeting the total 30 hours credit requirement. Candidates for the BBA degree should declare a concentration no later than the first semester of their senior year. The specific concentration requirements are listed below.

Accounting—21 Hours

The accounting concentration consists of these courses: Mgt 340, 341, 342, 346, 440, 443, 449.
   Mgt 343, 348, 444, and 445 are strongly recommended as electives. Transfer students selecting the Accounting concentration must complete a minimum of 12 hours of upper-division accounting courses, including 341, while in residence at the SSM.

Management Information Systems—21 Hours

The course requirements are Mgt 329, 337, 459, 460, 461, and two programming courses. The first programming course must be either CS 151 or CS 237. The second programming course must be either Mgt 327 or Mgt 331.

(Continued)

APPENDIX III   SUPER School of Management—(*Continued*)

Entrepreneurial Studies—15 Hours

The required courses are: Mgt 324, 346, 384, 493 (Internship), 495, and 496.

Financial Management—15 Hours

In addition to Mgt 326, required courses are Mgt 340 and four of the following: Mgt 426, 470, 471, 473, 474. In addition, Mgt 341 is encouraged.

General Management—12 Hours

Required courses are: One management course beyond the core from four different concentration areas (including entrepreneurial studies).

Organizational Behavior / Human Resources Management—12 Hours

Students must take four upper-division OB/HRM courses (Mgt 463, 464, 465, 466, 467, 490, or 493–Internship), one of which may be a graduate OB/HRM course. Other SSM courses or courses outside of the SSM may be substituted with department chair's prior written approval.

International Management—18 Hours

International Management students must take MGT 474 (International Financial Management) and MGT 483 (International Marketing), two elective concentration courses (6 credit-hours) must be taken from among the following courses: MGT 480 (Buyer Behavior), MGT 481 (Marketing Research), MGT 490, 491, 492, 493 (Special Topics in Management), or Economics 424 (International Economics), a minimum of two courses (6 credit-hours) must be taken in one of the two geographical emphasis options. Note that some of the eligible courses are cross-listed in more than one department (see department chair for details).

Marketing Management—15 Hours

Mgt 480 and 481 plus three upper-division or graduate marketing management concentration courses. Other SSM courses or courses outside SSM may be substituted with faculty advisor prior written consent.

Production and Operations Management—21 Hours

The course requirements are: Mgt 432, 434, 462, and three courses from Mgt 337, 459, 486, 488, ME 356, CS 452 or other courses approved by faculty advisor.

Travel and Tourism Management—18 Hours

The course requirements are: MGT 411, 412, 413, and 494, plus two courses from MGT 324, 462, 474, 480, 481, 483, 490 or 495.

APPENDIX IV   SUPER School of Management

SSM Advising Center Software and Hardware Inventory

Software:
  Licenses for 2 users MS-Office Professional
  Netscape Gold
  Netware (enables connection to SSM
    fileserver and laser printers, and SUPER backbone)

Hardware:
  2 PCs (ValuePoint 386/33)
    8 meg RAM
    200 meg hard disk
    2 floppy drives (3 1/2" and 5 1/4")
    MS PS/2 port mouse
    2 com ports
    1 printer port
  Laser jet 3 (local connection to one of the ValuePoints)

APPENDIX V SSM Advisement Summary

Date _____
Prepared By _____
Present College _____

Name _____ SSN _____ Phone _____
Mailing
Address _____

Admission: _____

| Xfer Hrs | English Writing Requirement | CLEP/AP | Concentration | Semester Admitted |

Initial _____ _____ _____ _____ Mgt/Econ: _____ _____ _____

Degr Hr   Hrs Attempt   Grade Pts   UNM GPA   Hrs Att   Gr Pts   GPA

Final _____ _____ _____ _____ Mgt/Econ: _____ _____ _____

Degr Hr   Hrs Attempt   Grade Pts   UNM GPA   Hrs Att   Gr Pts   GPA

Hours Required	Preadmission Requirements					Hours Earned
9	Humanities					
9	Social Sciences					
4	Laboratory Science	Hrs	Pts	Hrs	Pts	
0–3	English 102/ ACT/SAT/AP					
6	Soci 101/ Psych 105 & 200 - level					
6	Econ 200 Econ 201					
6	Math 121 Math 180					
3	Mgt 290					
6	CS 150 Mgt 202					
10–13	Electives	Total				
		GPA				
62 Total						

	Core		
	Econ 300 Mgt 308		
	Mgt 300 Mgt 309 or 310		
36	Mgt 301 Mgt 322		
	Mgt 303 Mgt 326		
	Mgt 306 Mgt 328		
	Mgt 307 Mgt 498		

30	Concentration: 12–21 hrs (vary depending on selection of concentration)	
	Electives: 6–18 hrs (depending on selection of concentration)	

128 Total hrs. required	The student is solely responsible for knowing the rules and regulations concerning graduation requirements and for registering in the courses necessary to meet specifications for the degree	Total hours earned

Student's Signature: _____

(Continued)

25

Semester

	Sem	Cum	Sem	Cum	Sem	Cum	Sem	Cum	Sem	Cum
CR/NC										
Adjustments										
Transfer hours										
CLEP										
Degree hrs										
Hrs attemp										
Grade points										
Cum GPA										
Mgt/Econ hrs att										
Mgt/Econ gr pts										
Mgt/Econ GPA										

Comments:

APPENDIX VI Graduation Eligibility Card

	For Office Use Only
A. _____ Name	Graduating Semester
B. _____ SSN	Concentration
C. _____ Current Address	Cum GPA Mgt/Econ
City State Zip Code	Points Mgt 398
D. _____ Phone #	Hours CS
E. _____ Permanent Address	Comments _____
City State Zip Code	
F. _____ Date of Birth	
G. _____ Sex Ethnicity	

APPENDIX VII   Admission Tracking Card

Date _____	College _____	
Name _____	SSN _____	
Address _____		
Local	*Permanent*	
Telephone _____	_____	
Local	*Permanent*	
E-mail _____	Concentration _____	

GPA:

Cum _____

Specific Req. _____

Mgt/Econ _____

Admission Status:

Letter _____		Needs _____
Admit _____	_____	
Refuse _____	_____	
	_____	
Ethnic _____	_____	
Age _____	_____	
Sex _____	_____	

Origination:

Transfer _____   UNM _____   Branch _____

Comments: _____

_____

_____

_____

_____

_____

_____

ANALYSIS MILESTONE I   Team Organization and Project Management

Recommended Due Date: Four Weeks after Class Begins

Member ID	*Deliverables*	*Grade*

Rosalinda Goldstein has just told you that your consulting team is one of two finalists to compete for the year-long systems analysis and design project. She has heard good things from some local business owners, but she is unsure if your team can handle this project in the SUPER environment. You are to write her a business letter to clinch the contract for your team.

Introduce your team members and their particular skills, describe your proposed plan of work, and chart your schedule. (Refer to subsequent milestones for general tasks and events.) How can you convince Ms. Goldstein that you're the right team? Show her that you've "heard"

(Continued)

ANALYSIS MILESTONE I   Team Organization and Project Management—*(Continued)*

Recommended Due Date: Four Weeks after Class Begins

Member ID	Deliverables	Grade
	her and demonstrate that you're competent to complete the analysis. Include the following attachments in your letter.	

(1) Using a Project Management software tool, develop a PERT or Gantt chart projecting your team's activities for the analysis phase of the contract (you'll be extending this into the design phase if you're successful in getting the contract). Identify the team's resources and milestones, and schedule each resource such that milestones will be accomplished on time. Consider your scarce resources to include your members and any software or hardware which you share. Be specific enough that your plan will be useful throughout the project for monitoring project status.

(2) An expectations management matrix that identifies measures of success for your project. All projects are evaluated with respect to time, cost, and performance—three goals which must be balanced and often involve trade-offs. Commit to the priority scheme your team believes is appropriate to this phase (the analysis) of the project.

Since Rosalinda Goldstein is a counselor and a manager and *not* an information systems professional, be sure that you describe your attachments well and in an appropriate tone. Remember what your objective is.

Assess your own group experiences from the past, write a brief contract (signed by all group members) detailing how your group will manage yourselves such that pitfalls are avoided and strengths are emphasized. Be *specific* as to the expected behaviors, unacceptable behaviors, consequences of inadequate performance, and the assignment of responsibility for group management actions. (This piece is NOT intended for your customer; it is solely for your group and the instructor.)

Grammar, spelling, organization, consistency, and readability will affect your grade.

ANALYSIS MILESTONE II   Data Flow Diagramming, CASE, and Project Management
---

Recommended Due Date: Four Weeks after First Milestone

Member ID	Deliverables	Grade

Your team has been awarded the contract to complete analysis and design work for SSM Advisement Center. This milestone begins the technical modeling necessary to convey your understanding of the current operations, and continues your project management focus.

Use your CASE tool to create a two-level DFD of the current SSM Advising Center operations. A two-level DFD includes a context diagram and its associated level 0 diagram, and provides a "forest" perspective of the current system. Be sure that the two diagrams are created within a single project and that the repository contains entries for all objects on both levels.

Use your CASE tool's automated "model analysis" to evaluate your project (include both levels in the "model analysis"). Study, explain, and correct the errors and warnings. Submit the output from the analysis and recommendations. (Note: this step can take a surprisingly long period of time.)

Using your project management software, update your PERT/Gantt chart with your actual progress through this milestone. Add task-level details as you become aware of them.

Write a letter to Ms. Goldstein to accompany the new DFD and updated PERT/Gantt chart. Be sure that your letter includes the purpose for submitting these documents to her (what value are these supposed to have for her, etc.), what you want her to do with them, and what types of feedback you want. Be certain that all technical models you include are well documented and self-contained.

In one page or less, identify one group-management problem you experienced thus far, the causes of the problem, and the steps taken to resolve it and ensure it does not recur in your group. Identify one positive group experience during this milestone, the causes, and how you can create a similar experience during the next milestone.

Grammar, spelling, organization, consistency, and readability will affect your grade.

ANALYSIS MILESTONE III   DFD, ERD, Repository, Project and Team Management,
Business Communication

Recommended Due Date: Six Weeks after Second Milestone

Member ID	Deliverables	Grade

Using a CASE tool, correct any errors indicated on your two-level DFD
from Milestone II and complete the DFD—modeling as many levels as
necessary for the current Advising Center.

Complete repository entries (a) three primitive processes, (b) all the
input and output data flows for these *three primitive* process, (c) all
data stores, and, finally, (d) *all* the data items included in *three*
(3) data stores from part c.

Expect that the work involved to create the repository entries will be
extensive, although not difficult. Be sure that data flows are defined
in terms of data elements or intermediate structures. If you define
any intermediate structure, be sure that its elements are defined.
Ensure that each data store is sufficient to support its inflows and
outflows. Primitive processes should be defined in structured English.

Use your CASE tool to prepare an ERD for the contents of all the data
stores. Complete repository information for the entities and relationships. Use the CASE tool "model balancing" feature to reconcile the
DFD and ERD.

Use your CASE tool's automated "model analysis" to evaluate your project (include both levels in the "model analysis"). Study, explain, and
correct the errors and warnings. Submit the output from the analysis
and recommendations. (Note: this step can take a surprisingly long
period of time.)

Prepare your final letter to Rosalinda Goldstein briefly explaining the
contents of this deliverable. Reconcile your actual performance, time,
and cost with your estimates in the PERT/Gantt charts from previous
milestones. In closing your consulting commitment, review the
progress, status, and necessary future work. Indicate what next steps
are appropriate for the Advising Center, especially with respect to
continuing work with your team; clearly indicate what next steps
your team will take.

Prepare a 10- to 15-minute presentation of your team's work for the
class. You are encouraged to use Presentation Graphics software for
this purpose. Your presentation should include team identification, a
brief summary of the case, your team's assumptions about the Advising Center; discussion of one process (use your DFD), and a critique of
one of the software packages you used for the project; your team's
division of labor and your conclusions.

(Continued)

Finally, each group member *separately* will critique the design process
you've completed. This critique should include one specific problem
and one specific positive group experience during Milestone III *and*
your personal roles in each. The critique should address both the
group process as a whole, tools or techniques you employed, and
should clearly indicate "lessons learned" and suggestions for future
team efforts. Critiques may be submitted on paper or through e-mail.
Direct this critique to the instructor, and *submit separately from the
milestone*. (Any critiques *included* with the milestone will be ignored.)

Grammar, spelling, organization, consistency, and readability will affect
your grade.

DESIGN MILESTONE I   System Level Design and Group Management

Recommended Due Date: Five Weeks after Class Begins

Member ID	Deliverables	Grade

Develop an executive summary of a new system. Using no more than two
pages, write a letter to Ms. Goldstein whom you may assume has
asked your team for recommendations. Identify the major strengths
and weaknesses of the current SSM's Undergraduate Advising Center. Your team must identify the issues from the perspectives of SSM:
its students (customers), staff and faculty, and external constituencies—and relate these issues to the stated strategic concerns of
Ms. Rosalinda Goldstein, Advising Center Program Manager. One
objective is to convince her that your team comprehends the problems
to be solved and the context within which the Advising Center operates. Indicate what types of changes your team envisions for the
Advising Center, and specify one set of priorities and evaluation criteria for alternative solutions for the new system.

As an attachment, prepare a logical DFD (context and level 0 only) of
the current system.

As a second attachment to this letter, describe two *feasible* alternatives.
Include hardware and software and be sure to acknowledge any of
your *customer's* stated constraints or preferences. Level of detail
should include specific hardware and software (e.g., spreadsheet,
database, LAN, etc.—include model #s and/or versions), as well as
personnel. Each component of the alternatives should be justified/
explained. Estimate both tangible and intangible costs and benefits.

(Continued)

DESIGN MILESTONE I   System Level Design and Group Management—*(Continued)*

Recommended Due Date: Five Weeks after Class Begins

Member ID	*Deliverables*	*Grade*

As a third attachment, and using Project Management software, develop a PERT or Gantt chart projecting your team's activities for the design phase of the contract. Identify the team's resources and milestones, and schedule each resource such that milestones will be accomplished on time. Consider your scarce resources to include your members and any software or hardware which you share. Be specific enough that your plan will be useful throughout the project for monitoring project status.

In a second letter, select one of the alternatives and justify your recommendation using the evaluation criteria and priorities/weighting you had specified above. In this letter, describe the proposed new system—highlighting the *differences* between this new system and the current one—in one page or less. Some teams use charts or tables to accomplish this task in a succinct manner. Remember that you're writing to the manager of the program and that she is concerned with the impact on customers, users, and managers in the organization as they relate to effective and efficient performance.

Develop a "to be" physical DFD and include automation boundaries to represent the target system. Focus on the aspects of the BBA program that are relevant to your work, but be sure your modeling includes the "big picture" for the program. Clearly indicate batch, on-line, manual methods, and the timing/frequency of processes within each boundary. Consistency and reasonableness are important. Justify automation boundaries by referring to system performance requirements; be sure boundaries are balanced through all the DFD levels.

Use your CASE tool's automated "model analysis" to evaluate your entire project (not just for a single level in the model). Since you may be doing two separate projects (that is, "as is" and "to be"), be sure to run this function for each. Study, explain, and correct the errors and warnings. Submit the output from the analysis and recommendations. (Note: this step can take a surprisingly long period of time.)

Describe security, backup, and recovery procedures.

Assess your own group experiences from the past, write a brief contract (signed by all group members) detailing how your group will manage yourselves such that pitfalls are avoided and strengths are emphasized. Be *specific* as to the expected behaviors, unacceptable behaviors, consequences of inadequate performance, and the assignment of responsibility for group management actions. (This piece is NOT intended for your customer; it is solely for your group and the instructor).

Grammar, spelling, organization, consistency, and readability will affect your grade.

DESIGN MILESTONE II   Input/Output Design

Recommended Due Date: Four Weeks after Milestone I

Member ID	Deliverables	Grade

Design five input/output/turnaround documents or screens. This means a total of five—in any combination.

Write input and output instructions for use by those who will be using the screens and forms; therefore, clarify when, why, how, and for whom the form/screen is to be used. Coding schemes, legends, and/or on-line help and/or explanations should be used liberally.

Follow design guidelines reviewed in class and in the texts. Grading will be based on these guidelines and the reasonableness and consistency of the designs in light of the assumptions you already developed in the project.

Develop a 3NF conceptual schema (ERD) to support (at least) the five screen/report designs (user views). You may use your CASE tool's ER diagramming capabilities or develop the schema with another tool.

Using your CASE tool, develop repository entries for all elements, processes, flows, and stores used in the five designs and the ERD. Repository entries should conform to standards in text and discussed in class.

Use your CASE tool's automated "model analysis" to evaluate your entire project (not just for a single level in the model). Since you may be doing two separate projects (that is, "as is" and "to be"), be sure to run this function for each. Study, explain, and correct the errors and warnings. Submit the output from the analysis and recommendations. (Note: this step can take a surprisingly long period of time.)

Prototype at least one of the five screens and reports you've designed.

Using your project management software, update your PERT/Gantt chart with your actual progress through this milestone. Add task-level details as you become aware of them.

Write a business letter to Ms. Goldstein summarizing the contents of this milestone. Indicate clearly why you're submitting this material and what you expect her to do with each of these things. Indicate the software you've used and the commands she must use to examine the prototype on her own computer.

In one page or less, identify one group-management problem you experienced thus far, the causes of the problem, and the steps taken to resolve it and ensure it does not recur in your group. Identify one positive group experience during this milestone, the causes, and how you can create a similar experience during the next milestone.

Grammar, spelling, organization, consistency, and readability will affect your grade.

Recommended Due Date: Four Weeks after Milestone II

Member ID	*Deliverables*	*Grade*

Design a dialogue chart, indicating the full structure for your proposed system. Be sure that the menu includes utilities (e.g., backup, restore). Dialogue charts should indicate "escape" sequences (e.g., to operating system, software shell, and other levels in menu) and help wherever appropriate. Use guidelines given in class, as they differ significantly from STD material in the text.

Using a DBMS or CASE tool, prototype your system design. The prototype should include at least three of the five designs from Milestone II *and any necessary navigation.* Ensure that the dialogue chart and the prototype are consistent.

Use your CASE tool's automated "model analysis" to evaluate your entire project (not just for a single level in the model). Since you may be doing two separate projects (that is, "as is" and "to be"), be sure to run this function for each. Study, explain, and correct the errors and warnings. Submit the output from the analysis and recommendations. (Note: this step can take a surprisingly long period of time.)

Write a letter to Ms. Goldstein outlining the completed design and the demo and implementation plan. Provide instructions for installing and using the prototype. Explain the differences between the prototype and a final system. Include your recommendations for implementation, training, and maintenance (who, what, when, where, $$, etc.). *Reconcile your results with your initial recommendations and promises.*

Your final design document will include all corrected milestones. Your three-ring binder should be submitted as a professional-looking piece. It should therefore be readable, well organized, *with one complete table of contents.* Your title page should include your names, signatures, and date submitted. Include a disk with the prototype SSM system and the CASE models. Selected screen prints included th your milestone enhance its readability.

Prepare a 10- to 15-minute presentation of your team's work for the class. You are encouraged to use Presentation Graphics software for this purpose. Your presentation should include team identification, a brief summary of the case, your team's assumptions about the Advising Center; demonstration of your system, your team's division of labor, and your conclusions.

Finally, each group member *separately* will critique the design process you've completed. This critique should include one specific problem and one specific positive group experience during Milestone III *and* your personal roles in each. The critique should address the group process as a whole, an assessment of the software you employed, and should clearly indicate "lessons learned" and suggestions for future team efforts. Critiques may be submitted on paper or through e-mail. Direct this critique to the instructor, and *submit separately from the milestone.* (Any critiques *included* with the milestone will be ignored.)

Grammar, spelling, organization, consistency, and readability will affect your grade.

THE ASHWORTH GROUP

David Erbach

"You look like you've been hit by a truck," sympathized Jean, David's secretary, as he returned from a meeting with Rob and George. "He can't be that bad . . . or can he?"

David Archer was director of information systems for the Ashworth Group, an independent securities broker based in Winnipeg, Canada. Rob Weaker was his boss, a former accountant who had become the vice president of operations. Rob's idea of a nice afternoon included the St. George Country Club's golf course. But it didn't include George himself; at least this one. Rob would have preferred the dragon.

George Li had quite a reputation, and coincidentally, the branch manager for the Scarborough branch of the Ashworth Group. Raised in Hong Kong, he had never lost the taste for the fast-paced life of that city. He was in Winnipeg for some marketing division meetings, and as usual, had taken time out to harangue Rob about the information systems division. George thought that anyone who wasn't in sales was a needless drag on the Ashworth bottom line, and his opinions about the IS division were well known in the company. They were expensive; they couldn't react fast enough; they couldn't deliver the simplest reports and queries in less than six months; and if they did, the answers wouldn't be right.

Rob was nearing retirement. He had received his CA and learned his craft some 30 years ago. In addition to IS, he was in

charge of accounting and finance, human resources, and corporate properties. He didn't really know enough about computers to handle the likes of George. He even had the gnawing feeling that, while George's style was disagreeable, there might be a grain of truth in what he said. When George came calling, Rob often called David in for reinforcement, as he had this time. The result was always the same.

David shook his head and smiled grimly to Jean. "You'd be surprised. Maybe George had too many pan-galactic gargle blasters at the warm-up last night."

David beat a hasty retreat into his office. Over his desk was a poster of Albert Einstein riding a bicycle beneath the trees and tranquil arches at some university somewhere. Under the picture were the words "Everything should be made as simple as possible. But no simpler." He wondered what Albert would make of the problems faced by his information systems division.

The Ashworth Group

The Ashworth Group is a regional stock brokerage company. It was founded almost 100 years ago by two wealthy entrepreneurs who foresaw that the economic development of western Canada would need a mechanism of capital formation. The firm grew up with the West, modernizing and transforming itself as the community around it grew. It had always retained its connections with the wealthy and entrepreneurial, who continued to form the core of its customers.

Gradually it became a modern brokerage company. While the heart of its business lay in the Canadian plains, it now had offices in

---

This case was prepared by David Erbach, University of Winnipeg, as the basis for class presentation and discussion rather than to illustrate either effective or ineffective handling of an administrative situation.

all major Canadian cities, and even a few in the American Sun Belt. These were designed to attract Canadian customers with enough money to winter in Florida.

But now the world was gradually moving away from it. Western Canada never developed the economic mass its founders had hoped and anticipated. The financial center of Canada remained in Toronto and, if anything, its dominance was growing. As communications technology became more sophisticated and widespread, the West became more and more dependent on services provided by banks and other financial institutions from the East. Ashworth was in danger of being left out in the cold.

The Canadian Financial Services Industries

It was traditional to say that the Canadian financial system consisted of "four pillars": the banks, trust companies, insurance companies, and brokerages. The original purpose of stock markets was to provide a place where new companies could sell shares to raise the capital needed for the start-up costs of new businesses. However, the banks had long played a role in underwriting new business ventures too.

By the '90s, it was getting harder to tell the four pillars apart. This was particularly true in the securities business. Stocks had become trading, as well as investments, vehicles. That meant that trading was a major source of income for securities firms, whose profits became heavily dependent on the overall economic climate. The need of securities firms to have deep pockets to help them ride out the ups and downs of the markets had caused some to be acquired by chartered banks.

The banks which had taken over independent brokers tried with mixed success to peddle new investment services to their vast base of retail customers. They didn't have the scale of expertise needed to deal with all these customers, so there was a trend to simple, low-cost services, such as mutual funds. These obviated the need for brokers to track individual situations too carefully. As long as the market kept going up, it didn't matter.

Because the markets had experienced a sustained rise during the '90s, there had been space enough for everyone, including firms like Ashworth which had remained independent. But the management at Ashworth knew that nothing lasts forever. They knew that the odds didn't seem to favor medium-sized firms. They were determined to find a means for their company to continue to remain independent and to prosper.

Information Systems at Ashworth

Ashworth, like many financial firms, had been an early user of computer systems. Since their firm's business largely consisted of information-based work, they had seen many opportunities. The earliest systems dated from the '60s. They were in accounting, used vast piles of punch cards, and were run overnight on a batch basis. Over time a portfolio of systems was developed, which covered needs ranging from payroll to providing summaries of the holdings of Ashworth's customers. In recognition of the range of computerized activities, a separate information systems department was established as part of the accounting division. Rob joked that he had been put in control of information systems because he had complained most loudly about it in those days.

By the '70s, most business computers used some form of time-sharing, and Ashworth was no exception. Terminals were placed on the desks of the brokers, first in the sales offices in Winnipeg and, later, using a network of data communications lines in offices in other provinces. These terminals allowed brokers to have up-to-the minute access to a customer's account, and greatly improved the sense of immediacy which brokers were able to bring to their discussions with customers. The novelty of the terminals even helped to lure customers into their brokers' offices more frequently. Without competition from the banks, and with the economy still stable and expanding, it had been a good time for the industry. Computers and leased data lines were expensive, but there always seemed to be adequate resources to finance the development, deployment, and operations of new systems.

The '80s brought changes on many fronts, and these had repercussions for Ashworth and other firms in the industry. Political crises in the Middle East and sharp increases in the price of oil brought a period of high inflation. Mortgage rates above 15 percent hadn't been seen in North America for generations. They seriously undermined ordinary people's confidence in money and investment. Then the price of oil plunged, throwing real estate into turmoil. Companies which had invested in office buildings in cities with oil booms found the rents from the surviving leaseholders weren't enough to pay the interest owing on the mortgage. Many individuals had borrowed to buy expensive houses, expecting to repay the loans with inflated dollars. Some found their salaries frozen and the value of their house less than the amount they owed. A few just gave up and walked away.

Meanwhile, the information systems department, now promoted to the status of a division, was trying to grapple with the emergence of personal computers, despite the abrupt halt which had come to its annual budget increases. Mainframes in glass houses had ceased to be admired. But

it wasn't that easy to integrate personal computers into a mainframe environment.

The Emergence of Personal Computers
This was the seed of David's troubles.

The President's Circle was the designation given each year to the 24 most successful brokers of the previous year. Officially the president's eyes and ears were on the front lines of the business, they also tended to be the company's prima donnas. One year a group of these marketing hotshots, led by George, spent their bonuses on some personal computers for home and business use. They bought word processing programs and spreadsheets like Lotus 1-2-3, and began to experiment with them. Gradually they developed reports, which they exchanged with each other and started to present to their customers. To create these, the brokers would combine information from their mainframe reports, their own personal records, Ashworth securities research reports, and the financial page of *The Wall Street Journal* or other financial publications.

The combination of text, tables, charts, graphics, and individualized presentation blew the customers away. These reports required quite a bit of work from the brokers and especially from their support staff. But in a high-end market, the time and expense required could be justified. Besides, they were fun, and no one said that about mainframe systems. George the dragon became George the PC guru.

George had no difficulty convincing Rob that personal computers represented the way of the future. However, at the same time, Rob and the other senior management were growing concerned about control issues associated with the information in these personal computers. The marketing spreadsheets were passed from hand to hand, and people in the head office barely knew they were there. They certainly didn't have any assurance that the information being presented was accurate. In a brokerage environment, there are significant risks associated with what brokers tell customers. George was a great salesman, but even his admirers didn't have much confidence in what he might say when schmoozing with customers.

So Rob directed David to get control of the personal computers. This wasn't easy. When IS was buying the hardware and writing the software for Ashworth mainframes, they had effective control of what was happening. With the assistance of the purchasing department, David had a fighting chance of controlling what was bought with company money, though it had transpired that several PCs were bought under the guise of "office furnishings."

But many personal computers were being bought with personal funds, and that could not be controlled in the customary ways. Gradually David had come to realize that he had to change his control model from bureaucratic to leadership. So IS had acquired personal computers, developed a bit of software, and substituted them for the terminals on their brokers' desks. These were providing much the same information the terminals did, but at least they gave the impression that IS was moving forward.

PCs were still pretty expensive, and the tougher economic times of the '80s helped by providing some natural restraint.

The Information Systems Annual Planning Exchange

Ashworth had a planning method which it went through each year. For most of the company, the plans were formulated during the first quarter of the calendar year, which corresponded to the first quarter of its financial year. This had the advantage of being after the year-end rush in the line divisions, but before people started to disappear for the summer holidays. However, IS formulated its plans during the fourth quarter. There were two reasons for this. Rob had learned from experience that it wasn't wise to make system changes during the rushed fourth quarter, so what was a rushed time in most divisions tended to be lighter in IS. Also, it allowed other divisions to know what IS was working on before finalizing their own plans.

The high point of the IS planning cycle was the Annual Planning Exchange, or ISAPE. Scheduled during November, it was a half-day meeting which David and his team hosted for Rob and the other senior management for an exchange of plans and ideas. The exchange began with a review of the IS plans for the previous year, progress which had been made, and problems which had arisen. Then they outlined specific projects which they intended to undertake during the next year, as well as their longer-term ideas for how emerging IS could best be applied to serve the company's needs.

These meetings were always spirited, partly because of the personalities, but partly because of the inevitable tension between IS and the lines. David knew from experience that it wasn't easy to build and deploy new information systems on time and on budget. He had been caught often enough so that he liked to be very careful in his planning. He wanted to ensure that he could deliver anything he promised, and that he could be confident of getting things right the first time. His experience had been that people would eventually forget projects which were late, or even over budget, but they would never forget mistakes.

The brokers lived in a different world. For them, the professional environment was a pastiche of rumors, factoids, instincts, and plausible guesses. Economic figures on everyone's mind one day might be forgotten a week later. What was a recommended buy one day could become a sell the next. The people in the marketing divisions understood that there were longer-term factors in play, but most brokers felt that these were, at best, marginally useful and, at worst, an excuse used to avoid the need to make decisions and get on with things. They expected to make mistakes, but expected to fix the mistakes next week. They viewed the long term as the next quarter.

Time to Take Stock

Back at his desk, David sat down to recover his composure after the meeting with George the Dragon. Neatly centered on the desk in front of him was the memo he had received from Rob the previous week (see Exhibit 1–1). The time was coming for the ISAPE. Despite misgivings, David generally enjoyed the meetings. They gave him his best chance to meet the line managers in a

---

EXHIBIT 1–1

To: David Archer, Director, Information Systems Division
From: Rob Weaker, Vice President, Operations
Date: August 15th
Re: IS APE

Dave, here are a few points from my notes of our recent Sr. Executives' Planning Retreat last week.

- Our current primary market of affluent individuals is stable and provides a good foundation for growth.
- Competition from banks and discount brokerages is putting us under margin pressure. We will have to lower our costs. Our customers may be loyal, but they're not blind.
- We must provide better services, even with lower costs. Our target will be 2 for 3. We will need to do for $2 in 5 years what it currently costs us $3 to do.
- Demographic strains on the public purse and social safety net will make investment success a key to ensuring people's financial futures. People will need to rely more on their own accumulated resources. This provides opportunities for us.
- The banks have access to a large inventory of middle-class Canadians, and we have a very small market share in that group. We would like to expand there.
- At the moment, our financial situation is healthy, but a significant market correction is inevitable. When the time comes, it will put financial pressure on all brokerages, including us.
- The correction will also provide opportunities. People have ridden the market up with index and mutual funds, and they won't like riding it down the same way. At that time, we will have an opportunity to convince people that more customized service is their best opportunity to handle their investment needs.

As you will be aware, if we are to deal with these issues successfully, information systems will have a critical role to play. I have scheduled this year's IS APE for November 15th. This will be an opportunity to ensure that our plans are properly coordinated with those of the line divisions.
Please prepare an outline of your proposed presentation for the APE. As usual, you should provide a divisional project plan for next year, and long-term technology plan for the next 3 years.
Give me a call when you are ready to go over your proposal.

---

context where people could explore ideas calmly. He knew it was also his best chance to help other divisions understand the difficulties he and his staff faced in building and maintaining complex information systems. Besides, he had a weak spot for the petits fours, which tended to be better than the doughnuts he and his team usually got.

David had sent a copy of Rob's memo to his management team, and called a brainstorming session the next morning. He had three managers who worked for him.

Doug Oakley, Operations Manager

Doug's job was to keep the mainframe computers and network, which linked the company's offices, running. It was an exposed and high-pressure job, because any problems were immediately evident to everyone, and many of the sources of the problems lay outside his control. Doug was a placid person, because no one with a nervous style could survive the situation. But, apart from the occasional operating system upgrade, he didn't like change. He viewed change as the enemy of 99.9 percent uptime.

Maria Melnor, Systems Manager

Maria's job was to keep the company's databases and systems running. She liked new technology, and tended to be quick about seeing opportunities. She often had interesting and unusual perspectives on information systems, and has a good intuition about how things would appear to other people.

Sandi Fernleigh, Application Development Manager

Sandi had the job of developing new applications. She and David would work with users to decide what projects had the highest priority. Once the work had been done, she would work with Maria to get them installed, and then pass them to Maria's group to operate and support. Sandi liked

new technology, but she tended to be cautious about it. She knew how far it is from the glowing pitch of a software vendor to a reliable, working application. She liked details, which was fortunate, because there were many of them for her to keep organized.

Dave and His Staff Discuss the Coming ISAPE

The next morning, David and his three managers meet in the IS conference room to discuss possible plans to present at the coming ISAPE. Marie has brought some doughnuts. They all take one.

Dave: You've all read Rob's memo. I confess I don't understand how we are going to reduce our expenses by one-third, while doing all the things that George and his dragons want.

Maria: It isn't every individual department that has to reduce its expenses. It's the company as a whole. Maybe technology costs will have to increase in order to reduce costs elsewhere. It's only an average cost. If the company as a whole could keep our expenses the same, but expand the business by 50 percent by going after the middle-class market, it would have the same effect.

Dave: I've never had much success convincing the line people that our costs might have to increase in order for theirs to go down. They just think we're building an empire. But expanding the business sounds better for everybody's job. If they decide to cut expenses, we might be part of it.

Doug: What is it that the people in the marketing offices actually want?

Maria: BMWs in every parking space.

Doug: Besides that?

Sandi: Well—they want to be able to monitor their customers' accounts better.

At the moment, they get up-to-date information about what is in the account, and the current prices of those items. But a lot of interesting information isn't there. Or if it is, you have to look too hard for it. For instance, we provide a summary of the value of the total portfolio. But we don't provide information about the profit or loss on individual stock positions.

Doug: Maybe they wouldn't want their customers to have that information?

Maria: Maybe, but why not? People expect to win and lose, as long as they win more than they lose.

Doug: Where would we get the cost data?

Maria: We must have it somewhere. After all, the accountants must need it when they're reconciling the original purchase transaction. Why can't we take the data and just pipe it into our reports?

Sandi: Purchase transactions are handled by one of our legacy systems. For years, we've had the idea to bring that sort of data together so people could use it better. But it's never urgent enough to make the cut when we're deciding which projects to keep.

Doug: We could also improve service there. I know what a bother it is to have to look up old purchase price information for income tax forms. Why can't we just provide it?

David: Most of you weren't around when we first deployed terminals in the marketing offices. But it had some interesting and unanticipated side effects. We thought we were just trying to give brokers up-to-date information so they could be more professional on the telephone. But the customers thought that an up-to-the-minute computerized report on their account was so amazing that it actually brought people into the offices just to see it. Our average sales

went up substantially that year. Also, there was a reduction in mistakes. Everybody learned pretty quickly that a mistake was likely to be discovered the next day, before everybody forgot who had done the work. So there was a big reduction in clerical errors, and that made the brokers happier than almost anything else. They were getting more quantity and better quality service at the same time.

Maybe there are some new opportunities here. What would it take to bring all this data together?

Maria: At the moment, it is mostly associated with the various individual systems which use it. They were developed with the individual systems in mind, not with sharing, and certainly not with slicing and dicing. For instance, the security cost data is associated with the system that clears our own accounts every night, not with the system that provides information about a customer account's current status.

It seems to me that there are various possibilities. One would be to develop a data warehouse of some sort. We have lots and lots of data coming from various sources. We could archive it more or less directly in whatever form it arrives. That would take relatively little work on our part.

Then our problem would be getting it out and combining it in various ways. We would need to concentrate our resources on the query and extract problem. We could probably provide much more timely service this way than we currently do. Maybe it wouldn't take us six months to get George a new report any more.

Sandi: Another approach could be to develop a companywide database that holds all the data we need in standard form. This has bigger up-front costs because of the data analysis you have to do. There would be a big conversion task too. But once those jobs were done, the extraction and analysis should be a piece of cake. We could probably find tools that would let brokers build their own reports for their own customers.

We might be able to get to the point that customers could dial in to our system and get information directly.

David: I wonder what the auditors would make of that one. Of course, they'd probably rather we did nothing. We don't have any trouble balancing the books now, and that's what they care about.

Doug: None of what we're talking about sounds like less money.

Maria: Unless we just stop our systems development altogether, and hope the hardware cost reductions will be enough to do our part in reducing budget costs.

David: I don't think we can count on that to be enough. Is there an alternative? What kind of efficiency gains can we get by continuing what we're doing, but doing it in better ways?

Sandi: That's hard to say. We systems developers are the biggest expense. At best, we tend to do more for the same cost, rather than the same for less. We try to use new tools which will enable us to get the job done faster. But I think there are limits. Even when a new tool gains us something on its own, it brings a new task in knowledge and system maintenance. Our people are already spread thin trying to be knowledgeable in what we've got. Somewhere, we are going to hit the limit of how much we can improve without a major shift in what we are doing.

The discussion continues while David takes the last remaining doughnut.

Doug: So, how should we proceed about this then?

David: We've come up with a range of approaches, from doing nothing, to a major overhaul of our systems development environment. I think that I would like the three of you to put together several scenarios about how we should approach our one-year and five-year plans. We'll get together in a week to review them, and select the one that seems best. I'll take that to Rob. If he approves, we'll spend another week examining the implications of that one. I'll refine it and put together an overview for ISAPE. While I'm doing that, you can think about strategies for your own areas which will fit into the overall plan. Of course, when the day comes, you won't forget to have the details about what happened last year, and how you will be continuing the projects which are currently underway, in case there are questions about that.

There being no more doughnuts, the meeting is adjourned.

Assignment Questions

1. What are the "four pillars" of the financial industries? Summarize the economic and competitive changes that are occurring in these industries. Which of these changes are likely to be stable over a 5-year planning period?
2. What is the market in which The Ashworth Group has specialized? What are the demographic and economic changes affecting that group?
3. What new markets are being targeted by the Ashworth senior management? What strengths and weaknesses does Ashworth have to develop those markets?
4. Describe the relationships between Rob and George, between David and Rob, and between George's division and

David's division. What are the sources of the tensions between the IS division and the marketing division?

5. What are the strengths and weaknesses of David's IS division? What are the difficulties David's management group faces in trying to help Ashworth achieve the "2 for 3" objective? What are the technical trends they need to consider?

6. Answer David's question: What opportunities are there for improved systems to provide better quality service for customers? What opportunities are there to lower the costs of IS services to the line divisions? What opportunities are there to apply new technology to lower the company's average cost of delivering services to customers?

7. Write a memo from David's managers to David outlining the strategic alternatives the IS division has available. Include the main advantages and disadvantages of each.

8. Based on your answer to question 7, write a memo from David to Rob proposing a five-year strategic plan for the division.

9. Based on your answer to question 8, write a point-form presentation to be made to the vice presidents' group at the ISAPE.

10. Deliver the presentation you have developed in question 9 to your classmates as if they were the group of Ashworth vice presidents. Deal with their questions. Don't forget the doughnuts.

THE APPLICATION OF GROUPWARE AT COAST GUARD HEADQUARTERS

Matt Zamary and Rick Gibson

Introduction

As is done in any organization, the Coast Guard conducts group meetings to generate ideas, make important decisions, and garner additional information to better understand and solve problems. Although the Coast Guard is not a typical business, its duty to serve the customer, the public, demands a high level of service. The Coast Guard's need for group activities is less of a response to economics forces, and more of a response to readiness constraints. *Semper paratus* (always ready) is the Coast Guard motto. The ability to respond decisively, promptly, and effectively is truly a matter of life and death. Whether it's responding to a search and rescue case or an oil spill, the Coast Guard makes use of group activities to improve its level of readiness.

This case was prepared by Matt Zamary of the U.S. Coast Guard and American University, and Rick Gibson, American University, as the basis for class presentation and discussion rather than to illustrate either effective or ineffective handling of an administrative situation.

Definition

Groupware has been defined as "Any information system designed to enable groups to work together electronically." This definition excludes technology that was not specifically designed to promote group work, such as telephones, word processing programs, and e-mail. Although some agree that an application such as e-mail is not groupware, many argue that it is. In fact, all members attending the conference entitled "How can we make groupware practical?" argued that e-mail is a form of groupware, and one attending conferee stated that e-mail has been the only successful form of groupware. To further convolute the controversy over what constitutes groupware, additional scholarly definitions include applications such as multiuser databases, network file servers, operating systems, and telecommunications under the auspices of groupware.

Same Time, Same Place Groupware

The most prevalent place- and time-dependent groupware is EMS (electronic meeting system). The most basic EMSs can allow group members to anonymously vote their agreement or disagreement. More advanced EMSs include features that help groups brainstorm ideas, organize thoughts, rank ideas, examine alternatives, and plan for implementation of chosen ideas.

Different Time, Different Place Groupware

On the other end of the groupware spectrum is different time, different place groupware. Among the most common types of different time, different place groupware are e-mail, message linking, and scheduling tools. Message linking allows users to link messages concerning one subject area or associated with a distribution list. Hence, this groupware feature creates a virtual repository for information, thoughts, and ideas as they pertain to specific subject matter. The usefulness of message linking dates back to the U.S. Department of Defense Advanced Research Project

Agency's ARPANET implemented in 1969. ARPANET, which ultimately evolved into the Internet, served as a message linking service for military researchers. It gave researchers the ability to share ideas with other professionals in a given specialty and get immediate input or feedback on thoughts and ideas. Scheduling tools have not received such wide use. The main reason scheduling tools fail to gain acceptance and use within organizations is that they are not seen as an improvement over "paper" methods. Additionally, such tools are only useful if all group players use the tool as designed; that is, if some group members do not use the scheduling tool, then the information available to the group as a whole will not be accurate, rendering it useless or unreliable. As discussed earlier, the ballots are still out as to whether e-mail is an accepted form of groupware.

Groupware in Use

The many uses of groupware have been explored through various research mechanisms. A survey of over 100 organizations found an increased commitment to the use of groupware and revealed that it is most frequently used for computer conferencing. One groupware product, Lotus Notes, is used by more than 5,000 companies, which translates to over 1.35 million users.

IBM was one of the first large organizations to successfully implement an EMS. The use of EMS at IBM has improved group performance by an average of 55 percent, with even greater reductions in project calendar time. Among the top success factors are organizational commitment, executive sponsorship, dedicated facilities, and extensive training.

Another example of the successful implementation of place- and time-dependent groupware is the IRS-Minnesota project.

The application of a group decision support system (GDSS) at an IRS office focused on quality management. Similar to the Coast Guard's TQM (total quality management) program, JQIP (joint quality improvement process) at the IRS focuses on process improvement. The GDSS system was designed to promote the standard features available with most EMSs, with the addition of quality methods familiar to the IRS end users. The GDSS (1) eased adoption of JQIP procedures, (2) allowed quality teams to apply sophisticated group decision models at critical times in their lives, and (3) helped team members and program coordinators to monitor the quality program and its progress. Similar to the elements that made the application of EMSs at IBM successful, the IRS-Minnesota project reinforced the importance and need for the support from organizational leaders.

It is important to note that the place- and time-dependent groupware discussed thus far are not a panacea for an organization's meeting woes. Several studies have shown that the successful application of groupware is situational and contextual. That is, the situations at both IBM and the IRS were ones that included the groupware developers as an integral part of the implementation process. From a contextual viewpoint, research supports the notion that users' reactions to groupware depend on how it is implemented and used in a particular organizational context. Organizational differences, such as implementation policy and ongoing training, may determine the groupware's success or failure.

An examination of different time, different place groupware from a broader organizational perspective reveals additional findings. Users reported the most value from tools that paralleled nonelectric activities (e.g., electronic messaging). Sending messages between group members was a func-

tion that was taking place prior to the implementation of groupware, hence users found electronic messaging to be a more efficient means of doing so. On the other hand, scheduling tools that included functions such as project tracking, reminders, directories, and expense tracking provided little value to users mainly because none of these functions represented tasks that people were doing. Such functions become viewed as tools that simply create more work. Organizations that have experienced the greatest gains with groupware went well beyond simply loading the software on end users' workstations. Clear relationships that relate groupware functionality to accomplishing specific work tasks is one recurring theme evident with businesses experiencing success with groupware. Another redeeming theme associated with groupware success is the explicit connection made between the social and technical aspects of groupware.

Coast Guard Project

To obtain data needed during the project initiation phase of a groupware development project, Coast Guard Headquarter's employees were asked to respond to questions. The employees selected were from three work groups: (1) the Marine Safety Office (MSO), (2) information resource managers (IRMs), and (3) total quality management (TQM) facilitators. The respondents were asked to rate two different forms of groupware: (1) same time, same place electronic meeting groupware; and (2) different time, different place electronic meeting groupware, with regard to specific usefulness when used in conjunction with various computer functions (e.g., databases, presentation graphics, etc.).

Different time, different place electronic meeting groupware was rated the most likely to be useful in the workplace. The TQM facilitators view groupware to be the most useful in supporting group work, followed closely by the IRM managers. The MSO respondents perceived groupware as likely to be useful, but less so than the other divisions. Respondents also viewed consensus building tools between meetings as less likely to be useful.

Assignment Questions

1. Based on the results of the survey of Coast Guard Headquarters' personnel, can it be inferred that the application of groupware would be useful?
2. Why were there differences in perceived usefulness among the three divisions?

Chapter 2

Requirements Analysis

This chapter describes how, using various fact-finding techniques, information may be gathered about what a new system should do. Two different approaches may be taken to determine requirements. First, the current system may be investigated to learn about the business environment. The good aspects of the current system should be candidates for retention. Naturally, the negative aspects will be identified and modified as requirements of the new system. The second approach is to ignore the current system and concentrate on what the new system should do when implemented. Proponents of this approach suggest that it takes less time and focuses everyone involved on the new system.

REQUIREMENTS DETERMINATION

A requirement may be defined as a feature that must be included in the new system. There are four areas in which requirements should be identified: basic, transaction, decision, and organizationwide.

Basic Requirements

In this area, the very essence of the system is identified. Here it is necessary to understand the process to be followed by the system. The purpose of the business activity should be identified. Also, in order to carry out this activity, it should be determined what steps are performed, where, and by whom. Further, it should be determined what data are used and what information is produced. Anticipated process timing and volumes should be estimated. The identification of any necessary system controls will complete the documentation of the basic system requirements.

Transaction Requirements

In this area, all the components of what constitutes a transaction are documented. The purpose of the transaction should be identified, along with who and what action initiates a transaction. Frequency, volume, and seasonal variation are other aspects that should be identified. It is also necessary to determine what data are required to process a transaction and if there are any conditions that may affect how a transaction is processed. The determination of what data are stored and what information is generated will complete the identification of transaction requirements.

Decision Requirements

This area addresses the issue of how the information generated by the system will be used. Thus it is necessary to analyze the decisions to be made using the information from the system. In order to be able to make effective decisions it is necessary to have suitable transaction-processing procedures in place. Although this is the emphasis placed on the development of the new system, it is wise to also consider the availability of information from other systems, both those internal to the organization and externally provided services such as public databases or Internet.

Organizationwide Requirements

It is also important to assess the implications to other departments that interact with the system being investigated.

FACT-FINDING TECHNIQUES

Various techniques may be employed here. It is necessary to know whether facts or opinions are being gathered. When investigating information systems, facts are usually gathered. Depending upon the circumstances, either may be valuable. There is also a level of accuracy associated with a fact. Again it is necessary to determine an appropriate level of accuracy.

Initially, access must be gained to the personnel who can provide the necessary facts. Department managers should be contacted first as a courtesy and then to obtain approval to communicate with members of that department. Senior personnel of the department will be able to provide an overview of the system. So more general, policy-oriented facts should be obtained from this higher level. Department operations staff will be able to discuss the area in detail because of their more intimate knowledge of the specific processes.

Interview

Conducting interviews can be a very time-consuming process. It may be difficult to arrange interview times because of the work schedules of those who should be involved. It is also very important to be prepared for the interview. There are a number of steps in the preparation for and conduct of the interview.

1. **Study Background Information:** It will be helpful to review any documents from previous projects as well as current (remember they may be outdated) procedure manuals and job descriptions.
2. **Planning the Interview:** Develop a list of questions, but do not necessarily stick rigidly to the script. Be flexible regarding scheduling. The location of the interview will be important. The workplace may have distractions or the interviewee may feel insecure outside a known environment. The level of questions should be appropriate for the individual; that is, policy-type questions should be directed to more senior management, whereas procedural detail questions should be asked of operations staff.
3. **Preliminary Interview with Department Manager:** This interview is conducted mainly as a matter of courtesy to obtain permission to interview staff in the department. Further valuable background information may be obtained. It is important to verify the terms of reference of the investigation and to discuss any areas of concern as seen by the department manager. The number of personnel within the department to be interviewed and the time requirements should be agreed on.
4. **Interviewing Department Personnel:**
   a. Starting the interview: A good first impression may be made by being prompt and appropriately dressed. Try to relax the interviewee, but do not take up too much time with social chat. Begin the formal part of the interview by explaining the purpose.
   b. Conducting the interview: Keep questions direct and avoid jargon unless it is in standard use by the interviewee. Listen carefully to the answers. Make neither assumptions nor suggestions. Although difficult, it is very important to be patient during quiet periods when the interviewee is thinking about how to respond to a question.
5. **Verify Findings:** Immediately after the interview, transcribe and expand the notes taken during the interview. Provide a copy to the interviewee and ask for verification. All findings should be cross-checked with other sources in order to determine their accuracy. Inaccurate findings will have to be resolved.

Questionnaire

If facts are to be gathered from a large diverse group, employing a questionnaire may be a more appropriate method. The standard questions will lead to results that can be statistically analyzed. Low response rates may be increased through some form of encouragement, such as a letter from senior management indicating the importance of a response.

Questionnaires are difficult to develop. Care must be taken to ensure that the answers to the questions asked will reveal usable information. It may be helpful to test the questions on a small group of personnel to determine whether the intended analysis can be carried out. Open-response questions may be appropriate for obtaining general ideas, but they will not allow the statistical analysis of closed-response questions.

Observation

This technique provides firsthand information about how activities are carried out. It provides an opportunity to assess the characteristics of a process. The observer can document personnel movement and interruptions, as well as attitudes toward work pressures. It is important to ensure that the act of observation does not affect the process. Further, the observation period should cover both peaks and valleys inherent in the process.

Record Review

Records represent evidence of a business event. The movement of records may be charted. It is important to measure volume of records processed as well as seasonal variation, processes involved with any special cases, and error procedures that exist.

Document Review

Documents describe the business area. They are represented by organization charts, policy manuals, operating procedures, and company instructions. It is important to be aware that the description in the document may not be an accurate representation of the current processes.

The Role of Sampling

Sampling can be used in a more efficient application of all of the above techniques, but should only be used when appropriate. It can help reduce the time and cost to gather facts. It is important to note that easy-to-reach samples may not be representative of the entire population.

THE CASES

Canada Construction Services Payroll Software

Ron Craig

> This case focuses on the make/buy decision. The situation involves a payroll system that has encountered problems because of its age. Also, the current system does not take advantage of current technology. These problems may potentially cause a walkout of the company's construction workers.

Systems Analysis and Design at Stratford General Hospital

Yolande E. Chan and Richard J. Simm

> This case presents a situation involving recommendations from the steering committee pertaining to the strategic plan for investments in new technologies at Stratford General Hospital. The committee was confident that the plans would enable the hospital to streamline and improve the efficiency of many of its manual processes. The plan outlined an integrated approach to managing the information within the hospital. A development project is presented and describes the initial stages of implementing the medical laboratory information system (MLIS) using an "off-the-shelf" application package.

Stakeholder Analysis and Diffusion of Innovation as Requirements Determination Tools

Barry A. Frew and Susan Page Hocevar

> This case describes an organization's attempts at early analysis of user requirements. Whereas traditional user requirement studies focus on functional analysis and uses data flow and data relationship tools, this study focuses on stakeholders. Instead of data analysis tools it uses stakeholder analysis; strength, weakness, opportunities, and threat (SWOT) analysis; diffusion of innovation surveys; management of technological change techniques to determine what the system should look like; and it presents a plan for implementation.

Billboard Corporate Accounting System

Bruce Johnson

> This case presents the requirements determination process for a new information system. The manager of systems and programming of the company

struggles through the requirements determination with a user who seems less than committed.

Billboard Charts

Bruce Johnson

> This case presents the problems of requirements determination from a different perspective. In this situation, the corporate management has bypassed the information systems department regarding the acquisition of an information system. Corporate management does not support the IS department because of past failures and a lack of understanding of appropriate roles within the firm. This process further contributes to problems with the determination of requirements.

CANADA CONSTRUCTION SERVICES PAYROLL SOFTWARE

Ron Craig

It was a lovely July morning but Joseph Wirekai was not happy today. He had just talked with his site manager in Quebec, who told him workers were threatening to walk off the job in an hour if all of them did not receive their pay checks (half a dozen new workers had been taken on last week and their paychecks had not been prepared). And this was not the first time workers had threatened to walk off a project because of payroll problems. In the past year alone

there had been two work disruptions and several near disruptions.

Joseph sympathized with these employees. He knew people counted on their paychecks. But he wished they would be a little more tolerant today—he had his hands full with other important things. Payroll was a chronic problem because CCS's computerized payroll system was archaic. Joseph looked forward to a meeting that afternoon to deal with payroll automation. Now he had further ammunition to get things rolling quickly! Last year management had not listened to him when he said that replacing the payroll system should be a top priority.

Meanwhile, he had to find out why the new workers had not received their paychecks, get the problem corrected, and phone the unions involved. A walkout at the Quebec site would cost his company tens of thousands of dollars per day, and they had a tight schedule to meet.

Background

Canadian Construction Services (CCS) is a wholly owned subsidiary of a large international firm specializing in the design, manufacture, erection, and maintenance of reactors for chemical manufacturers. The company focuses on erection of new facilities and overhaul. Although over half its business comes from Canada, CCS is often involved in projects in Europe, Asia, Central and South America, and elsewhere. CCS erects its own equipment and equipment of competitors, providing a turnkey service for the client. In addition, the company services and repairs all types of equipment to provide proper customer support on their parent's manufactured goods.

Competition comes from two sources. There are only a few firms involved on the design/manufacturing side, and all of them are large. Each has a construction arm. There are a larger number of firms who are solely involved in construction services. In good times, the manufacturing firms concentrate on the largest projects, leaving the least attractive smaller jobs to others. But when times are tough, they go after almost all available work.

Joseph Wirekai has been in the heavy construction industry all his working life, and with CCS for the past 11 years. He is now director of site operations and works out of CCS's head office in Toronto.

The Canadian construction industry is highly unionized and relatively labor-driven. Some unions are more militant than others, but none wants their pay delayed by even a few hours. It is important that checks be issued on time—otherwise an entire job site could be shut down. On some of the larger CCS projects, like the Quebec site, the cost of a labor walkout could be tens of thousands of dollars per day.

Current Payroll System

The current payroll system is a combination of manual and computerized procedures. The computerized part comprises some three dozen programs, written in three languages over two decades. It was developed entirely in-house by programmers who are either no longer with the company or have moved to other positions, and it runs in batch mode on the CCS mainframe located at the head office in Toronto. There is very little documentation available for the system, and none for many of the programs. PL/1, one of the programming languages, is no longer used within the firm and most of CCS's programmers are not familiar with it.

The following procedures are followed in preparing each payroll run:

1. Initial employee payroll data is manually reported at the job site as employees are hired on from local union halls.
2. At the end of each workday, foremen turn in a "push card" (which lists job description, employee number, hours worked, and project number) to the timekeeper.
3. Each morning the timekeeper takes the push cards from the previous day and prepares a "daily time sheet" for each project number. The time sheet lists, by job type, the employee number, trade class, hours worked, and any travel or bonus time. These are totaled and approved by the supervisors and the customer.
4. Every Monday morning the timekeeper prepares a "weekly work report." The report summarizes and totals by day of the week the number of hours of standard time, overtime, and bonus time expended on each project for both tradespeople and supervisors. To the report are added all other job charges,

which are approved by the customer's on-site rep, then sent to the CCS head office (to be used for customer billing).

5. Every Tuesday the timekeeper manually prepared a paycheck for each site employee. A copy of the check stub is sent to the head office, to be totaled and reconciled with the weekly work reports. Paychecks are handed out on Wednesday morning.

Problems with the Current System

As CCS has grown over the past two decades, the payroll system has not kept pace with company developments and external changes. The current system is quite inflexible and is not fully automated. It now consists of some three dozen programs, written in three different languages (COBOL, RPG, and PL/1). The MIS department at CCS no longer supports PL/1, so programs written in that language are left alone (or, if absolutely necessary, a contract programmer is hired). Over time the code has been patched so many times that it has become a classic example of "spaghetti code." Any changes require the involvement of a minimum of three people. One manager estimates that maintaining the software costs CCS at least $60,000 a year in addition to operating costs.

The current system, a batch program run on the CCS mainframe, does not allow installation at construction sites. It is centrally run and requires manual records sent from the sites. Thus it does little to meet the needs of site activities. With the recent downturn in the economy, construction services have increased from less than 20 percent to more than 50 percent of CCS's total business. It is critical for the company to have timely information on the financial status of each contract. But the current system is designed to have daily data feeding into weekly files which in turn feed into monthly files. The monthly files are then used to prepare contract status reports. Ongoing financial information is often not available until 4 to 6 weeks after the relevant time period and, when costs run awry, management is not aware of the problem soon enough.

Another major problem with the program is that many of the fields are too small for current needs. An example of this is the federal income tax field: when the payroll system was initially developed, entries to a maximum of $999.99 were allowed (much more than was needed at the time). Now this field length is inadequate, as it is not unusual for workers to earn up to $4,000 or more per week and owe more than $1,000.00 in federal taxes. Fixing the problem is not a simple matter of increasing the field size, as the maximum record length has now been used. Any increase in field size will require an increase in record size, which will require changes in all programs that read these records as well as changes to the database's physical structure.

Special procedures have been developed to handle problems such as the inadequate federal income tax field length. The procedures are cumbersome and error prone because they are done manually. For example, in the case of federal income tax, the entire payroll is run. Checks are issued for everyone, but some are incorrect. The incorrect checks are canceled (those with federal tax greater than $999.99), and reissued manually. After this, the database must be updated to reflect the corrections.

Overall the system is very unreliable. Typically there are software problems every week. Programs often do not run through due to field size limitations and various other program faults. It has become the accepted practice to first run the payroll and then fix the payroll.

CCS uses an older IBM mainframe, with disk drives that IBM will soon no longer support. The maintenance cost of the current system is sufficient to cover the leasing and maintenance costs of a new system. Regardless of what is done with the payroll system, CCS plans to move to a new hardware platform next year.

Everyone recognizes that the payroll system has reached the end of its useful life. However, the MIS department is small and has several other projects underway. It has no slack resources. People would have to be taken off current maintenance and development activities if CCS decided to push through the payroll revision. Besides, just maintaining the system takes up enough of the department's resources already. Last year, it was decided that two other projects would receive priority this year, ahead of payroll. These projects are well underway, but will not be completed until year-end.

Users of Payroll Data

The payroll system does a lot more than just provide paychecks to people. Its primary purpose is to ensure that people receive the correct pay and that appropriate deductions are made and forwarded to various groups (government, insurance companies, unions, etc.). But the system also provides data used by other departments at CCS and other computerized applications.

Personnel makes extensive use of the system to ensure that union agreements and provincial labor regulations are followed. Twelve unions are used on most projects, and CCS is active in five provinces (with occasional work in the remaining five). A number of reports are required by certain provincial labor departments, and agreements with trade unions require regular reporting of numbers of tradespeople employed. Union dues are automatically deducted and forwarded to the appropriate union.

Accounting and finance incorporates the payroll information into the monthly profit and loss statement and balance sheet which goes to senior management. As part of financial statement preparation, the work-in-progress accounting module receives payroll information.

Project management is important to CCS, and the current payroll system provides data for it. The current project management system does not provide all the detail that managers want, and consideration is being given to upgrading (either enhancing it, or replacing it). Consideration of changes to the payroll system would have to include the possible future impact on the project management system.

The Meeting

Joseph spent the rest of the morning sorting out the current crisis. He grabbed a sandwich and coffee at lunch, then spent an hour preparing for the afternoon meeting. The general manager of CCS, Roy Britton, had called the meeting to develop a plan for improving payroll services.

Several people were already there when Joseph arrived, and he greeted each of them. Susan Bish, MIS director, was seated at the table, along with one of the programmer/analysts (Walt) who spent much of his time on the current payroll system. Because several other departments were involved, they all had people at the meeting. John was there from personnel, Kim from finance and accounting, and Trevor from project management services.

Roy walked in and called the meeting to order.

Roy: Thanks for taking time to come today. We're meeting so we can develop some general objectives and an action plan for improving our computerized payroll system. You all know it's been a problem in the past, and we've put off doing something about it for long enough.

Joseph: You can say that again! We just had a problem at the Quebec site, with the workers threatening to walk off the job because some of their paychecks weren't ready this morning. I got things sorted out, but it took me two hours. And it almost cost us big dollars. It's time to stop complaining and start acting. I told you all last year that this should be our top priority.

Roy: Joseph, I know your area ends up with more problems than any other because of the payroll system. But all of us are fighting fires more frequently because of it. This afternoon we start doing something to prevent these fires. I've asked Susan to tell us what our options are.

Susan: As you all know, our Payroll System was developed for an earlier time. It no longer works well, and it's too difficult for us to maintain. Everyone involved in its initial development is long gone, and there is very little documentation for it. On top of that, the hardware we use for it will be replaced soon, so we have no choice but to change the system. I've prepared a summary of our options. Here's a copy for everyone.

Susan handed out a single page (see Appendix I) to each person, and spent the next 35 minutes talking about the alternatives. There were many questions as she went through the list. Several people thought it would be a good idea to buy packaged software, and Susan indicated the pros and cons of doing this.

Susan: I need to point out that our department has everyone committed to various projects at present. Most of our time is spent on maintaining the hundreds of programs in regular use at CCS. We have a few programmers and analysts working on the new cost accounting system and the marketing support system. These were agreed to last year as the priority items. If we suddenly start working on a new payroll system, I'll have to pull people off the other two projects, or hire more people.

While you may think that buying an outside software package would solve our problems, there's more to it than that. First of all, we have to be very careful to ensure that the package meets our current and future needs. And even if the software does, my department needs to be involved in the selection and installation process—that takes time!

Roy: Thanks, Susan, for your presentation. We know what the options are, and some of the major advantages and disadvantages of each. Doing nothing is not on the list, and we know action must be taken.

I agree that buying a package looks very attractive. But I also respect Susan's concern about not rushing into this without realizing the possible consequences. Susan, how do you recommend we proceed?

Joseph: Just a minute, Roy. We need this done, and we need it done quickly. Buying a package that runs on a micro will solve our problems, and solve them quickly. Why, I'd be willing to look after it, so there wouldn't be any need for overburdening MIS with additional work.

Susan: I wish it was that easy, Joe. If packaged software is the best alternative, it will be faster and cheaper than the other options. But, and I emphasize this, we still need to identify all our payroll needs before we can compare them to what the various packages have to offer. It may be that we can't find something that matches our needs completely; we may be forced to change the way we do things.

The analysts in our department are trained to work with users, to help them identify and document all their requirements. We need to have a written list of requirements, so we can carefully compare them to what the various packages have to offer. Otherwise, we could very likely be sold something that would create new problems for us, and particularly for your department.

Joseph: I'm all for changing the way we do things if it's for the better. Just because we've done something in the past doesn't mean it's the best way to continue. Our payroll problem is a good example.

But I agree that we don't want to jump from the frying pan into the fire. I'm just so anxious to get this payroll situation cleaned up so I can get back to my proper job.

Roy: I think it's clear that we can't make a decision today. Susan has shown us our options, and buying a ready-made package may well be the best thing to do. However, we need to identify our requirements clearly before proceeding.

Susan, you'll need help on this. It's too early to decide what additional resources your department might need, or where they will come from. But we can't drop the other projects that are underway.

Can we spend some time considering the general requirements of our payroll system? If we can identify the major objectives we want to set for ourselves and this project, we can give further consideration to our options.

The group spent the next hour talking about individual department and company-wide objectives for the payroll system. There were lots of complaints about the current system, but Roy kept things moving.

Appendix II lists the objectives finally agreed upon.

Roy: I think we've come up with quite a comprehensive list of things we want to see from the new payroll system. I'll have the list typed up and sent out with the minutes of this meeting. The last thing we need to do today is develop an action plan—where we go from here, and the major steps in getting us there.

The group focused on immediate actions that could be started this week, and the assignment of responsibility for them. It only took three-quarters of an hour to complete; their results are shown in Exhibit 2–1. Since it was so important for his department, Joseph volunteered to work with the MIS department in preparing a project plan. He was determined to resolve the payroll problems once and for all.

EXHIBIT 2–1   Action Plan

---

1. Finalize general objectives
   Confirm agreement with the objectives with each department involved. Complete this week.
2. Select alternative
   Decide whether to develop software in-house or make an outside purchase. Decision to be made in one month.
3. Definition of inputs and outputs required
   For the final project plan, we need to take a close look at what we need in the way of inputs generated on the construction site (time sheets, start/stop notices, etc.), as well as the output or reports that we will require from the system.
4. Final project plan
   This plan should include a detailed schedule as well as the resources required, key documentation points, and project milestones. Joseph and Walt will take responsibility for this.

Roy: We've accomplished a lot this afternoon. Several of you have things to get busy on. We'll meet in a month's time to finalize and make/buy decision. I'll be in touch weekly with everyone involved, and so will Susan. Thanks for coming to the meeting, and for your help.

The Next Step

Joseph went back to his office, reflecting on the meeting, the extra work he had taken on, and how nice it would be to have a payroll system that worked. A proper payroll system was currently the key need for his department. And getting it up and running as quickly as possible would make life easier for him. Without the recurring payroll problems that took up so much of his time, he could concentrate on some projects he had in mind to improve cost control at CCS construction sites. He wished they could just find a software package that would do everything they needed, put it onto a micro, and be finished with it. But was it that simple?

APPENDIX I   Alternatives

1. *Restructure the current system.* This could solve some of the software problems such as "spaghetti code" and inadequate field size. In addition, software maintenance would be simpler. This alternative would not eliminate some of the other deficiencies of the payroll system (such as lack of portability to remote construction sites). The current program is designed for batch processing and would not accommodate real-time on-line processing. In addition, it is not designed to be a multiuser system.
2. *Service bureau.* CCS uses the Bank of Montreal to handle salaried payroll, and this is very satisfactory. This service (or other similar ones) could handle many of the functions for site payroll, but it is weak in two areas. It cannot handle retroactive pay requirements, or the short turnaround required (e.g., it is not unusual to get a call on a Friday afternoon, and need the system set up and ready to go by Monday morning; a tradesperson hired midweek must be paid the following Wednesday).
3. *System used by American branch (American Construction Services).* ACS developed their own mainframe-based system which is satisfactory for their needs. The problem with using this system in Canada is that it is not set up to handle Canadian tax requirements, and correcting this would require in-house programming. In addition there would need to be constant updating as tax laws change. There would also be differences in the treatment of the various unions. Finally, with CCS moving to a new computer system in the future, it might require additional modifications for the new operating system and hardware.
4. *Reengineer the current system.* Develop a new set of custom programs which would meet all of CCS's needs. CCS could contract out the development of a payroll system, or ask their information services unit to develop the application. Currently the MIS Department has an 18-month project backlog.
5. *Packaged program.* If a suitable package could be found, it might be the fastest option. Depending on how closely the capabilities of the package matched CCS needs, modifications of the package may or may not be required. Alternatively, CCS might change their way of doing things to meet the capabilities of the package.

APPENDIX II   General Objectives of CCS Construction Payroll System

---

1. Reduce payroll production cost

   Any new system should reduce the cost and effort required to maintain the field payroll. CCS is uncompetitive because:
   a. It takes too long to sign tradespeople onto the payroll.
   b. Too many timekeepers are required on a job in order to maintain the current system. Some competitors appear to spend one-tenth the time CCS does maintaining similar-sized payrolls.
2. Improve payroll accuracy

   Correct calculation of all checks, including personal, union, and government remittances automatically.
3. Reduced sign-on time when using system

   The objective would be to have a sign-on time of less than 1 minute per employee. Much of the construction start/stop employee documentation could be maintained on a resident file accessed by the employee's SIN or similar number.
4. On-line access

   On-line access is required at both the construction site and head office.
5. Dial-up access

   To provide communication between construction sites and head office via telephone.
6. Multiple site capabilities

   On a continuous basis should be able to issue payroll checks from the regional offices in Vancouver, Calgary, Toronto, Montreal, and Halifax.

   For a large construction or maintenance project, CCS would establish a site payroll with the computer system on location. The system should provide for at least 12 sites including the regional offices.
7. Daily pay

   A daily pay capability is required.
8. Interface with WIP

   For accounting purposes, the payroll system must be capable of interfacing with the WIP accounting module.
9. Project management interface

   The payroll system input (e.g., worker time sheets, etc.) must be designed to support an eventual project management system that would provide similar reports to those currently generated.
10. Security

   The system must provide a proper audit trail, part of which is the capability to print a daily workforce report within 30 minutes of shift start.
11. Handle multiple trades

   The system must be able to handle multiple trades in all Canadian provinces. Currently 12 trades are used on a regular basis.

(Continued)

APPENDIX II   General Objectives of CCS Construction Payroll System—*(Continued)*

---

12. Head office trade file maintenance

    Interpretation of the various agreements for each of the trades with the various locals would be supported by a combination of head office personnel and payroll departments. This would eliminate the current problem when the local timekeeper on a job has to interpret the proper rates of pay from the local agreement.

13. User friendly

    The system must be easy to use, user friendly, and not unwieldy.

14. Documentation

    All software and procedures must be properly documented, and existing documentation removed from the manuals.

15. Schedule

    It is essential that the new system be in place by January 1 of the coming year.

Assignment Questions

1. What are the business and information system issues in this case?

2. What factors and considerations should CCS take into account in deciding upon the best course of actions? Describe these and indicate whether they are of primary or secondary importance. For each alternative CCS is considering, use these to summarize the advantages and disadvantages.

3. What software packages are currently available for the construction industry? Is CCS likely to find one that meets its needs?

4. Based on the facts of the case, critique the management planning and decision-making process at CCS.

5. Given existing technology, would it be cost-effective to provide the connectivity (communication needs) specified in the requirements? Also, what type of computer system might be best suited to handle the new payroll system? What general hardware specifications and network services would you recommend?

SYSTEMS ANALYSIS AND DESIGN AT STRATFORD GENERAL HOSPITAL

Yolande E. Chan and Richard J. Simm

Part A of Systems Analysis and Design at SGH

Philip frowned as he skimmed the memo which prefaced the report from the Information Systems (IS) Steering Committee. The concern over escalating health care costs for the hospital and the province as a whole was outlined, as was the plan to temporarily close an entire ward on the third floor. This was apparently the first phase of a series of cost containment initiatives and strategic investments in new technologies at the Stratford General Hospital (SGH).

The steering committee had prepared recommendations pertaining to the strategic plan for information systems at SGH. While concerned with the political ramifications of investments in new technologies in light of ward closings and downsizing, the committee was confident that the plans would enable the hospital to streamline, and improve the efficiency of, many of its manual processes. The plan outlined an integrated approach to managing the information within the hospital.

With this in mind, Philip's attention shifted to his responsibilities as the charge technologist (charge tech) for the histology, cytology, and biochemistry departments of SGH's laboratory. Schooled in England,

Philip joined SGH in 1971 and had been the charge tech for over 18 years. Philip was responsible for the daily work flow of his departments—including quality control and assurance, introduction of new tests, evaluation and coordination of equipment and medical supply purchases, continuing education, staffing and departmental communication, and test production—as well as long-term laboratory planning. In addition, Philip was responsible for teaching the laboratory technologist interns from the college program with which the hospital was affiliated.

As Philip printed the workload list for the day's scheduled biochemistry tests he pondered over how the professional requirements of delivering are and clinical laboratory services had far outstripped the ability of any paper-driven system to support them. Concerned over both the efficiency and effectiveness of the laboratory, Philip wanted to move quickly on the steering committee's recommendations.

The SGH Laboratory

A medical laboratory is a facility where tissue, cells, blood, body fluids, and other biological specimens are tested, analyzed, and evaluated. Precise measurements are made, and the results are calculated and interpreted.[1]

The laboratory at SGH was a regional laboratory, as it served as the medical laboratory

[1]Norma J. Walters, Barbara H. Estridge, and Anna P. Reynolds, *Basic Medical Laboratory Techniques* (New York: Delmar Publishers, 1990), p. 1.

for 10 other smaller hospitals in the region. These included the hospitals in Clinton, Exeter, Goderich, Hanover, Kincardine, Listowel, Palmerston, Seaforth, St. Mary's, and Wingham.

The SGH laboratory was comprised of six clinical departments:

1. Histology
2. Cytology
3. Biochemistry
4. Hematology

5. Immunohematology
6. Microbiology

A brief overview of each department and their corresponding functions is presented in Exhibit 2–2.

Laboratory Services at SGH

Laboratory services began with a request for tests by a practicing physician. Only a physician could request laboratory testing

---

EXHIBIT 2–2   SGH Laboratory Departments

Histology
Histology procedures concentrate on detecting tumors and other abnormalities in tissue. In this department, the technologist prepares the slide whereas the pathologist views the slide, and writes the final report.

Cytology
Cytology procedures look for malignant cells primarily in pap smears but also in other body fluids or aspirations.

Biochemistry
Most tests in biochemistry are performed on blood serum, the liquid portion of blood after clot formation. Procedures include analyzing all body fluids (serum, plasma, cerebrospinal fluid, plural fluids, urine, and joint fluids) for specific chemical content. Some major tests performed include glucose, total proteins, cholesterol, and triglycerides.

Hematology
Hematology procedures concentrate on counting various components of the blood, including the white blood cells, red blood cells, and platelets. All of these counts are performed using automated systems. Other procedures include the observation of cell size, shape, and maturity level.

Immunohematology
Otherwise known as blood bank, this department provides blood products to patients. These include whole blood, packed red blood cells, fresh frozen plasma, platelet, and white blood cells. Procedures performed in blood bank include ABO and Rh typing, cross-matching for transfusion and antibody screening.

Microbiology
Disease-causing microorganisms, obtained from the patient's blood, urine, or other body fluid, sputum, or wound, are isolated, observed, and identified in this department. After the organism is grown, susceptibility testing—exposing the organism to different antibiotics—is performed. The microbiology department has traditionally been less automated than other departments.

Adapted from Jacquelyn Marshall, *Fundamental Skills for the Clinical Laboratory Professional* (New York: Delmar Publishers, 1993), and Norma J. Walters, Barbara H. Estridge, and Anna P. Reynolds, *Basic Medical Laboratory Techniques* (New York: Delmar Publishers, 1990).

for a patient. Hence, a specimen could reach the laboratory, primarily, in one of three ways:

1. Through patients with *inpatient* status (i.e., with the patients admitted in the hospital).
2. Through *emergency*.
3. Through patients with *outpatient* status (i.e., patients go to the laboratory and technologists or lab assistants perform the tests).

Because SGH was a regional health service provider, the laboratory also received specimens via courier from other hospitals.

The laboratory at SGH was staffed with four pathologists, 24 technologists and technicians, nine lab assistants—two of whom were part-time—and six clerical staff. As well, there were two management positions in the laboratory (see Figure 2–1).

The pathologist—a physician who is specially trained in the nature and causes of disease—was the director of the laboratory. The technologists and technicians were primarily responsible for performing all specimen testing, analysis, and interpretation. Lab assistants were primarily responsible for specimen collection, test result entry into the existing database system, and general assistance in the laboratory. Clerical staff were responsible for data processing and office operations.

Test results from biochemistry, immuno-hematology, cytology, hematology, and, microbiology could be signed off[2] by the charge tech and transmitted to the requesting physician. Only abnormal results needed to be reviewed by a pathologist. With tests performed in histology, all results had

to be reviewed by a pathologist. The pathologist would then dictate a final report for transmission to the requesting physician.

The organization of the laboratory, in relation to the hospital as a whole, is presented in Figure 2–2.

Database Management in the Laboratory

The existing laboratory information system (LIS) was a legacy system, coded in a 3GL, dating back almost 14 years. The system provided database management functions for biochemistry, hematology, and microbiology. It was developed in-house using WANG architecture and consisted of seven dummy terminal-keyboard units distributed throughout the laboratory with a central processor. Aside from its processing limitations, the system was also limited in its ability to provide timely results and statistics for the technologists. Furthermore, the LIS was *not* interfaced with any of the laboratory instruments or equipment, or with the central hospital information system (HIS). This presented an obstacle to the efficient and effective delivery of medical laboratory services.

A separate stand-alone system—comprised of three 386 personal computers networked over a local area network with a file server—was used for the production of pathologists' reports. WordPerfect, Lotus 1-2-3, and Harvard Graphics were available on this DOS-based system. Output devices included both a Panasonic impact printer and a Hewlett-Packard LaserJet 4. This system did not interface with the existing LIS, or with the central HIS.

The Future of Information Systems in the Laboratory

Philip had arranged to meet with the coordinator of laboratory services, Graeme

---

[2]"Signing off" is a process whereby the charge tech or the pathologist reviews the test results and, if clinically acceptable, initials the report.

FIGURE 2–1   SGH Laboratory Organization Structure

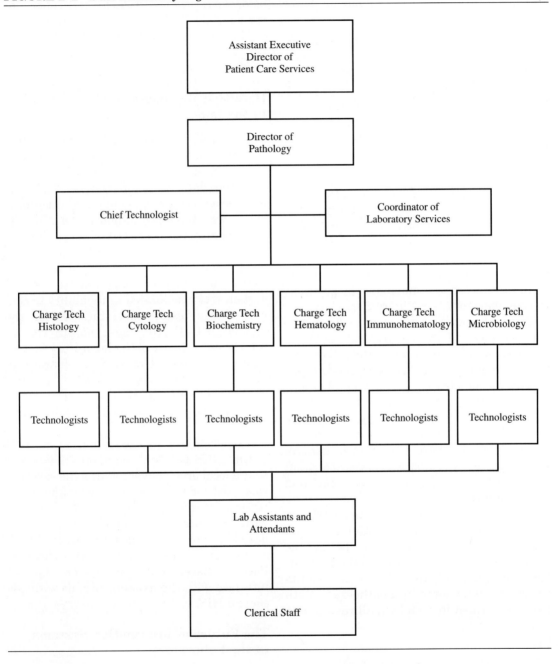

FIGURE 2-2 SGH Organization Structure

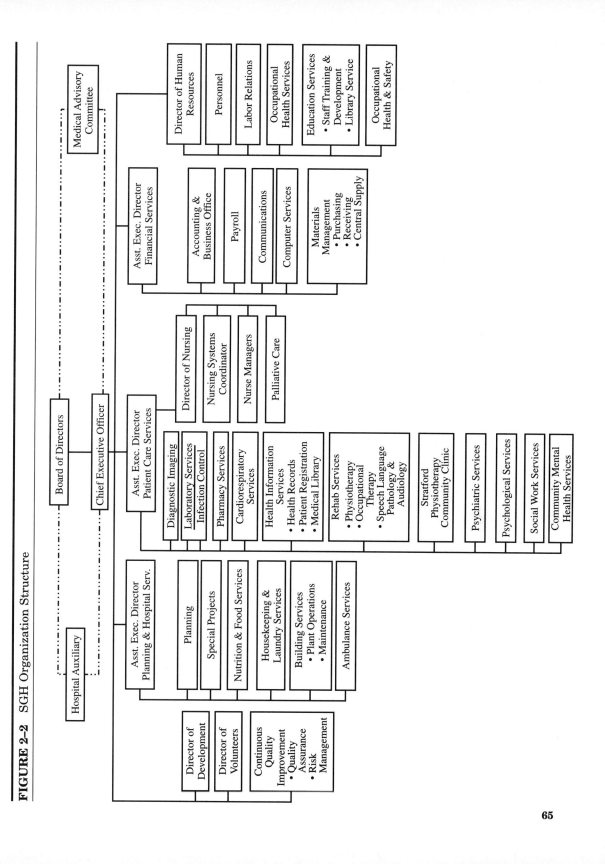

Johnson, later that afternoon, to discuss the future of IS in the laboratory. At the request of the steering committee, Philip was to act as the laboratory's representative throughout the duration of the project. This was to ensure that needs of the laboratory would be accurately identified. Also in attendance would be a project analyst from the IS consulting firm selected to manage the development and implementation of the system.

Over the past 8 months, under the direction of an independent IS health care consultant, Graeme had evaluated many LISs in the province, including those at University Hospital, Victoria Hospital, and St. Joseph's Hospital in London. The purpose of these visits was to gain insight into issues surrounding advanced LISs, as well as their benefits, and thus formulate an effective strategy for the new LIS at SGH.

As outlined in the IS Steering Committee's report, the laboratory had been selected as the first department in the hospital to undergo a series of systems development projects. The laboratory was identified as one of the departments with the greatest potential for savings through automation. The possible benefits to the laboratory and the hospital as a whole from automation were identified, in the report, in the following areas:

- Processing test requisitions.
- Preparing workload lists.
- Processing admissions, transfers, and discharges.
- Distributing results.
- Developing costing information.

Additional time-saving benefits could be realized in quality control and assurance practices, and in generating statistical analyses.

Philip decided to review the proposals that had been submitted for the systems development project in the laboratory. While he strongly believed that the new LIS would provide the laboratory and the entire hospital with a means to ultimately improve the level of service within the region in a cost-effective manner, there was still some concern over the project, especially with respect to the following:

- Verifying vendors claims and features.
- Ensuring that the system added value rather than merely "putting wheels under manual processes."
- Expansion options and limitations.
- Adherence to standards for the LIS under current health care legislation.

With this in mind, Philip thought about the scope of the proposed hospitalwide IS project. This would be no meager project—the budget had been set at Can $3.5 million. As outlined in the laboratory's request for proposal (RFP), the development project consisted of four primary components:

1. The *core LIS,* comprised of the individual departmental systems.
2. The *automated laboratory instrument interfaces.*
3. A *Clinical Decision Support System* (CDSS).
4. A *hospital information system* (HIS) *interface.*

Hardware architecture was to be based on Digital Equipment Corporation's (DEC) VAX line of superminicomputers. Terminals and printers included DEC's VT320 series and Hewlett-Packard LaserJet 4 series, respectively.

The RFP had also outlined parameters for development and implementation. Phase I involved developing a system for *biochemistry,* implementing it, and then integrating it with the existing HIS. Once the technology had "proven itself," the remaining components of the core LIS (i.e., the systems for the other departments in the laboratory) could be implemented. The reasoning behind this approach was twofold. First, this would enable the laboratory to reduce the risk associated with replacing a paper-intensive system with an electronic one. Secondly, Graeme was unsure of its potential impact on the laboratory's existing staff. He wondered whether there would be a need for additional staff. While many vendors claimed that advanced LIS solutions freed up technologists' time, Graeme had observed that, in other hospitals, additional staff were often required to effectively deliver patient services.

The Next Step

Although considered a medium-to-small laboratory, the laboratory at SGH had grown significantly in terms of responsibility over the past 10 years. While Philip enjoyed the challenge associated with providing laboratory services, the demands for timely reports and statistics had become almost unmanageable lately. There were too many administrative details to process manually. While the existing system had mechanized the paper system once used, there were still many inherent limitations in the existing LIS. Philip was greatly concerned over the use of his time in the laboratory. He was eager to move quickly into phase I, replace the legacy system, and provide greater value to the hospital via the improved laboratory delivery of patient services.

Assignment 1

Project Assignment Guidelines
Assignments may be completed by groups. It is recommended that all project submissions include the following standard items.

- A *cover page* with the project title, each team member name, the course identification, and the date of submission.

- A *table of contents* that lists the items being submitted.
- A *cover letter* or *memo* to explain the purpose of each component and any special features of the components that are not obvious from the submitted material.
- A *completed peer evaluation form* or *memo* that indicates relative *individual* project assignment contributions.

All assignments are of an incremental nature. Thus, it is important that all project assignment material is available when assignments are being reviewed and graded. It is recommended that groups prepare a project binder to contain all submitted assignments. This binder can be kept by your professor in a secure area. Creation of a similar binder or file that contains copies of submitted assignments and working documents is recommended for use by the project team.

Deliverables
Your team of IS consultants has been selected to manage the first phase of the *biochemistry* systems analysis and design project at SGH. Assume that a detailed system design is required in 10 weeks. Your initial task—and this assignment—is to prepare a plan of action for the project team. How are you going to proceed? What information do you need to collect? Whom do you wish to interview?

In the action plan you submit, include objectives, tasks, a timetable or schedule, and team member responsibilities. Be sure to include any approval checkpoints required and indicate who would be involved at each checkpoint. Draw on the knowledge you have gained in other courses and your personal experiences to supplement the material in the case.

Part B of Systems Analysis and Design at SGH

The Information Requirements

That afternoon Philip attended the scheduled meeting with the coordinator of laboratory services, Graeme Johnson, and the project analyst from the IS consulting group undertaking the project. The IS Steering Committee had received the green light on project funding for the new laboratory system from the chief executive officer and the board of directors. The medical advisory committee had also endorsed the IS strategic plan.

The purpose of the meeting was to provide a starting point for phase I of the systems development project slated for the laboratory—the medical laboratory information system (MLIS). The goal of the meeting was to accurately identify the system requirements for the MLIS, even though the new MLIS would be an "off-the-shelf" package. The package would provide an opportunity to "reengineer" existing manual and automated processes. However, the plan was also to request minor modifications to the package to meet the specific requirements of the laboratory and SGH.

The meeting commenced with Philip expressing his concerns over the existing system: "There are two major problems with the existing system—its capacity and processing speed; we must be able to handle more work and with shorter turnaround times. As well, there are other secondary limitations. If these are not remedied in the new system, this entire process and project will have been pointless.

To have any real advantage over the existing system, this proposed system must reach two objectives. First, it must reduce the time technologists spend on administrative detail, perhaps by eliminating previously undertaken procedures. Secondly, it must produce accurate results in an efficient manner—processing speed is vital.

Furthermore, the system must have many of the standard features—Graeme will provide you with details of the requirements; he's reviewed many systems." Philip turned to Graeme.

"This includes on-line patient admission and patient information queries, test requisition entry, automatic specimen accessioning, and on-line results entry. As well, the system must be able to produce daily worksheets, test result reports, cumulative test summaries, statistical reports, and management reports. Without question, the system must also provide a means for the charge tech to enforce quality control.

Finally, there is a great concern for errors in the transposition of test results in the system. Because of the limitations of the existing system, many test results—in biochemistry for example—are manually recorded on a standard requisition sheet (see Exhibits 2–3 and 2–4) and then batch-processed. Ultimately, I would like a system that allows the technologist to enter the results in real time. Wherever possible, test results would be downloaded directly from the testing equipment. Having a direct equipment and instrumentation interface with the laboratory information system would also significantly reduce time spent graphing cumulative lab summaries, performing statistical and trend analyses, and processing paperwork."

The analyst probed Graeme for the details of the requirements: "I guess a logical place to start is with patient information. Under our existing system, we—the laboratory—have to input this data ourselves, which subsequently is stored separately from the patient information in the HIS.

The new MLIS, beginning with the biochemistry system, must interface with the central HIS. The laboratory, more than most

EXHIBIT 2–3 Biochemistry Multirequest Test Requisition Form

STRATFORD GENERAL HOSPITAL | Multirequest Requisition

Imprint Plate (print if no plate) | If Stat Attach Sticker

Other Hospital

Diagnosis

Specimen	Mo	Day	Time
If Urgent Print Phone No / Collected By			
Ordered by Dr.			

Date _____ Ward No. _____

Name _____

Address

City _____ Postal Code _____

Sex _____ DOB _____ Hospital _____

Health # _____

Check Test(s) Requested

#	Screen 1-Biochemistry	#	Screen 1-Biochemistry	#	Screen 3-Hematology
1	Blood Sugar-Fast	37	Digoxin	8	Differential-Poly
2	Blood Sugar-PC	38	T3 Uptake	9	-Stab
3	Urea	39	T4	10	-Lymph
4	Creatinine	40	TSH	11	-Mono
5	Electrolytes-Sodium		**Screen 2-Biochemistry**	12	-Eosin
6	-Potassium	1	Blood Gas -pH	13	-Basop
7	-Chloride	2	-pCO	14	-Meta
8	-Total CO	3	-pO	15	-Myelo
9	Calcium	4	-Bicarb	16	-Comment
10	Phosphorus	5	-Saturation	17	-Comment
11	Magnesium	6	Protein Electrophoresis	18	-Comment
12	Total Protein	7	Acetaminophen	19	Platelets
13	Albumin	8	Ethanol	20	ESR
14	Urate	9	Lithium	21	Retic
15	Cholesterol	10	Dilantin	22	PT
16	Triglycerides	11	Saucylate	23	PT-Control
17	HDL Cholesterol	12	Theophylline	24	PTT
18	Bilirubin-Total	13	Gentamicin-Trough	25	PTT Control
19	-Direct	14	Gentamicin-Peak	27	Fibrinogen
20	AST	15	Ammonia	28	FDP
21	CK	18	Hb A 1C	29	Thrombin Time
22	LD	19	Osmolality-Serum	30	LAP
23	CK-MB	20	Osmolality-Urine	31	LE
24	LD-1	24	Cortisol	32	Mono Test
25	GGT	25	HCG-s	33	RA
26	ALP		**Screen 3-Hematology**	34	CRO
27	ACP-T	1	CBC-WBC	35	Streptozyme
28	ACP-P	2	-RBC	36	ASTO
29	Amylase	3	Hemoglobin	37	ANA
30	Iron	4	-Hct	38	IgA
31	TIBC	5	-MCV	39	IgG
32	Vitamin B-12	6	-MCH	40	IgM
33	Folate-Serum	7	-MCHC		
34	Folate-RBC				
35	Ferritin				
36	Alt				

Test(s) not listed above, enter on miscellaneous form LA-007.

EXHIBIT 2–4   Miscellaneous Test Requisition Form

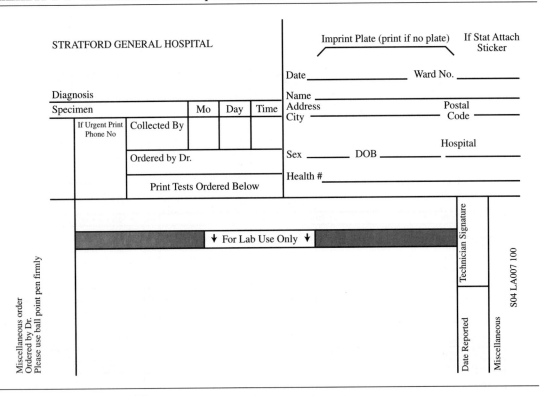

other departments in the hospital, necessitates a high level of real-time interfacing with the HIS. Major time savings will occur through automatically processing admission, transfer, and discharge information. Having a second interface for results reporting will save time preparing the results and distributing them back to the nursing units. Furthermore, additional cost savings can be realized from reducing the average length of stay through better turnaround time for laboratory results.

So, while we'll need input windows to capture patient information for outpatients and specimens received from other hospitals, all inpatient information should be passed through the HIS to our MLIS." To illustrate this, Graeme displayed a standard patient admission form (see Exhibit 2–5).

Philip continued the discussion: "Information about the requesting physician and the specimen type must also be tracked."

Philip reached for the carbonless two-copy SGH multirequest requisition form for biochemistry tests (see Exhibit 2–3).

"In the top left corner, you'll notice that we capture the name of the requesting physician and his or her telephone number in case the test results are urgent, the diagnosis of the patient, and the specimen type. In the case of biochemistry test requisitions, this would be primarily *blood, urine, cerebro spinal fluid, feces,* but could also be *other body fluids.*

As well, it is important to know who collected the specimen and the exact time of collection. In most cases, specimens are collected by the lab technicians or the lab

EXHIBIT 2–5   Stratford General Hospital Admission Form

STRATFORD GENERAL HOSPITAL

46 General Hospital Dr. Stratford
NSA2V6   519-271-2120

FACE SHEET

Patient's Surname	Patient's First Name	Patient ID Number

Address	Home Phone

Postal Code	Date of Birth yy mm dd	Age	Sex

Register Number	Admission Date yy mm dd	Time	Health Number	Mar Stat	Alternate or Previous Name

Residence Code	Type	Amo.	Lang	RTS	RFP	Language	Religion

In Emergency Notify - Name, (Relation), Address, Phone

Responsibility For Payment & Other Insurance Data

Accom.	Requested	Assigned	Room No.	Rate	Transferred From

Family Physician	Admitting Physician

Discharge Date yy mm dd	LOS	Admitting Diagnosis

(For Coding Use Only)

	Nomenclature
Most Significant Condition Which Causes the Greatest Length of Stay (LOS)	
Other Important Conditions Which Significantly Influence LOS and/or Treatment	
All Conditions Arising <u>After</u> Admission Which Influence LOS and/or Treatment (Complications)	
Procedures	

Discharge Summary (Date Dictated ☐ MM DD)	Patient Service
	Coder _____
	Date _____

Transferred to	Reason for Transfer

CHART COPY

HR00 1 93-04

Died   > 48 Hrs. ☐
        < 48 Hrs. ☐

Most Responsible Physician

assistants. Remember too, that this is a regional laboratory; hence, we have to know where to send the results if we receive a specimen from another hospital.

While there is no defined space on this form for physician's comments, these comments are vital and must be captured. Sometimes physicians will scribble quick comments along the margins, but in most cases, they will append a small note."

Philip then pointed to the bottom two-thirds of the requisition form: "The information under the headings 'Screen 1—Biochemistry' and 'Screen 2—Biochemistry' will be the information at the core of the system (see Exhibit 2–3)."

Graeme nodded at Philip and interjected: "Don't let the headings that Philip just referred to confuse you. They correspond to screens in our existing LIS."

Philip continued: "Under the 'Screen 1' and 'Screen 2' headings there are 40 and 25 separate tests, respectively. These are the most commonly performed tests in biochemistry. Other tests not listed specifically on this form are entered on the miscellaneous requisition form." (See Exhibit 2–4.)

"A very important piece of information, the means to track a specimen throughout each department in the laboratory and the different tests, is the lab accession number (LAN). This is a six digit number assigned to each specimen when it enters the laboratory.

We also want to know the time at which the test was started, the time at which it was completed, the responsible technician, and the charge tech who signed off the report. This information is predominately for internal use. We use it to generate management reports and calculate the productivity of our staff.

Finally, we track the results of each requested test and any comments that the technologist has made during the testing procedure. Eventually, the results are stored in patient history database files."

The analyst prompted Philip and Graeme for any final thoughts. There was a pause. Philip leaned back in his chair, took a deep breath, and pressed his fingers together in a prismlike fashion. "When considering an MLIS, it is not enough to look only at the laboratory as a separate function within the health care system. It is important to understand how the laboratory adds value in the chain of delivery in ways such as the reliable and accurate determination of test results, and the interpretation and efficient transmission of these results.

The new MLIS should focus on where we add value, and further enhance that value."

Graeme concluded the discussion: "Ultimately, we would like to have a system whereby every health care professional in the region has a PC on his or her desk. Not only would this represent an improvement to many of the manual processes now in place, it would allow health care professionals to focus on their core responsibilities. This day is not so far off as it seems. I feel we are moving in the right direction."

As Philip and Graeme left the table, they felt assured that they had accurately identified the goals and information requirements for the MLIS, and that the database design phase could begin.

Assignment 2: Entity–Relationship Data Modeling

Deliverables

In order to design the MLIS database, prepare the following items:

1. An entity–relationship diagram depicting the entities that will need to be tracked in the laboratory database, and the relationships between these entities.

2. A table of detailed attributes for each entity identifying the primary key and any foreign keys. All tables are expected to be in third normal form, except for those where you explicitly indicate that third normal form conditions are being violated and explain why this is necessary (e.g., to improve the practicality of the design).

Part C of Systems Analysis and Design at SGH

Obtaining and Storing the Information
Now that the requirements had been identified and the database structure had been designed, the next step was to identify the processes to accurately obtain, store, and update the data, and print the necessary reports for the biochemistry system.

Specimen Testing in Biochemistry
Processing of Patient Information
The first step during the biochemistry testing procedure, as with all other laboratory testing procedures, begins with collecting relevant patient information, as well as their status (inpatient, emergency, or outpatient).

Processing of Test Requests
In the case of an inpatient, a physician obtains the SGH multirequest requisition form (Exhibit 2–3), fills in the relevant information, and ticks off the appropriate tests. The laboratory is notified and the patient provides the specimen. In general, a lab assistant goes to the appropriate ward, signs the requisition, leaves the back copy, and collects the specimen.

This process is similar in the case of a patient admitted through emergency. In the case of an outpatient, the requesting physician fills out the requisition form, notifies the laboratory of the tests, and sends it, or has the patient deliver the form.

In the laboratory, the specimen is triaged (i.e., sent to biochemistry) and assigned a LAN. The LAN is a six-digit number with the first two digits representing the day of the month and the remaining four representing the specimen number for that day.[3] For example, 170189 represents the 189th specimen collected on the 17th day of the month. The LAN is then stamped on the requisition form.

All information from the requisition form is then entered in the existing LIS. This includes data on the patient, the requesting physician (see the top left box in Exhibit 2–3), and the requested tests. Furthermore, general comments are also entered in the system. For example, in the case of diabetic patients, it is important to know the time of their last meal or insulin intake when performing tests and interpreting results.

At this point, a workload list is printed from the LIS. The workload list indicates the number and type of tests to be run for each specific LAN. An example workload list for the Paramax—a biochemical analyzer—is presented in Exhibit 2–6. The required tests are then programmed in the Paramax and the necessary tests are run.

Entering Test Results
If the results are urgent, they are entered on the original requisition form, reviewed by the charge tech, signed off, and telephoned to the requesting physician. Otherwise, these results are entered into the LIS.

Reporting Test Findings
Once the results have been entered in the LIS, a final report (see Exhibit 2–7) is printed and reviewed by the charge tech.

---

[3]Because the life span of most specimens is just a few days and test results are transmitted immediately, only the day of the month information is needed.

EXHIBIT 2-6   Paramax Analyzer Workload List

Cup	IDS	X	CAN	Patient name	FB	PC	URE	CRE	SOD	POT	CL	CA	PHO	MAG	TPR	ALB	URA	CHO	TRI	TBI	AST	CK	LD	GGT	ALP	AMI	IRO	AL
1				S-1 OC																								
2				S-2 OC																								
3	26857	OP	93					R							R													
4	26858	OP	94					R							R													
5	27804	OP	101		R		R	R	R	R	R				R					R	R	R	R	R	R			
6	27806	H	102		R		R	R	R	R	R							R	R	R	R	R	R					
7	27807	H	103		R		R	R	R	R	R									R	R	R	R	R				
8	27808	H	104		R		R	R	R	R	R				R						R		R					
9	27809	H	105		R		R	R	R	R	R				R													
10	27810	H	106			R	R	R	R	R	R											R						
11	27811	H	107		R		R	R	R	R	R																	
12	27812	H	108		R		R	R	R	R	R																	
13	27815	H	109		R		R	R	R	R	R															R		
14	27818	H	110				R	R	R	R	R																	
15	27819	H	111		R		R	R	R	R	R																	
16	27822	H	112				R	R	R	R	R																	
17	27825	H	113				R	R	R	R	R																	
18	27827	H	115		R		R	R	R	R	R																	
19	27838	H	116		R	R	R	R	R	R	R																	
20	27839	H	117				R	R	R	R	R	R	R															
21	27840	H	118			R	R	R	R	R	R	R	R		R													R
22	27842	H	119		R		R	R	R	R	R	R	R		R													R

EXHIBIT 2–7 Biochemistry Final Report

BIOCHEMISTRY FINAL REPORT

DEPARTMENT OF PATHOLOGY STRATFORD GENERAL HOSPITAL J.M. VETTERS M.D. FRCP(C) - DIRECTOR

REPORT DATE

PATIENT NAME   87 F   H   W4N   OR.TAMC/ARCI
PATIENT NUMBER
COLLECTED 97 06 16

TEST	SI RESULT	FLAG	REF.VALUE	CALCULATED	RESULTS
F 8S	5.8 mmo1/L		(3.8– 6.4)		
UREA	13.0 mmo1/L	H	(3.5– 7.0)		
CREAT	99.0 umo1/L		(50.0–110.0)		
SOD	132.0 mmo1/L	L	(135.0–145.0)		
POT	4.5 mmo1/L		(3.5– 5.0)		
CL	100.0 mmo1/L		(99.0–108.0)		
TCO2	28.3 mmo1/L		(23.0– 33.0)	An. Gap = 8.2	(8–12)
AST	76.0 U/L	H	(0.0– 45.0)		
CK	131.0 U/L	H	(12.0–170.0)		
LD	241.0 U/L	H	(94.0–172.0)		
CK-MB	4.7 ug/L		(0.0– 5.0)		

PATIENT NAME   REPORT PRINTED–97 06 16 10:17

The report identifies the acceptable ranges for the results and flags high, low, and panic (extreme) values, which are printed in red. After the charge tech has reviewed each result, the report is signed and sent to the office for sorting and mailing.

At any time, the charge tech can also print management reports indicating the number of tests run and other relevant statistics.

The Close of Phase I
As phase I of the MLIS neared completion, Philip reviewed the process and the IS consulting firm's deliverables. He pulled from his file the SGH vendor evaluation tool for the biochemistry system (see Exhibit 2–8) and mentally scored the new system against each of the functional requirements. Philip had been pleased with the work to date and was eager to have a fully designed and implemented MLIS.

EXHIBIT 2–8   Biochemistry System Vendor Evaluation Tool

Vendor Demonstration Scoring Functional Application: Laboratories—Biochemistry

Functional Requirements	*Vendor Score*	*Comments*

1. Key requirement: order entry features

   1.1 Demonstrate the system capability of retrieving patient demographic information from the ADT/CPI—display date of birth format, bar code or accession number to identify blood specimen, time, and place bar code generated.   0 1 2 3 4

2. Key requirement—workbench processing/results capturing

   2.1 Demonstrate how the additional tests (liver profile, CPK-MB) are ordered and recorded on the same blood specimen.   0 1 2 3 4

   2.2 Demonstrate the work list generated identifying tests to be performed by: 0 1 2 3 4
   - Workbench
   - Lab section
   - Test procedures
   - Test priority number
   - Accession number
   - Patient name
   - Patient location

   2.3 Demonstrate the method of reassigning the work list to a different analyzer.   0 1 2 3 4

3. Key requirement—results reporting/inquiry

   3.1 Demonstrate that the results for urinalysis, chemical and microscopic, appear together on the same screen.   0 1 2 3 4

Instructions	*Rating Scheme*
Circle ONE number on the rating scheme for each requirement.	0 = Not available 1 = Inadequate/poor 2 = Average 3 = Good 4 = Excellent

---

EXHIBIT 2–8   Biochemistry System Vendor Evaluation Tool—(*Continued*)

Vendor Demonstration Scoring Functional Application: Laboratories—Biochemistry

Functional Requirements	*Vendor Score*	*Comments*
(3 *continued*)		
3.2 Demonstrate the ability for TDM/TOX reference ranges to include a therapeutic range and a toxic range.	0 1 2 3 4	
3.3 Demonstrate the ability to automatically enter default results.	0 1 2 3 4	
3.4 Demonstrate the ability to graph protein electrophoresis results.	0 1 2 3 4	
3.5 Demonstrate the reporting of results after results have been verified: all tests ordered for a given patient during an encounter.	0 1 2 3 4	
3.6 Demonstrate the flagging of abnormal results and verification that the results have been seen.	0 1 2 3 4	
4. Key requirement—quality control		
4.1 Demonstrate how the system generates statistics using the following calculations: mean, standard deviation, population mean, population standard deviation, regression analysis.	0 1 2 3 4	
4.2 Demonstrate how the system flags abnormal results with a corrective comment.	0 1 2 3 4	
4.3 Demonstrate how the system uses the Westgard rules.	0 1 2 3 4	
4.4 Demonstrate how the system allows overriding of the Westgard rules.	0 1 2 3 4	
4.5 Demonstrate that the system has the ability to access more than one level of quality control at one time.	0 1 2 3 4	

Instructions	*Rating Scheme*
Circle ONE number on the rating scheme for each requirement.	0 = Not available 1 = Inadequate/poor 2 = Average 3 = Good 4 = Excellent

Assignment 3: Data Flow Diagrams

Deliverables

Create data flow diagrams to describe required system processes. Include the following:

1. A statement of purpose for the *medical laboratory information system* (MLIS).
2. A context (or level 0) diagram for the new system.
3. Leveled data flow diagrams.
4. Amended database definitions if any new data requirements are discovered during your analysis.

Assignment 4: User Interfaces— Windows and Reports

Deliverables

Design the MLIS user interface.

1. List all the windows that will be provided in the new information system. If there is a hierarchical relationship between them, draw a dialogue/tree diagram to show the sequence in which windows can be accessed.
2. Design and print windows to enter patient information, test requisitions, and test results.
3. Design a biochemistry report listing the results of several tests that have been carried out for one patient.
4. Design a biochemistry report listing the results of one test that has been carried out for several patients.

5. Include amended documents from previous systems analysis and design stages if you discover new data or processing requirements.

Assignment 5: Project Implementation and Evaluation

Deliverables

Prepare a brief report to address either question 1 or 2:

1. Assume that you have completed the design of the MLIS, the newly designed automated system for the laboratory. Describe how you would go about implementing this new system. Discuss objectives, tasks, and a tentative timetable. Highlight the strengths and limitations of your plan.
2. Conduct a brief postimplementation review to describe your experience with this systems analysis and design project. Address the following:
   a. The particular strengths/benefits and weaknesses/limitations of your design for the MLIS.
   b. Key lessons learned in the analysis and design process. What might you do differently in your next system project? What particular skills have you gained?

STAKEHOLDER ANALYSIS AND DIFFUSION OF INNOVATION AS REQUIREMENTS DETERMINATION TOOLS

Barry A. Frew and Susan Page Hocevar

Executive Summary

This case describes an organization's attempts to analyze user requirements using nontraditional methods. Traditional user requirement studies focus on functional analysis and use data flow and data relationship modeling tools. This study focuses on stakeholders' analyses and diffusion of innovation surveys to determine what the system should look like and to form the basis for an implementation strategy and plan. This case focuses on the user-identified requirements of general interoperability, e-mail connectivity, and database access connectivity.

Vice Admiral Bowes became the champion for the implementation of a Naval Air System Team Wide Area Network (NAVWAN) system. He viewed this infrastructure upgrade as critical to the success of the competency aligned organization. He established a demonstration/validation team to perform the systems analysis, design, and implementation of the NAVWAN. This team identified several prototype implementation sites to be used to both validate the functionality the NAVWAN and provide data to support a full-system implementation.

The ultimate goal of the NAVWAN system is to enable people at different geographic sites throughout the Naval Air Systems Command (NAVAIR) community to directly communicate with one another. Initially, functional requirements were perceived to be electronic mail, electronic file transfer, and electronic directory services throughout the activity. The task of the reader, at the close of this case, will be to critically analyze the process described and to analyze the data provided to generate recommendations supported by this analysis.

Background[1]

The Naval Air Systems Team (NAST) is the component of the United States Department of Navy responsible for delivering aircraft and related systems to be operated, based, and supported at sea. To that end, this organization employs 42,000 civilians and 4,500 military personnel[2] at commands and bases throughout the country. Examples of products provided by this organization include air antisubmarine warfare mission systems, aircraft and related systems for aircraft carriers, maritime and air launched and strike

---

This case was prepared by Barry A. Frew and Susan Page Hocevar, Navy Postgraduate School, as the basis for class presentation and discussion rather than to illustrate either effective or ineffective handling of an administrative situation.

---

[1]This case is derived from V. R. C. Bayer (1995). A related case (Hocevar, Frew, and Bayer, in press) focuses on the use of stakeholder analysis and SWOT analysis as tools for effective change management.

[2]Data from fiscal year 1994 report of NAST. Hocevar, Frew, and Bayer in Cases on Information Technology Management in Modern Organizations. Liebowitz, Jay and Mehdi Khosrowpour (Eds.), Idea Group Publishing, 1997.

weapons systems, and training in the operation and maintenance of these systems.

In April 1992, NAST, then headed by Vice Admiral William C. Bowes, initiated a significant organizational restructuring as part of a large-scale change effort to enhance organizational effectiveness. The structure changed from that of a traditional functional hierarchy to a competency aligned organization (CAO) which is a modified matrix organization that established dedicated integrated program teams located at 22 different sites across the country. These teams are comprised of personnel from relevant functional competencies and coordinate activities that often span multiple command locations. In order for the teams to work jointly on projects, they must efficiently communicate. A wide area network (WAN) was identified as a critical infrastructure requirement for the success of these teams.

As part of this effort, NAVAIR sponsored a research effort to conduct a stakeholder analysis at one of the prototype implementation sites. This analysis was designed as an alternative to the traditional design phase for a new information system implementation. The Department of Navy has traditionally used a waterfall method. This method begins with a requirements analysis and is followed by analysis, logical design, physical design, implementation, and maintenance (Hoffer, George, and Velacicho, 1996). The requirements definition phase has historically focused on the data being manipulated and on the business functions being performed. The focus of this case is on the different view of requirements resulting from the use of stakeholder and diffusion of innovation analyses. The data gathered and presented in this case were derived from interviews with representatives of each of the critical stakeholders at this implementation site. This case provides an example of the different types of information that result from analyzing requirements with these tools. Traditional system requirements tools result in functional-based information and typically did not contain broader stakeholder issues including interoperability, database connectivity, and e-mail requirements. The case data provide information to be used in generating a set of recommendations to be presented to the validation team and ultimately to Vice Admiral Bowes.

The Miramar Naval Air Station (NAS) is located in Southern California just north of the city of San Diego. The Naval Air Station chain of command is similar to other air stations and includes a commanding officer, executive officer, supply officer, aviation intermediate maintenance officer, administrative officer, security officer, and a staff civil engineer. At this base command, there are also several tenant activities. Tenant activities have their own chain of command, but they are located at the NAS and they rely on the NAS to provide infrastructure support including supply, facilities maintenance, and administrative services. NAS Miramar and the tenant activities who are participating in the NAST are potential users of the NAVWAN. (An organization chart is presented in Figure 2–3.)

Stakeholders

A stakeholder is defined as an individual or group who can affect or is affected by the achievement of a given mission, objective, or change strategy (Freeman, 1984; Freeman and Gilbert, 1987; Roberts and King, 1989). Stakeholders with significant interests in the implementation of the NAVWAN were initially identified. From this group each was asked who they felt the most significant stakeholders were and from that list 12 were selected. With inputs from multiple significant stakeholders it is believed that the resulting information is less biased and

FIGURE 2–3

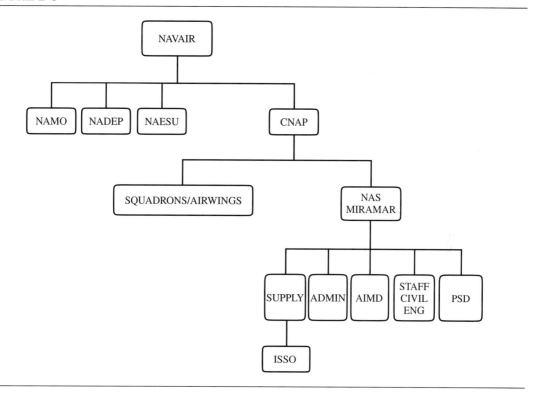

more complete. From the perspective of site-level implementation, NAST and the NAVWAN demonstration/validation team represent external stakeholders. Internal stakeholders include the departments within NAS Miramar and the tenant activities. Each stakeholder and the general mission of their organization is presented below. While the Department of Navy uses "alphabet soup" acronyms, a translated title for each of these stakeholders is presented in quotes and these will be used in the presentation of data in the case. The official organization title and acronym is also included:

a. *Validation team.* The NAVWAN demonstration/validation team was established by VADM Bowes. This team is led by the program manager responsible for the NAVWAN implementation at headquarters, Naval Air Systems Command. [NAVAIRSYSCOM]

b. *Maintenance office* is responsible for all aspects of naval aviation maintenance and administration programs. [Naval Aviation Maintenance Office: NAMO]

c. *Maintenance depot* provides intermediate-level aviation maintenance support for Pacific Fleet aviation activities. Intermediate-level maintenance reflects a more complex maintenance action that is beyond the capability of squadron and station organizations. [Naval Aviation Depot, NAS North Island: NADEP]

d. *Pacific Region aviation command* promulgates policy and asset management direction to all Pacific Fleet aviation activities. [Commander, Naval Aviation, Pacific: CNAP]

e. *Supply department* is responsible for all logistic and supply support required by the squadrons and tenant activities of NAS Miramar.

f. *Intermediate maintenance department* is responsible for all intermediate maintenance services required by the squadrons at NAS Miramar. [Aviation Intermediate Maintenance Department, NAS Miramar: AIMD]

g. *Administration department* is responsible for all postal and administrative services required by NAS Miramar personnel and its tenant activities.

h. *Civil engineering department* is responsible for all facilities maintenance, construction, hazardous waste management, and environmental conservation required by NAS Miramar and its tenant activities.

i. *Personnel* is the activity responsible for all personnel and disbursing administration for NAS Miramar and tenant activity personnel. [Personnel Support Activity Detachment, NAS Miramar: PSD]

j. *Aviation squadrons* are two aviation-type wings that are responsible for administration of all operational, maintenance, and administrative support for the squadrons located at NAS Miramar. There is one stakeholder representative for both commands. [Commander Fighter Wing Pacific: COMFITWING; and Airborne Early Warning Wing Pacific: COMEAWWING]

k. *Engineering support facility* is the activity responsible for providing technical support and maintenance training to organizational activities throughout the Pacific Fleet. [Naval Aviation Engineering Support Unit: NAESU]

l. *Information systems department* is responsible for providing information technology support to NAS Miramar and tenant activities. [Information Systems Support Office, NAS Miramar: ISSO]

Method

For purposes of gathering the data for this case, representatives of each of the stakeholder groups were individually interviewed in regard to the NAVWAN implementation.[3] Each of the selected stakeholders was personally interviewed (see Bayer, 1995, for elaborated discussion of methodology). Interviews took place in the stakeholder's office at times determined to be best for them. Each was asked a set of 15 standard questions and completed a five-question survey. Responses were recorded on tape and supplemental notes were taken by the interviewer. Each one-on-one interview lasted an average of 90 minutes. Each interview contains a common base set of questions with appropriate, unique follow-on questions pursuing issues particular to individual interviews. The following are the base set of questions.

1. Identification of the stakeholder.
   a. What is the name of the command representative?

---

[3]The responses are only attributable to the representative and may not reflect the opinions of the chain of command. Any mention of the stakeholder command should be attributed only to the stakeholder representative and *not the organization.*

b. What is the general mission of the command?

c. What role does information technology play in accomplishing the command's mission?

2. What are the functional requirements of the stakeholder's information systems?

a. Office automation (word processing, file transfer).

b. Communications (e-mail, message traffic, bulletin boards, Internet access).

c. Decision support systems (spreadsheets, DBMS, SQL).

d. Workstations (graphics, engineering drawings, project management).

3. To your knowledge, what are the current capabilities of the NAVWAN?

4. How does the NAVWAN's capabilities meet or facilitate achievement of your functional requirements?

5. Does use of the NAVWAN constrain the accomplishment of your functional requirements in any way? (For example, duplication of effort.)

6. Will the NAVWAN facilitate interconnection of existing information systems with commands beyond the NAS? If so, what other commands and for what purpose?

7. What other benefits do you expect to derive from interconnectivity with the NAVWAN? (For example, news groups and research information.)

8. What is the anticipated response of the users at the site to the NAVWAN?

a. Positive aspects? For example, increased knowledge or communication.

b. Negative aspects? For example, information security.

9. Do the users at your site understand the capabilities of the NAVWAN?

10. What motivation exists for them to use it? Is it important for their job performance?

11. Will you provide training to the users on the capabilities of the NAVWAN?

12. Will interconnectivity of current and proposed systems with the NAVWAN increase the productivity of the users? If so, how is this accomplished?

13. Does it directly support the mission of the activity? Is it supported by the chain of command?

14. Are there any barriers to the NAVWAN implementation at this site?

15. How will you overcome these barriers?

Interview Results

The information presented below represents a subset of the data gathered from the interview process described above. A complete report of the findings can be found in Bayer (1995).

Current Technological Environment

All of NAS Miramar offices are currently connected on an ethernet local area network (LAN). Each stakeholder has implemented LANs in an autonomous way and the systems used at stakeholder activities are not well integrated. These stakeholders have diverse missions and responsibilities. The NAVWAN is intended to be a conduit for them to communicate at the local, metropolitan, and global levels. This improved communication will better support the information requirements of the competency aligned organization. Also important, are the improved integrated communication capabilities offered to the larger Navy organization.

Although their missions differ, many of the above-listed stakeholders in the NAVWAN have similar information technology requirements. Because of the NAVWAN open-systems architecture, stakeholders do not expect it to significantly constrain their mission accomplishment. In fact, all of the stakeholders anticipated significant benefits from interconnectivity with an array of Department of Defense, federal, academic, and civilian organizations.

Interfaces and Interconnectivity

Interoperability seems to be the greatest constraint to the NAVWAN implementation. The demonstration validation team has not been able to overcome these interoperability problems at all the sites. Because they want to take advantage of the existing architecture, they cannot standardize everything to one system. They continue to have problems migrating the existing systems at the 22 NAVAIR activities to the four protocols selected for NAVWAN implementation. "It is technically feasible, but there may be some performance issues that we'll need to measure and correct," summarizes the validation team.

Air Station department heads and the information systems department were concerned about the LAN interface with the WAN. These stakeholders believed the LAN to be too limited in its capabilities. Currently the LAN uses category three coaxial cable and twisted-pair copper wire. This cabling infrastructure limits the speed of WAN transmissions. "If the performance of the WAN is limited by the LAN, people will not be that impressed, because it is definitely not high speed," according to the information systems department representative.

The engineering support facility is concerned that the NAVWAN will become one of many communication systems that must be periodically checked. Currently they must read the message traffic, check the fax machine, review electronic mail, answer the phone, reply to voice mail, and access bul-letin boards. They are overwhelmed by the number of existing communication tools. Consequently, the engineering support facility fears they will miss important messages because they are busy responding to another system. The frustration of having to log on and log off several systems was evident in the comments of the engineering support facility representative:

> The number of mailboxes with my name on it is ridiculous. I have to check them every day; sometimes several times a day. If they're going to bring the NAVWAN online, they need to eliminate some of these other systems and make everybody use it, instead of just adding another mailbox. Logging on and off all these systems . . . it's just too much.

The aviation squadrons representative also hopes that the introduction of the NAVWAN will consolidate current systems. In this command, not all personal computers are connected to the local area network or have modem capability.

> If a person wants to do word processing, they can use a Zenith 286 computer. If they want to send e-mail, they must find a computer on the local area network. If they want to access a bulletin board in another command, they need to find a computer with a modem.

All three functional capabilities are available somewhere, but not all are on any single computer. The LAN computers don't have modems and the Zenith 286 computers do not have network interface capability. Using multiple platforms to perform functions that could be performed on one platform is inconvenient and inefficient. "Providing NAVWAN access to everyone will hopefully eliminate this inefficiency," sums up the aviation squadron's response.

Previous comments were oriented toward a technical ability to be connected. Another aspect of interconnectivity is who is being connected and to whom or what are they connecting. "If the wide area network connectivity was coordinated on a Navy-wide basis, the NAVWAN would definitely be more beneficial because then you wouldn't need to figure out who is on the network and who isn't," said the administrative department stakeholder. She went on to say, "If you could eliminate the hassles of the Navy message system and put everyone on the NAVWAN, then you would really be helping us out!"

Although Internet access was not one of the initial functional requirements of the system, it quickly became an interest of all the stakeholders. During the presentations by the demonstration/validation team, it was repeatedly requested. Although stakeholders are interested in wide area connectivity between MILNET addresses, they were definitely more interested in Internet access.

Connectivity to On-Line Databases and Legacy Systems

The maintenance office representative is also a member of the NAVWAN demonstration/validation team. He views "easy-to-access corporate data with reduced or eliminated duplication of data risk" as the most significant benefit. He believes the users will "appreciate Internet access most, and the same or increased service at a reduced price." As part of the NAVWAN team, his job is to convince potential users that these benefits will outweigh the costs.

From the maintenance depot's perspective, the constraint of no access to the Internet is a big issue for the users. "This is a big requirement, which we want to provide, so we're looking for two large gateways for Internet access through a commercial source." The maintenance depot felt the functional requirements of the NAVWAN for the users would not be satisfied until Internet access was provided. Although it is not

an original functional requirement, it quickly became an issue with the potential users who consistently requested it during briefs and interviews.

Connectivity to on-line databases and legacy systems required by outside activities was also a common connectivity concern. Pacific region aviation command is most interested in running the naval air logistics command management information system (NALCOMIS) on the NAVWAN to the squadrons. This legacy system was developed many years ago to track maintenance data on airframes operated by NAVAIR. The validation team, maintenance office, and aviation squadrons also support this concept because "NALCOMIS is the only system most squadrons have at this time." By combining the NALCOMIS and NAVWAN initiative, Pacific region aviation command states, "they can both take advantage of existing resources and couple their assets for combined benefits. Coordination of this effort would greatly reduce the duplication of effort that is currently occurring."

Several stakeholders, including the supply department, intermediate maintenance department, personnel, and aviation squadron, require access to real-time database management systems (DBMS) particular to their missions including aviation maintenance, administration, and logistics information. They would also like the DBMS to have a structured query language allowing employees to make ad hoc inquiries and updates of logistics and maintenance material control data.

As expressed by the engineering support facility, "Unless all NAVAIR systems are accessible via the NAVWAN, it becomes just one of many systems available." The validation team determined that the initial functional requirements of e-mail must include an integrated user directory and simple file transfer. They did not intend to meet all the user functional requirements at the outset. NAVWAN functionality is seen by the validation team to be evolutionary. NAVAIR will continually evaluate user's functional requirements and add functionality in layers. "The next layer will use existing assets more and employ commercial off-the-shelf applications to minimize the development effort," says the validation team representative. "We will continue to address emerging requirements and try to merge requirements into the NAVWAN that will address multiple protocols," was the validation team assessment of the NAVWAN future capabilities.

E-Mail Improvements

The intermediate maintenance department is also dissatisfied with the current e-mail system provided on the LAN and felt the NAVWAN would be used more if the current e-mail system was improved. The maintenance depot, the intermediate maintenance department, and the supply department were the most enthusiastic about the possibility of the NAVWAN to improve e-mail throughout NAVAIR activities because they rely heavily on information and support from other NAVAIR activities to perform their jobs. E-mail communication and on-line database access will make their jobs much easier to perform by eliminating other less efficient modes of communication and reducing the delay time for aviation maintenance and supply management information.

The validation team also warns that e-mail is a democratizing agent in the organization that may affect the chain of command. If an airman wants to send the commanding officer e-mail, he can do so without asking his supervisor or division officer. Lastly, the validation team is concerned that business is depersonalized by not requiring face-to-face contact intracommand . . . people just send e-mail.

Diffusion of Innovation Survey Results

Following the interviews, each stakeholder was given a simple survey to provide a representation of how each perceived the project's innovation characteristics. Technical innovation may have obvious advantages over current systems, yet these innovations may not be readily adopted by implementers and users. Often, there is a lengthy period between the time in which an innovation becomes available and the time in which it is adopted. As a consequence, a common problem for inventors is how to increase the speed at which their invention is adopted. This speed, known as the diffusion rate, can be predicted using Rogers's (1983) paradigm. Rogers's research has found that the rate of diffusion of an innovation is determined by several attributes:

a. *Relative advantage* of innovation to current technology.
b. *Compatibility* of innovation with values, experiences, needs of potential adopters.
c. *Complexity* of innovation (i.e., difficulty of use).
d. *Trialability* of innovation (i.e., extent to which it can be experimented with).
e. *Observability* of innovation (i.e., are results visible, observable to others).

Stakeholders were asked to rate these five characteristics from high to low. The following five questions formed the basis of a diffusion of innovation survey:

1. Rate the level of relative advantage of the NAVWAN to your current information systems.
2. Rate the level of complexity of the NAVWAN for the average user.
3. Rate the level of observability of the NAVWAN by potential users.

4. Rate the level of trialability of the NAVWAN by the average user.
5. Rate the level of compatibility of the NAVWAN with the average user's current job.

The results of the diffusion analysis is displayed in the following Table 2–1.

Summary

Technologies needed to support the NAVWAN are available in the marketplace. The only technology-oriented concerns, therefore, are whether the correct combination of technologies can be determined, acquired, implemented, and maintained within this culture and resource environment.

Interview responses to the NAVWAN initial capabilities were generally positive but somewhat skeptical. Some of the stakeholders believe it would be technically infeasible to provide wide area connectivity across several platforms and multiple interfaces. Standardization of interfaces and platforms was repeatedly advocated to facilitate the implementation process.

TABLE 2–1 Diffusion of Innovation Frequency Distribution

	Low	1	2	3	4	5	High
1. Relative advantage				1		3	8
2. Complexity		1	3	2	5	1	
3. Observability		3	2	3	2	2	
4. Trialability			1	2	1	8	
5. Compatibility			1	3	2	6	

References

Bayer, V. R. C. *Analysis of Naval Air Systems Command Wide-Area Network Prototype Implementation.* Unpublished master's thesis, Naval Postgraduate School, Monterey, California, 1995.

Freeman, R. E. *Strategic Management: A Stakeholder Approach.* Boston: Pitman Publishing, 1984.

Freeman, R. E.; and D. R. Gilbert. "Managing Stakeholder Relationships." In *Business and Society: Dimensions of Conflict and Cooperation,* eds. S. P. Sethi and C. M. Falbe. Lexington, MA: Lexington Books, 1987, pp. 397–423.

Hocevar, S. P.; B. A. Frew; and V. R. C. Bayer. "Implementing a Wide-Area Network at a Naval Air Station: A Stakeholder Analysis." In *Cases on IT Management in Modern Organizations,* eds. M. Khosrowpour and J. Liebowitz. Hershey, PA: Idea Group Publishing, 1997.

Hoffer, J. A.; J. F. George; and J. S. Valacicho. *Modern Systems Analysis and Design,* Menlo Park, CA: The Benjamin/Cummings Publishing Company, 1996.

Roberts, N. C.; and P. J. King. "The Stakeholder Audit Goes Public." *Organizational Dynamics.* Winter 1989, pp. 63–79.

Rogers, E. M. *Diffusion of Innovations.* 3d ed. New York: The Free Press, 1983.

Assignment Questions

1. Develop a recommendation for the NAVWAN implementation using the data from the interviews as well as the results of the ratings of the diffusion characteristics of NAVWAN. The goal of the recommendations should be to improve the productive impact of NAVWAN to stakeholders. Each recommendation should be justified in terms of the data presented in the case and relevant course material.

2. Develop a proposed strategy for requirements definition that integrates what you consider the most effective aspects of the data-gathering mechanisms used in this case along with the traditional methodologies. Assume that you have been named as the team leader for the demonstration/validation team that is

responsible for systems design and implementation planning for a system at a new site. Outline the strategy that you would use drawing, as appropriate, on the methods implemented in the case as well as traditional methods.

3. Improve the wording of the diffusion innovation questions. How have your changes improved the data analysis and usefulness of the answers?
4. Analyze the data from Table 2–1. What conclusions can be drawn?

BILLBOARD CORPORATE ACCOUNTING SYSTEM

Bruce Johnson

Johnson sat in his office exhausted. It was almost quitting time on Thursday, the 11th of the month. Eric Accrue, the accounting department's liaison with the information systems department has just informed him that the final step in the month-end accounting process had run successfully and the books were closed for last month. This indeed was good news. Eric's boss, Billboard's comptroller, would now be off of Johnson's back—until the beginning of next month. And the department, particularly the data center, could begin to return to normal. But at this very moment everything was in disarray. Customers, whose processing had been delayed while the accounting system hogged the computer, were upset. Johnson's systems and programming staff was demoralized and exhausted from the constant pressure required to push the accounting runs through. Systems development work that had been promised had been delayed—again. And worst of all, it would all happen again next month. Nor was Johnson happy with finishing the closing on the 11th.

Granted that this was better than the 13th (a Friday no less) last month, but the goal had been the 9th and they could have made it—if Eric had not taken two days off to go sing with the symphony chorus.

Bruce Johnson was manager of systems and programming (S&P) for Billboard Publications.[1] He had been with the firm just under a year. Prior to that he was a consultant to Billboard. As a consultant he and the firm he was with had successfully designed several systems, including sales reporting, catalog preparation, and closed-end book club. Billboard subsequently made Bruce an offer that he could not refuse to become manager of systems and programming. But Billboard's management had not lived up to the terms of the agreement. Johnson did not have the resources or flexibility to solve Billboard's many information systems problems. He and his staff were continually fire fighting and being whipsawed as priorities changed as often as daily, and occasionally even more often, based on the "squeaky wheel gets the grease" philosophy of priority setting practiced by Billboard's management.

This case was prepared by Bruce Johnson, Xavier University, as the basis for class presentation and discussion rather than to illustrate either effective or ineffective handling of an administrative situation.

[1]For background information about Billboard Publications, please refer to the Billboard Charts case.

The first problem Johnson tackled after becoming S&P manager was the monthly accounting closing. At the beginning of every month, Billboard's accounting and data processing departments went into panic mode as they attempted the month-end closing required to produce the monthly profit and loss statements. The accounting system was antiquated. It had been developed for a prior generation of hardware and software and no one really understood how it operated. Usually it had taken until the 20th of the month to close the books. Only occasionally, when they were lucky and a month ended on a Friday, had they been able to close by the 15th.

Johnson took several actions that improved and sped up the closing. He overhauled the closing operation using the existing computer programs and manual operations. This systematization included taking advantage of the priority and multitasking capabilities of Billboard's new computer system. In addition, as much processing as possible was done at night or on weekends with critical personnel scheduled to be available during this processing. A critical path schedule was laid out each month at a marathon meeting of the accountants and systems professionals. Johnson and his staff were continually on the lookout for ways to simplify, speed up, and further rationalize the month-end accounting marathon—anything to reduce the month-beginning madness. While this did reduce the time, stress, and panic it was still very far from satisfactory. And, in truth, there still was a great deal of stress as both the accounting and information systems departments were held hostage each month until the books were closed. But this was not the ultimate source of Johnson's dissatisfaction.

Johnson, knew that neither he, the departments, nor the company could survive with the level of panic required by even the improved closing procedures. So he immediately began trying to implement a long-term solution. As soon as possible, even while overhauling the existing closing procedures, Johnson established a project to produce the requirements for a new accounting system. A team consisting of himself, members of his S&P staff, and key accountants was formed. They began to analyze the requirements and capabilities for an up-to-date accounting system. Prior to the first meeting of the project team, Johnson reproduced a copy of the requirements and design notebook that had been recently produced for the closed-end book club system. He changed the name of the project on the cover, title, and table of contents pages. At the team's first meeting, Johnson handed out to each participant this thick notebook with "Billboard Accounting System Design Specifications" on the cover, title, and the table of contents pages. As soon as everyone had a chance to glance through it he said. "Here is a completed design document with all the requirements for a system. This is good news and bad news. The bad news is that it is not our accounting system, it is for the closed-end book club system we developed last year—I have just changed the project name—the rest is for the book club system. The good news is that we are not starting with a blank page. All we have to do as a team is to replace these specifications, bit by bit, with the specifications for our new accounting system. We can use the computer, the word processor, itself to help us record our understanding of our requirements and how to implement them as they develop—and we can continually update them and distribute copies to each member of the team. Thus we will not know the terror of a blank page. In addition, these book club specifications will give us a clear idea of what we have to do."

This approach to developing a requirements and design document had worked for

Johnson before. In fact, Johnson believed strongly that the word processor was one of the best system design tools ever invented. The use of a word processor facilitates the capturing of thoughts and ideas in their infancy and then enables them to be fleshed out, incrementally, as they develop into a full-fledged understanding. This, he thought, is a vast improvement over the days of typewriters and typists. In those days analysts had reason to be reluctant to record their thoughts or the specifications until they were fully developed—which of course they never were—since change was so burdensome. This meant that documentation and likewise the project itself lagged.

But his optimism soon faded. Month after month the (reduced) panic produced the accounting statements and yet nothing was accomplished toward a long-term solution. The design team made minuscule progress toward a modern accounting system. In fact, some months the team, as a whole, never met at all. The accountants, of course, could spend no time thinking about the new system during the first part of each month. Until the books were closed and the financials were produced they were swamped with debits, credits, accruals, adjustments, and the like.

But even when the monthly crisis was over the accountants were seldom available. In fact, it was next to impossible to get a critical mass of the accountants on the "team" together at one time. There were multiple reasons for this lack of availability but the results were the same—no progress toward a long-term solution. There did not appear to be any way out of this monthly crisis. Actually, the monthly crisis appeared to be one of the problems. Once it was over the accountants sort of split. Some just took time off. Some were at other sights. Johnson could do nothing about the accountants' unavailabil-ity for these reasons. But, often one or more of the accountants were off investigating accounting packages—in Florida, California, or some other desirable location. Johnson was truly frustrated by this.

Johnson tried in vain to convince the comptroller and the accountants—specifically Eric Accrue—that looking at existing accounting packages was a waste of time until they had a set of specifications to compare them to. And since the accountants did not have specifications, these boondoggle trips were actually delaying the day when Billboard would have a modern accounting system and the monthly panic would end. But they did not listen and continued to bask in the sun in the name of the project. In addition, no "information" from any of these "investigative" trips was fed back into the project. And, what is more, neither Johnson or other S&P team members were involved in any of these trips. They were hostages back at the home office fighting fires.

Thus, even if Johnson had the resources and stable priorities to implement such a system he could not do so for the lack of specifications. As he wearily locked his office, full of unextinguished project fires, and headed for his car he said to himself, "How can I ever get off of this merry go round?"

Assignment Questions

1. Can a successful system ever be developed without user involvement?
2. Was Johnson's rationalization of the existing month-end closing part of the reason he could not get specifications for a new system?
3. Should Johnson have refused to partake in the month-end closing unless the accountants spent time on the task force?

BILLBOARD CHARTS

Bruce Johnson

"But Bill, I can't believe you have done it again! What about all of our meetings and discussions?"

"Yes, I know, Bruce, but I and other management are under pressure to assure continued operation of the charting system in case something happens to Ed or Susan. Thus we have hired ABC Consultants, from downstairs here on the 10th floor, to document the charting system so that it could be carried out in their absence."

"I know of your concern and I support it," said Bruce Johnson, manager of systems and programing (S&P), from his office in Cincinnati. "But why not use S&P personnel from here in Cincinnati to help Billboard kill two birds with one stone: develop a modern-interactive charting system and assure its continued operation independent of a few key personnel?"

Johnson, who was an engineer by training, had been manager of systems and programming for almost a year. Prior to that he had worked for a consulting firm on the Billboard account developing an open-order bookclub system and a catalog production system which were now in operation. He brought to Billboard a range and depth of experience in on-line, interactive, database-oriented systems. But as an engineer and technical person he tended to be apolitical. He often called a spade a spade.

This case was prepared by Bruce Johnson, Xavier University, Cincinnati, OH, as the basis for class presentation and discussion rather than to illustrate either effective or ineffective handling of an administrative situation.

"We just can't do that, Bruce," responded Bill Evans, vice president of sales, from his office on the 19th floor of Billboard's corporate offices in New York City. "We can't spare your people from the priority projects that they are already working on. Nor can we bring enough analysts up to speed fast enough to do this internally."

Evans had been with Billboard for almost five years. He originally was with one of the publications that Billboard acquired. He rose to the position of vice president of sales primarily due to his extensive contacts in the industry. Billboard's computer operation reported to him through Dave Reinhardt, data processing manager, who was Johnson's boss. Evans was experienced in dealing with computer systems but had almost no technical knowledge of how they worked or what was required to develop and operate them. He was a conciliator and tended to react to the most recent squeaky wheel. This caused Johnson and his staff of programmer–analysts a great deal of consternation as priorities shifted on a day-to-day basis making it very difficult to make progress on the many projects that they were working on.

Johnson, seeing that again he was getting nowhere, signed off and disgustedly hung up the phone. Evans was doing it again. He had authorized ABC Consultants from New York City, no less, to "document" the charting system which took place in Los Angeles. Johnson had tried, unsuccessfully, many times to convince Evans that since the charting system was so far out of date it was essentially useless to document the system as it exists. Such an effort was a total waste of the corporation's funds.

Billboard Publications, while headquartered in New York City, had their main operating facilities, such as computer operations, warehousing, and publications, in Cincinnati. While the *Billboard Newspaper* itself was published in Cincinnati, its editorial offices were in Los Angeles which also was where the actual charting data was produced.

Billboard (officially BPI Communications) a publications conglomerate has published its flagship publication *Billboard Newspaper: The International Newsweekly of Music, Video and Home Entertainment* since 1888. It has worldwide operations consisting of, but not limited to, magazine, catalog publication, and book publication (Watson-Guptil Publishers), book club operation, airplane music (Music in the Air), and the like. It has a loosely run, artistic, sales-oriented, culture which has had a difficult time adapting to the disciplined requirements of computerized operation. So while Billboard has a stable of computer applications most of them automate manual operations and are oriented toward cost reduction and not toward obtaining a competitive strategic advantage.

The *Billboard Newspaper* publishes lists of the top selections in a wide variety of music types and categories. This is called charting. The charting data is collected and processed in Los Angeles and sent via courier to Cincinnati for publication independent of the company's central computer operation. Producing the lists uses an antiquated system that is literally made up of punched cards, rubber bands, chewing gum, paper clips, and, above all, unique expertise contained only in the minds of a few key personnel in Los Angeles. Johnson has not been to Los Angeles to review or observe the existing charting system in action. While Evans goes to L.A. regularly, he has never specifically investigated the charting system while he was there.

Granted, the charting system is an undocumented, antiquated, accident of history that is subject to failure if key personnel with unique knowledge of the system are hit by the proverbial truck. But, what strikes Johnson as even more critical to the company's success is that the charting operations fails in any way to take advantage of the company's modern well-managed computer data center in Cincinnati.

Management in New York City correctly worries about the vulnerability of this key process. While Johnson is sympathetic with management's desire to document this important process he is, however, skeptical of management's ability to manage such a process so that it will produce the information and security desired; hence he feels that their response is incorrect. Management, on a regular basis, has hired, at premium rates, local and national consultants to produce detailed documentation of the charting operation. This has been done independently of the systems and programming group who regularly protest this action. Johnson knows that there have been several such projects predating his time with the firm. These multiple efforts have produced nothing but expense. And as yet no procedures independent of the key personnel in L.A. exist. Based on knowledge gleaned from talking to Evans and other executives, Johnson has no expectations that this time things will be any different. The net result is that several rounds of this "documentation" have produced only expenses that could have been better spent modernizing. No useful documentation has been produced. The company continues to limp along with an outdated and undocumented process that is vulnerable to misfunction or malfunction.

In addition, Johnson has discussed, pleaded, and argued with Evans and other executives about the advantages of a modern up-to-date redo of the charting system.

Several times he has proposed a project to determine the requirements of such a modern up-to-date charting system. He has suggested that a team of analysts and charters be formed to determine how charting can be done with the help of a modern interactive computer system. The basic difference between Johnson's approach and Evans's approach is that Johnson's approach stresses how charting should be done given a blank slate and today's technology, whereas Evans only wants to "document" the system as it is. Johnson has great expectations regarding the synergy that could develop given the Billboard's charting expertise, the computer systems expertise of his staff, and the capabilities of Billboard's computer facilities. Documenting the current accident of history system, even if it were successful, would produce little of value that would help overcome the current systems deficiencies.

In fact, as Johnson leaned back in his chair after hanging up from his call with Evans, he recalled a prototypical meeting attended by himself, Evans, Dave Reinhardt, and Joe Slake, the manager of the department in Cincinnati that publishes the magazine and hence the charts themselves. In addition, Sam Duncan, the publisher of *Billboard Newspaper,* was available by phone from his office in Los Angeles. The meeting started out with Johnson presenting his proposal for a study project (see Exhibit 2–9—Attachment 1: Proposal for a Study to Determine the Feasibility and Initial Design of a New Cincinnati Computer-Based Charting System).

"Given six person-months of effort over the next six months we could determine the nature and feasibility of replacing the existing charting system, with its inherent dangers and risks, with an up-to-date modern system that could take advantage of our state-of-the-art computer facilities together with the expertise of our analysts here in Cincinnati and the expertise of Ed and Susan and others in L.A. This would be a significant step toward both reducing our risks from the system as it now stands and taking strategic competitive advantage of new technology and current knowledge, neither of which are really utilized in the current system."

"Oh Bruce," said Evans "you are always wanting to study things and develop new systems. We already have a charting system . . . all we need to do is to document it so that we can continue to produce the weekly charts if something happens to Ed or Susan. I don't see the competitive strategic advantage of a new system, particularly given the likely cost. A chart is a chart is a chart."

Joe Slake stirred animatedly in his chair and spoke out: "I disagree with that Bill. Sam and I have discussed many times the delay inherent in gathering the data in L.A. with our primarily manual methods together with the difficulties and costs encountered with getting the data to Cincinnati in a timely manner. We think the type of system Bruce here is proposing will reduce the delay in getting the chart data into the newspaper by at least a week. Think of what a strategic advantage that would be to our readers and advertisers, not to mention Billboard."

Dave indicated that he agreed with Johnson's proposal and stated that the facilities in Cincinnati could handle such a system with minor additions of hardware or staff. Ed and Susan also stated that they and their cohorts would eagerly welcome such a new system. It would make their jobs much quicker and easier. They also stressed the competitive need for additional charts which, while discussed for some time, were not being published due to lack of resources and capabilities.

Evans hurriedly left the meeting to catch his plane back to New York City. On his way

---

EXHIBIT 2–9   Attachment 1: Proposal for a Study to Determine the Feasibility and Initial Design of a New Cincinnati Computer-Based Charting System

---

Objective: To determine the feasibility (costs) of replacing the current primarily manual outdated charting system with a new system utilizing the Cincinnati data center, telecommunications, and other potentially viable technologies together with Billboard's proprietary knowledge of charting and the skills of Billboard's systems analysts.

Goals: (1) To take advantage of current technology for competitive advantage. (2) To reduce (eliminate) dependence on a limited number of key personnel to assure continuity of operation so as to protect the corporation.

Participants: From systems and programming in Cincinnati: Bruce Johnson, Alan Schneider.
From magazine publication in Cincinnati: Joe Slake
From charting in Los Angeles: Ed Clementia, Susan Riker.
Ex officio: Sam Duncan, Publisher *Billboard Newspaper,* Los Angeles.
Time line: Six months from authorization and funding.

Approximate cost: Salary and wages (existing personnel) $35,000. Travel $11,000. Other $3,000. *Total cost:* $49,000.

Deliverables: Report outlining high-level design and ongoing operation. Resource budget (personnel, software/hardware, costs, time required, etc.)

---

out he said, "I will consider what has been said and presented here today and get back to you in a week or two after I have consulted with the other officers in New York."

As Johnson contemplated his just completed phone call with Evans, Dave Reinhardt walked into his office. Dave had a familiar look on his face indicating that another change in direction for the information systems department had just been instigated by the folks in New York. Dave's look along with meetings such as the one he just recalled caused Johnson to think of his overloaded schedule and that of his staff and wondered what action he should or could take. "How should I handle this," he said quietly to himself, as he nodded to Dave to take a seat. He further thought "I am so discouraged at picking up the pieces after Evans and others when I know how to avoid the crises if I could only get up-front control of the systems."

Assignment Questions

1. What was the level of involvement of S&P? Why weren't they involved more?
2. What was Johnson's frustration all about?
3. How did the current system come about?

Chapter 3

System Specification and Design

This chapter presents a great deal of information about system specification—which is a statement of what the new information system will do—and design—which describes how the new information system will operate. A number of tools and techniques are described here which may be employed to improve the efficiency of this stage and, hopefully, to improve the quality of the resulting information system.

SYSTEM SPECIFICATION

It is necessary to create a statement, agreed upon by both user and systems analyst, that describes what the new information system will do. The statement should contain a number of sections, of which the major ones are described as follows. One section should present the problems of the current information system. Another section should describe the new information system requirements. A further section could describe any current restrictions that might limit the choice of a new information system. The completed document not only will represent agreement between the parties involved, but also will be available to provide guidance and resolve conflicts as the project progresses through subsequent stages of the SDLC.

DESIGN

In this stage a description of how the system will operate is developed. Various tools and techniques may be employed to describe the components of the new information system. Specific alternative solutions should be identified and the "best" one should be chosen for development, based upon the current environment.

Tools and Techniques

The following paragraphs define and provide a brief description of the various tools and techniques that may be employed to describe the components of the new information system.

1. **Entity analysis:** This analysis brings into focus the objects that are significant to the business through the production of an entity–relationship diagram (ERD), which shows the meaningful relationships between entities. ERDs consist of entities and relationships. Entities define a category of unique objects of importance to the information system and relationships show how entities are associated with each other. Also, as part of this entity analysis process the attributes of an entity will be identified. Attributes, which are the descriptive components assigned to each entity, will be used late in the generation of the data dictionary and, eventually, in the development of the database that will support the information system.

2. **System modeling:** A system model is a representation of an information system using tools such as data dictionary, data flow diagrams, and process descriptions.

   a. Data dictionary (DD): The data dictionary provides a common source of reference. It is meant to describe the data used by the information system. Entities in the data dictionary may be data elements or data structures. A data element is data that will not be decomposed further into any other logically into any other meaningful data item. Data structures are meaningful groups of data elements.

   b. Data flow diagram (DFD): The data flow diagram is primarily a graphic tool that shows what happens to data as they flow through an information system. A data flow diagram is constructed using four components. A source destination is outside the boundaries of the information system and either supplies data or receives data from the information system. A process represents work that must be carried out and describes the transformation of data that pass through the process. The flow represents a parcel of data that moves between the processes, as well as to and from any source/ destination. The parcel of data is described in the data dictionary. A data store represents a repository of data and is employed when data are held for a time, or when data will be accessed in a different order from the way they entered the information system. Data flow diagrams describe the information system by presenting different levels of detail within the process symbol. The top, most general, level is called the context diagram. The lowest level includes processes referred to as functional primitives, which means that the process will not be further partitioned using data flow diagrams;

however, the activities involved in the functional primitive will be described in more detail using the tools described in the following process descriptions section.

c. Process descriptions: Process descriptions provide a detailed description of the rules governing the work to be carried out by a process. Three tools may be used here.

   (1) **Decision tree:** Decision trees are graphic documentation tools that sequentially present conditions and the subsequent actions to be taken. Although there are a number of different types of decision trees, the type used here is called "nested decision logic" because the action to be taken depends on the result of the evaluation of the conditions existing in the data presented to the process.

   (2) **Decision table:** Decision tables employ a method of concisely specifying the decisions rules to use when evaluating certain conditions, and the resulting actions to be taken based upon the result of the evaluation.

   (3) **Structured English:** Structured English presents text in a visibly logical format. A sequential structure may be used to present a linear progression of tasks. A decision structure may be employed to show successive actions to be taken based upon a decision. Decision structures usually employ the *If . . . Then . . . Else* construct. The more sophisticated case structure may also be used to depict a series of mutually exclusive choices.

OTHER METHODS

There currently exists a series of tools, techniques, and methods that may also be applied to the activities of the SDLC stages and which will contribute to improving both the efficiency of developing the information system and the resulting quality of the information system. These various approaches are described in the following subsections.

Prototype

This approach involves the development of a model representation of the proposed information system. The modeling approach may be iterative or throwaway. Prototyping provides rapid feedback, helps delineate requirements, reduces the time before the user sees something concrete from the system design effort, and brings about meaningful user involvement.

Computer-Assisted Software Engineering (CASE) Tools

These are tools that may be used to assist the systems analyst by supporting in some way the various stages of the SDLC. Front-end CASE tools provide support to the initial SDLC stages relating to problem identification and requirements determination. Back-end CASE tools support the production of the information system. Integrated CASE tools represent a combination of front-end and back-end CASE tools.

Application Packages

An existing information system may be acquired, usually from a software development company, to adequately address all the requirements for the new information system. Acquisition of such software should result in less time to complete the SDLC stages and improved quality of the information system.

End User Development

This approach is another way to reduce the time required to develop an information system because the user becomes directly involved in the design of the solution. The strategy adds to the total number of persons working on the various SDLC stages.

Outsourcing

This approach involves acquiring the services of an external organization to perform a certain function usually performed within the company. Although this concept can be applied to any part of a company, with regard to information systems development it typically refers to acquiring external services to perform any or all SDLC stages.

Business Process Reengineering (BPR)

This concept suggests that a broader perspective be taken when considering the development of an information system. So, instead of simply trying to generate a solution that will be more efficient, a more effective solution should be sought. This approach requires that those involved in the information system development process reevaluate what the system is supposed to do as well as how it will be done.

Knowledge of Information Technology

As the knowledge of information technology becomes more widespread throughout society, the ability to apply the underlying concepts to the resolution of business problems becomes more commonplace; thus, it is possible to involve more individuals in solving more business problems through the application of information technology and the development of information systems.

COST/BENEFIT ANALYSIS

Cost/benefit analysis is a method of comparing the costs and benefits, on an equal basis, of each acceptable design alternative. This analysis is conducted when enough information is available to compare design alternatives. Thus, procedure details must be known for each alternative. Also, the amounts for each component of the cost and benefit categories must be known or capable of being estimated. Methods used to compare alternatives include break-even point analysis, payback analysis, rate of return, and net present value. The "best" alternative is not only the alternative that provides the most benefit for the least cost, but also the one that is appropriate for the current economic and industry environment of the organization.

INFORMATION SYSTEM DESIGN COMPONENTS

An information system may be designed by concentrating on specific components of the system. These components are output, database, input, control, and codes.

Output Design

Output is the main reason for the development of an information system. Useful information is essential to gaining acceptance of the information system. Output can be presented in the form of hard copy reports or screen displays. Each of these alternatives may include text and/or graphics. In all of these cases the use of color can enhance the presentation of the information.

Database Design

Data storage in the form of a database is considered by some to be the heart of the information system. The two major considerations in database design are data availability, ensuring that data is available when the user wants it;

and data integrity, ensuring that both accurate and consistent data are stored in the database.

Input Design

The goal of this stage of the SDLC is to determine the input process so that transactions can be quickly and accurately entered into the information system. Business transactions are recorded on source documents which contain data that change the status of a company resource. In some cases these transactions may be entered directly into the information system through some form of source document automation. The quality of the input will determine the quality of the output.

Control Design

Procedures must be designed to establish and maintain control over the physical movement and quality of data. Control procedures must ensure the accuracy and reliability of data processed by the information system, and check on the accuracy as data move from one function to another. Both manual and automated procedures will require some processes meant solely to ensure that the information system and its data are under control.

Code Design

A code may be defined as an ordered collection of symbols designed to provide unique identification of an entity. Codes should be designed both for optimum human-oriented use and machine efficiency.

THE CASES

Cincinnati Health Department

Bruce Johnson

In this case an organization decides to acquire a package through the services of a software vendor. The package seemed to meet all the functional requirements, both a perfect match and affordable. A request for proposal (RFP) is issued and all seems to be progressing well when a problem arises regarding data storage capacity.

Laurier Phone System (A and B)

Ron Craig

> Installation of a new digital phone system has gone poorly. It is the busiest time of the year and people are upset. The acting vice president of finance and administration must make immediate decisions and develop a plan to correct the situation.

South Dakota Worker's Compensation

Bruce White

> This case presents a situation about the processing of worker compensation claims. Alternative methods are considered in an attempt to improve the work flow and processing of claims.
>
> The Department of Labor for the State of South Dakota is a state agency charged with handling the labor-oriented issues for the state. One of the functions of the Department of Labor is to handle worker's compensation claims. The workload has been increasing and the Worker's Compensation Division is experiencing space problems. Over the years the workload has grown so that the current system of handling worker compensation claims has been stretched. The material is stored in file folders in several rows of file cabinets. Various alternatives are considered in light of the identified requirements and the constraints of the specific situation.

Holly Hotel

Gordon C. Everest

> In this case the student is asked to prepare a data model. A high-level data modeling scheme should be used. The use of a data modeling case tool would also provide good experience. The problem, to which the data modeling concepts are to be applied, relates to the operation of a hotel. The hotel management desperately need computer support to keep track of rooms, facilities, reservations, guests, the usage of allied services, and billings. Such computerization would enable them to better serve their customers and guests, and make more efficient use of their facilities and staff.

Systems Analysis and Design at Trundles

Len Fertuck, Yolande E. Chan, and Richard J. Simm

> This relatively comprehensive case is based upon the operation of an exclusive restaurant. The case starts with the students developing a project plan.

The case then proceeds through the determination of information requirements, the documentation of systems design using entity–relationship diagrams and data flow diagrams, and the preparation of user interfaces. Finally, an evaluation of the project is conducted.

Ms. Ehree Hospital

Len Fertuck, Yolande E. Chan, and Sherry L. Jack

This is another relatively comprehensive case based this time on a patient care system of a hospital. As in the previous case, this case commences with the students developing a project plan and then proceeds through the determination of information requirements, the documentation of the system design using entity–relationship diagrams and data flow diagrams, and the preparation of user interfaces. The case is concluded with the preparation of a project evaluation.

CINCINNATI HEALTH DEPARTMENT

Bruce Johnson

Andy Anderson's, spirits took a nose dive as he read the words, ". . . defaulting on the contract." After a year of requirements determination, study, design, development of a request for proposal, award of contract, and sizable expenditures, the task force he led was now without a viable option for the Cincinnati Health Department's Health Care Information System (CHD–HCIS). Though he had already been informed of the default by phone, the letter made its stark reality come to life. As Andy reread the letter he

thought back over events related to the project trying to assess where his outstanding team of analysts had gone wrong. But he knew that he had to focus on the future and the decisions that he must now make. He quickly reviewed the events of the past year or so.

A thorough request for proposal (RFP) had been written by his team of analysts from which a bid for an off-the-shelf (OTS) system was received that was a perfect match to the functional specifications, was affordable, and conformed to the political realities. The team had visited the vendor and via observation, demonstration, and in-depth questioning determined that: "Yes, the OTS system met the functional specification." The team was ecstatic.

A contract was signed and it was believed that work was underway when word came

This case was prepared by Bruce Johnson, Xavier University, Cincinnati, OH, as the basis for class presentation and discussion rather than to illustrate either effective or ineffective handling of an administration situation.

by phone and now via the letter from the vendor's parent corporation making it official: they would not install the system and thus they were defaulting on the contract. As Andy saw it, as a result of this default, the health department's timetable for installing their HCIS was in serious jeopardy.

He believed that the task force had designed and specified a system that would meet the department's needs for the foreseeable future. Many who had been involved, in addition to Andy, such as the health commissioner and the members of the board of health, were aware of the importance of having such a system in operation. But now, where were they? He remembered the meeting at which the task force really hit stride and how well they proceeded from that point on in overcoming the complex relation between the Health Department and the City of Cincinnati and melding the temporary group into a cohesive task force.

As Bruce Johnson introduced himself and his firm to the members of the Cincinnati Health Department Automation Task Force, he noted that some of them did not appear to welcome him. This was particularly true of Andy Anderson, assistant health commissioner for administration, to whom the task force reported. While members of the task force were knowledgeable regarding health care administration and computers some felt that they needed additional expert professional help in the area of database design which they had come to see as an important aspect of the project. They had prevailed on Andy to invite Bruce, as a representative of his firm, to one of their meetings to pursue engaging his firm to help the task force with database design issues even though Andy and others felt that adding new members to the task force at this time would be counterproductive.

Bruce briefly introduced himself and his firm and then began asking questions to help him understand the nature of the project the task force was undertaking. After initial introductions and pleasantries, Ginny Gunderson, Andy's assistant, said, "We have a large federal grant to develop a health care information system that, among other things, will tie together our 11 clinics so that clients' records (charts) will be up to date and available regardless of which clinic or clinics they attended."

Johnson took notes while he listened intently. When Ginny finished and turned to him, he asked "What exactly do you mean by health care?" This question caused puzzled looks on the faces of the participants including Derek Brower, a consultant from Chicago, who was leading the task force. Derek turned to Andy, then to Ginny, and finally to Bruce and said, "Well, we had not gotten that basic. Our starting point has always been the existing chart and client records." After several moments while the group pondered Johnson's question and Brower's response, Johnson opened his briefcase and pulled out a paperback dictionary. He read the definition of *health* and of *care* to the amazed group assembled around the table. Andy, particularly, was flabbergasted. Here was a computer techie with a dictionary in his briefcase going back to the beginning reading basic definitions in his effort to understand the project. As the discussion continued, Andy's opposition to adding Bruce and his firm to the task force soon faded and he became an avid supporter of the idea. By the time that the meeting broke up the task force members were convinced that precise meanings, as demonstrated by this dictionary exercise, were important to the project and that precise definition of the meanings of their data would be essential to the design of their database.

Within a few meetings, Bruce became a full-fledged member of the task force. He became aware of the multifaceted nature of the project and the players. Not only was the project itself large and complex but the relationship between the health department and the City of Cincinnati was a significant factor in how they could proceed.

Johnson confirmed that the health care information system would have to be an on-line, interactive, database system. The clients of the 11 health care centers came from a highly mobile population. Thus the need to access up-to-date charts and to record services from multiple locations was paramount. The complexity of medical records, the variety of services offered, the intricacy of reimbursement schemes, the need for rigid security, reasonable response time, etc., meant that the functional specifications for the system were multifaceted and demanding.

The Cincinnati Health Department is a quasi-independent agency of the City of Cincinnati, governed by a board of health that appoints a physician as health commissioner. In some ways, the health department is independent of the city. However, in one very important aspect, from the task force's point of view, the health department is very dependent on the city. The department's purchases come under the jurisdiction of the city's purchasing regulations. Thus, for a project this size, full-scale competitive bidding was required. However, since the city had a blanket contract with Control Data Corporation, Control Data hardware, software, and services could be acquired as an add-on to the blanket contract without competitive bidding. Early in the project the decision was made to, if at all possible, operate any system developed or acquired on a Control Data computer, since acquiring hardware by another vendor would require an elaborate, costly, and time-consuming competitive bidding procedure that would draw the project out increasing its costs and thus reducing its benefits.

The task force investigated multiple options to fulfill its charge to install a health care information system for the department. The task force's first choice was to acquire, with as little adaption as possible, an existing system that would meet the department's functional needs and run on Control Data hardware. Their second choice was to adapt an existing system even if it ran on "foreign" hardware. Since, based on their initial search, finding an existing system did not seem too likely, consideration was given to developing a system in-house as their third choice.

During the requirements and initial design phases, the activities were the same independent of which option was chosen. While they were determining requirements, designing the system and its database, and producing functional specification, Bruce was studying and gaining experience with Control Data's database software. Control Data's database software was CODASYL-based, using a network approach. The schema data declarations generated ready-to-use data record declarations in COBOL which was the language of choice for the system in case an in-house development was required.

From time to time, the task force felt quite constrained by being limited to Control Data equipment. But when faced with the onerous procedures required by the competitive bidding process they concentrated their efforts on using Control Data hardware. Since the task force had limited people resources they were hopeful of finding an existing system that could be tailored to meet their needs. The task force was also aware of its temporary nature, having been pulled together for the duration of the project. Thus an actual in-house implementation of such a system appeared to be beyond their means.

About this time a very serendipitous event occurred—at least it appeared to be so at the time. A health-screening system used by a consortium of companies in New York came to the attention of the task force. They carefully studied the literature on the system and talked at length by phone to customers and vendor personnel. This system supplied by American Health Corporation (AHC), a subsidiary of Control Data Corporation, appeared to meet the developing specifications of the CHD–HCIS. And the system ran on Control Data hardware!

As a result of this positive initial evaluation of AHC's screening system the team went to NYC to view its operation firsthand and to further question its users and the vendor. They watched it in action. And again they talked to customers as well as vendor personnel. Not only did the system appear to be just what they needed but it also ran on Control Data hardware. In fact AHC was a subsidiary of Control Data.

The team returned from New York ecstatic. They concentrated their efforts on developing an RFP which simultaneously spoke to the functional specifications they had been developing and the characteristics of the system they had seen and observed. The RFP was for the software system only. Control Data hardware would be acquired through the city's blanket purchase agreement. After the RFP was issued they anxiously waited for the response period to end. During this time there was not much task force activity but they did continue to meet and hone their understanding of the health department's ongoing requirements.

When the deadline for RFP responses arrived there were only two respondents: AHC and Alfa Zin Corporation from California. Alfa Zin was quickly disqualified as their system did not run on Control Data

hardware and it fell short of the specifications in several key areas: namely the number of sites that it would handle and its medical record handling capabilities were severely limited. AHC was awarded the contract. The euphoria resulting from this effort was short-lived however and it soon turned to devastation when AHC defaulted on the contract.

As Andy gathered members of his task force together they pondered what, if anything, they had done wrong, and what they could or should do now to get the project back on track. One thing that they were very anxious to find was: Why had AHC defaulted after bidding from, what appeared to the task force to be, an unassailable product?

Postmortem

The task force subsequently determined that the default was actually precipitated by Control Data, the parent, because the underlying architecture of AHC's system could not handle the long-term data storage needs of the CHD–HCIS. AHC's system, as a screening system, only held each individual's medical record until the results of all the tests performed on that individual were gathered and a report, relating to a given screening visit, was issued. As soon as this was verified, all the data relating to that individual was deleted. The CHD–HCIS required that the medical record for an individual be stored for an indefinite time. It was not a matter of the absolute storage required; that could be handled with extra hardware storage devices. It was a matter of the "address space" in the proprietary database manipulation code underlying AHC's system. The number of bits provided for the data address was insufficient to access the storage capacity required for the CHD–HCIS.

These limitations in the address space architecture would require AHC to entirely rewrite the underlying database storage and accesses portions of their system to handle the health department's requirements. This implied significant losses on the contract which Control Data was not willing to underwrite. While the personnel from AHC had planned to proceed with this rewrite, they were prevented from doing so by their parent corporation who held the purse strings.

The task force felt betrayed and professionally derelict that they had not uncovered the fatal flaw in AHC's system. Furthermore they were very angry that the city did not hold AHC's feet to the fire and instead had let them default with no signif-

icant penalty. AHC and Control Data forfeited their bid deposit (an insignificant amount) leaving the health department without a system and with a large expenditure of money and, even more importantly, of time. But since the city's purchasing regulations came under the purview of the city and therefore, city council, there was nothing more the health department could do beyond pressuring the city, which turned out to be of no avail.

Assignment Questions

1. Who were the decision maker(s); what role did he/she/they play?
2. What were the constraints?
3. What were the alternatives?

LAURIER PHONE SYSTEM A

Ron Craig

"Why can't I get an outside line," Ralph wondered out loud. It was 8:00 A.M. on the first day of classes at Wilfrid Laurier University and Ralph was checking his cellular phone voice mail. He redialed, and after a couple of tries got through. "I hope everything is alright with the phone system," he thought.

He swung his chair around and logged onto e-mail. Among his many messages were two about the phone system upgrade. The univer-

sity was upgrading from an older analog phone system to a modern digital one. August had been a hectic month and not much had gone according to plan. Schedules had slipped as unexpected problems surfaced.

During the past week the major "cutover" had been completed. In preparation the new switch[1] had been installed right beside the old one, and some external lines were connected to it. Gradually users were moved from one system to the other. The final cutover was an overnight job, and involved removing all remaining external lines from the old switch and making it a slave to the new one. The cutover had not gone smoothly, and Northern Telcom engineers had to be

[1]Exhibit 3–1 explains the technical terms used in this case.

EXHIBIT 3–1   Terminology

Analog signals:
  These involve a continuously varying electromagnetic wave; older phone systems were designed entirely for analog signals. Signal distortion increases with distance.

Central office exchange (CO):
  Telephone company switching station for a district. Contains switching and control facilities. The first three digits of your seven-digit phone number reference a particular CO.

Channel:
  A communication path. Through technologies such as multiplexing, a high-capacity (bandwidth) channel can be divided into several lower-capacity channels.

Digital signals:
  These involve discrete sequences (0, 1 states). Voice signals represented this way can be treated as any other computer data. It is easy to keep a digital signal "clean" while it is transmitted vast distances.

FX line:
  Foreign exchange line. Allows a user to call a distant location without incurring any charges other than for a local call. Based on leasing direct lines to another city.

ISDN:
  Integrated systems digital network. A standard that integrates digital transmission and switching technology to support both voice and data (video, graphics, text, etc.) communications.

Switch:
  Allows interconnection of any two circuits (lines) connected to the switch. The basis for routing phone calls. Switches are used internally in organizations (PBX—private branch exchange), and by the telephone company (e.g., central office).

Tie line:
  Connects or "ties" two switches (or other communication equipment) together.

Trunk line:
  Voice lines connecting to a switch. This can be from a Bell Central office, or between on-site switches.

WATS:
  Wide area telephone service. A fixed monthly fee is charged for a fixed number of hours of circuit usage. A form of measured use service. Bell now includes this type of service as part of their "Advantage" portfolio.

---

called in (electronically) to diagnose the problem. What had been expected to be a three- or four-hour job took 10 hours. However, allowance had been made for potential problems, and the installation crew was happy to have completed their task before the university opened in the morning. The system was now working cor-rectly according to their diagnostic testing. Users were experiencing some ongoing problems, but it was not clear if these were due to their inexperience or to technical problems with the system.

Almost half the campus was now on the new switch, which was Laurier's connection to the outside world. The other half would continue to use the old switch, but were now routed through the new one when dialing outside or to the other half of the campus.

The original plan was for everything to be done during August, the quietest month on campus. The conversion required new wiring in many areas, delivery of new phones to every office and room that was being converted, training of staff "trainers" (one person from each major area, who would provide training to others), and finally the conversion from the old switch. The actual switch conversion had been scheduled for the last weekend in August, allowing a week for teething problems to surface and be remedied before students returned after Labor Day and classes started the following week. The first week of classes is the busiest time on campus; August provided the quiet time needed to make the changes while offering the least disturbance for staff and faculty.

The e-mail messages did not shed much light on Ralph's problems in getting an outside line. Installation of new phones was proceeding. It was taking longer than expected to connect people, and the original schedule served only as the sequence in which departments were being upgraded. A small department might only have four or five lines, and larger departments two or three dozen. Some departments were losing their phone service for several hours during the conversion.

It did not take long to realize that the system was not working correctly. By 9 A.M. people were calling Ralph, sending him e-mail messages, and coming to his office. People on the west end of the campus, who were still on the old switch, were having trouble connecting to the rest of the campus and beyond. When they did not get an external line, they were being disconnected unexpectedly. The two groups most affected were the senior administration (the president and

vice presidents) and the School of Business and Economics. Certain departments in the arts and science faculty were having problems, as was the business office. In the middle of a call to the United States, the president's line was cut off. Ralph started to use his cellular phone, from his office, for all external calls.

Ralph tracked down the university's telephone technician, who was working with Bell personnel on the conversion. Bell technicians were already working on the problem, which seemed to involve the connection between the remaining part of the old switch and the new main switch. People on campus who were directly connected to the new switch were not experiencing the same problems as those still on the old switch.

Phone System Background

In the early '80s Laurier was among the many organizations that stopped renting phones from Bell and invested in its own phone system. The university had purchased a Tie Mercury switch, along with hundreds of phones for campus users (faculty, staff, and students). External lines were still rented from Bell, but the university was responsible for the maintenance of its internal system.

Initially the local distributor of the system provided maintenance services and this worked well. System software was occasionally upgraded, providing additional features for users. Over time, though, the company lost market share, and eventually both the manufacturer and the local distributor went out of business. When the local distributor shut down, Laurier hired the technician who had been providing service for the university system. Many other local organizations (including a local hospital) had purchased similar equipment, and the people responsible for these various systems kept in touch with each other. As the systems aged, they even shared spare parts on occasion.

Phone responsibilities at Laurier rested with the purchasing department. This arrangement had gone along relatively smoothly for the past number of years, and no one had reason to question it. The purchasing manager, to whom the technician reported, had no background or expertise in telecommunications, and relied upon the technician for technical decisions. Overall, the Laurier phone system had functioned well for many years and costs were very reasonable.

By the early '90s the telcom scene had changed dramatically. Digital systems had become the new standard. Bell was in the process of upgrading its remaining analog central offices, and had recently converted the last of its regional equipment to digital. Fiber-optic lines were being laid on high-traffic routes. Many local firms had exchanged their old phone systems for modern digital ones or were contemplating such a move.

By this time Laurier had some experience with digital systems. Expansion of one part of the campus in the late '80s led to the addition of a Northern Telcom digital switch (a Meridian M21). This switch served people in the east end of campus, and connected to the main Tie Mercury switch. The university's telephone technician was sent to Northern Telcom for advanced training on the Meridian digital switching technology.

With a phone system that was becoming obsolete, and not upgradable, the university considered the alternatives. Ongoing growth resulted in increased phone usage on campus, which began to push the capacity of the current system. It was becoming more difficult to maintain the system, and there was considerable concern about what might happen if the main switch failed. More than ten thousand calls were

processed daily through it, both internally and externally. There were also safety and security concerns, as the telephone is the usual way of contacting emergency services both on or off campus.

A new digital system would be more efficient and effective. It would include features like voice mail and an auto attendant to take incoming calls on a 24-hours-per-day, seven-days-per-week basis (reducing or eliminating the need for switchboard operators). Maintenance costs would decrease. The new system would be upgradable, allowing new features to be added as available, and system capacity to be increased as needed.

Investigation of alternatives had been going on for more than a year. Price was a major concern, as early proposals carried a cost in the million dollar range. By the end of June 1993, when the university had closed its books for fiscal 1992–1993 and initial financial (although not yet audited) statements had been prepared, a decision was made to allocate $300,000 from the year's surplus for phone upgrading. This decision was subsequently approved by the board of governors on July 28, 1993. The upgrading would be done in two stages (spreading the cost between fiscal years). The budgeted $300,000 would cover the first phase, while the second phase was anticipated to cost an additional $150,000. Figure 3–1 shows the original centralized configuration proposed by Bell, and the final distributed configuration that was implemented.

Two contracts were signed with Bell on July 26, for a total cost of $301,635. Bell had started detailed work on the project on July 21, and had developed a 45-step critical path. This project plan identified activities, start and completion dates, and prime responsibility. Sandy, Laurier's telephone technician, was to be the project manager.

FIGURE 3–1   Switch Configurations Considered for Laurier

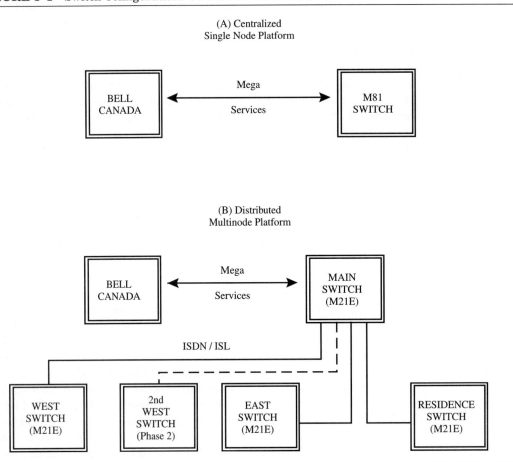

(A) Centralized
Single Node Platform

(B) Distributed
Multinode Platform

According to the project plan, cutover to the new system would occur on August 31.

The residence phone system, serving some 1,200 students, would be taken over by the university (it was currently rented from and maintained by Bell), and long-distance lines would be used mainly by university faculty and staff during the day and by students in residence during the evening and on weekends. Students would be charged Bell rates for long distance, less a 15 percent discount. Revenues from this charge would help pay for the phone upgrade, and students would benefit from lower long-distance charges. The change would require a switch for the residences, tie lines between the residence switch and the main campus switch, and installation of digital phones in all residence rooms. Since voice mail would be a feature of the new system, it could also be made available to students at an additional monthly cost. A nearby university charged their residents $12 per month for voice mail.

The Acting VP

Ralph was filling in for one year for the vice president of finance and administration. He officially moved into the office on August 1, and had spent the preceding two weeks with the VP. Ralph had just returned from a sabbatical in Australia, and the VP was now on his own sabbatical. It was not easy to get hold of the VP now, and Ralph clearly understood where the decision-making responsibility lay.

Planning for the phone conversion had been completed prior to Ralph's arrival, and he was so busy familiarizing himself with his new job that he was pleased to leave things to the individuals involved. That approach had not lasted long—on his first day in the new position he was told that $65,000 of additional equipment was required for the conversion to proceed as planned, and it would take two weeks for the equipment to arrive, and that the cutover schedule was in jeopardy. He authorized the additional purchase (uncertain where the funding would come from), then commenced to find out how this oversight had occurred and what could be done about it.

Upon his return in July, Ralph had been excited when he first learned of the planned phone upgrade. He knew that digital systems followed the ISDN standard and would handle both data and voice signals, which could reduce the use of modems across campus. It should be easy to provide computer access in all residence rooms. Voice mail would be provided. He was told that everyone on campus would have access to it. Students in residence would be charged a monthly rate, which would generate revenues for the university. Faculty and staff who were on the part of campus that would still be serviced by the old switch would also have access to voice mail. This meant that

the administration (of which he was part) and the School of Business and Economics (heavy phone users) could soon make use of this feature even though it would be another year before their switch was upgraded.

While Ralph's formal education was not in MIS or telecommunications, he had taken on some computing responsibilities when he joined the School of Business and Economics in 1979. He had introduced microcomputers to the school and the University in the early '80s. He had furthered his MIS education by attending comprehensive faculty development workshops during the summers of 1986 and 1988 (these sessions were sponsored by the American Association of Collegiate Schools of Business and were aimed at developing competent MIS faculty from Ph.D. holders who had not received formal education in the area). At both of these he had learned more about the telecommunications side of information systems. He had no experience with the operating details of phone systems, and he had no experience evaluating and purchasing them. Now this was changing. He liked to think of bad experiences as a learning tool, as a method of developing "scar tissue"; his favorite formula for competence was "ST/TSA $\rightarrow$ 1" (i.e., when the ratio of scar tissue to total skin area approaches one, you are competent). While he still did not feel competent to deal with the problem, he was becoming well informed and developing that much-needed scar tissue.

More Problems

By the end of the next day Ralph had a better understanding of the situation. Bell technicians had identified several problems. Apparently the new digital switch was so much faster than the old analog Tie Mercury switch that it gave up waiting for signals. Consequently, users who were still on the old switch and had to go through the old switch to the new one in order to get an outside line, were being abruptly dropped in the middle of conversations. A possible solution was to break the 24 bidirectional tie lines into two sets of unidirectional lines—half coming in and half going out. That way, the digital switch wouldn't assume that momentary inactivity on the tie line meant the conversation was over. If needed, more tie lines could be added between the switches, to a maximum of 32. From a queuing perspective, it is more efficient to have bidirectional tie lines. However the choice was now between less-than-optimal efficiency and unsatisfactory service.

Students had moved into residence (almost 1,200 of them, plus dons), and many didn't have their phones. In August it had been discovered that the wiring diagrams for the residences were inaccurate. This meant that every phone installation required "toning" of the lines before correct connections could be made. One person would work from the room, sending a signal down the line, while another worked in the wiring room, identifying the correct line and making the proper connection to the wiring block. Original plans had been to simply sweep through the residences, remove the 586 old analog phones, change the connecting plugs, and plug in the new digital phones. A one-week job for one person had become a three-week job for a crew. To expedite things, the work was contracted to Bell (at a cost of some $33,000). It was now the first week of classes and two residences were still unfinished. It was expected they would be completed by week's end. Needless to say, students who had already paid their residence and phone fees for the term were quick to complain.

Unfortunately first-year students had been told early in the summer that they could bring their own phones and answering machines. The residence staff had not found out about the phone upgrade until August, and did not realize then that analog and digital equipment is incompatible. So students were plugging in analog devices and "freezing" their lines. Correcting frozen lines meant manual intervention every time, as a technician reset the software instructions in the residence switch. Even disconnecting the digital phones produced the same problem, as students in one apartment-style residence moved the phone from the common area to their bedroom when they wanted to make a private call.

As more residence phones were successfully converted, busy signals were common during the day and evening. There simply were not sufficient tie lines between the residence switch and the main switch to handle the volume of calls. The new switches operated on the ISDN standard, with 1.544 Mbps channel structure (primary access). One channel was divided into 23 voice channels (B channels, 64 kps each) plus one signaling channel (D channel, 64 kps). There was a single primary channel between the two new switches, and this could be expanded to two primary channels, adding another 24 voice channels (since the signaling channel was already in place). If this were done, the M21E switches would be at their physical limit.

The problem with the residence phones also affected people phoning in (especially parents anxious to check on their son's or daughter's status during the start of term). Particularly annoying for them was being connected to the main university switch (and incurring a long distance charge) then getting a busy signal when they dialed the residence extension number.

And students were not the only ones to complain about problems. Typical of Ralph's e-mail was a message (see Exhibit 3–2) from one of the deans.

EXHIBIT 3–2   E-Mail Re Faculty Concerns

Date: Tue, 14 Sep 1993 10:51:18-0300 (EDT)
From: alan drurrey F <adrurrey@mach1.wlu.ca>
To: ralph creichton <rcreicht@mach2.wlu.ca>
Subject: Telephone system (fwd)

Hi Ralph . . . the kind of messages that I have received for the last week . . . maybe a SOS should go out from your office . . . thanks, Alan.

—————Forwarded message—————
Date: Tue, 14 Sep 1993 08:52:54-0300 (EDT)
From: jill mccormick F <jmccormi@mach1.wlu.ca>
To: "alan drurrey (sbe)" <adrurrey@mach1.wlu.ca>,
    "rob leslie (sbe)" <rleslie@mach1.wlu.ca>
Subject: Telephone system

I am sure that you have been inundated with complaints but I would like to add my concerns.

Since the conversion of a week or two ago, our phone system has been hopeless. We can't assume that we will get an out line, callers can't get through to us, and we are getting cut off midconversation. As an example, I got cut off two times in 5 minutes on a phone call from Idaho yesterday. As usual, I had to resort to going downstairs and using a pay phone to complete the call.

If this was temporary, I suppose I could live with it. However, things show no signs of improving—a caller yesterday was apparently told by switchboard that "there are now less lines to the Peters Building" and the implication was that the problem would continue.

I think we need to recognize the conditions that academic programs staff have been facing—a phone system that doesn't work during registration, and a second-rate academic software system that is not living at all up to promises.

I appreciate that there is likely little that can be done but some enquiries about the "real" situation would be appreciated.

Thanks, Jill

Complaints were also received from faculty and staff who were modem users. Most computer users on campus were directly connected to the main computer, while a few people used modems for connection to external systems. A general notice had been sent out to the university community in August about the implications of the change, but many modem users had not realized how it would affect them and so had not notified telephone services. It was possible to leave analog lines in place, so that modems could still be used, but this required an analog/digital conversion card on the switch (incurring additional costs and taking up a slot).

Adding to the confusion was a dramatic increase in calls to the switchboard from people with questions or complaints. In addition, the daily number of calls to and from the university was up over 50 percent from September of 1992.

Action Required

It was now late Tuesday afternoon. Ralph had more than a dozen major projects to manage, and now there was the phone system. People were upset and demanding answers. Here he was, only weeks into a new position, and apparently the sky was falling. Fortunately the president had been supportive and was leaving it to him to solve things, without adding additional pressure.

Assignment Questions

1. Recommend a plan of action to Ralph. Consider both the short-term (immediate) and longer-term (a six-month) horizon.
2. What do you think went wrong, and why? What could have been done to avoid the problems?
3. Discuss the organizational, economic, technical, and managerial issues in this case.
4. What lessons can be drawn from the case?

LAURIER PHONE SYSTEM B

Ron Craig

"Well," said Ralph, "I think we have all the information we need to make a decision. We need to do a sensitivity analysis of our options, and that should be easy. Then we'll see whether or not one option stands out from the others."

This case was prepared by Ron Craig, Wilfrid Laurier University, as the basis for class presentation and discussion rather than to illustrate either effective or ineffective handling of an administrative situation.

Copyright © 1996 Wilfrid Laurier University. Distributed through Laurier Institute, School of Business and Economics, Wilfrid Laurier University, Waterloo, Ontario, Canada N2L 3C5. Please address enquiries to the Coordinator of Management Case Sales.

Background

Upgrading the university phone system from an older analog[1] system to a modern digital one had not gone according to plan (see the Laurier Phone System A case for more information). The plan had called for development of a distributed system of three switches. Two switches were now in place, but performance was unacceptable for many users. The third switch was to be added during the summer, replacing the remaining analog switch. Figure 3–2 shows the existing campus phone system configuration, including switch type and location, number of users on each switch, and lines attached.

[1] A glossary of technical terms can be found in Exhibit 3–1 of the Laurier Phone System A case.

FIGURE 3–2 Current Configuration

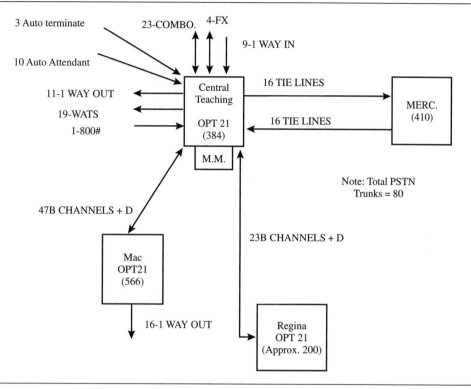

Many unexpected problems had arisen during the August–September 1993 initial changeover. While the problems affecting daytime phone use by faculty and staff had been resolved, there were problems remaining in the university residences. During the evening, people in residence had great difficulty accessing a line. Moreover, outside callers would get through to the main university switchboard, then hear a busy signal when they dialed a residence extension. Parents, in particular, were frustrated with the long-distance charges and lack of access to their sons and daughters. Residence staff had concerns about safety—in an emergency it might not be possible to use the phone.

In early November, more than halfway into the fall term, the problems persisted.

Bell had completed line monitoring studies and analyzed the results. Even this process had not gone smoothly—a monitoring computer failed during the first two-week test and the study had to be repeated. Since line usage varied by time of day and day of week, it was important to have a two-week history before drawing conclusions. The repeat study had to be delayed until after the Thanksgiving holiday weekend.

Bell's line availability analysis showed that blockage on the residence lines occurred routinely after 7 P.M. on weeknights. Demand for local lines peaked between 7 and 11 P.M., and was heavy until 1 A.M. Residence long-distance usage peaked during the midnight to 1 A.M. period (even though the highest long-distance discounts kicked in at 11 P.M.). The Brampton FX trunks were overloaded during the afternoon and evening, while the WATS trunks were only overloaded between midnight and 1 A.M. The availability analysis also showed that the tie trunk between the main switch and the Regina switch was more than adequate (12 trunks needed, 23 existing).

The availability data had to be interpreted carefully. When blockage is occurring, phone users may try repeatedly to get a line, exacerbating the problem and contaminating the data. As well, resident had undoubtedly changed their calling patterns in response to the problems they encountered, so there was a significant "hidden" demand. With these qualifiers, the data showed when blocking occurred.

Bell made a presentation to the university in November, recommending a $225,000 multistage solution for both the residence and other campus phone problems. At that point, Ralph decided to find a consultant who could work with the university to solve this problem. He had talked with Nikki, director of computing services, the previous month and she had used her e-mail network to ask her counterparts at other Ontario universities for recommendations. So he had some names. A few calls to his own counterparts provided him with backgrounds on people who ran the phone systems elsewhere. Then he called some of these managers and asked about their experiences with consultants. Trent University had used a person from KPMG and recommended him highly. Ralph contacted this person, was impressed with his knowledge, and subsequently verified all the references provided (some from the private sector and others from the college and university environment).

In late November an initial meeting was held with the consultant, Mike. Ralph now had a project team together—the manager responsible for telephone services, the direc-

tor of computing services, and himself. Also in attendance was Sandy, Laurier's sole telephone technician.

The meeting proved extremely productive. Two issues were on the table—what could be done to alleviate the immediate problems, and what should be done for the longer term. Mike knew the questions to ask Sandy, and Sandy knew the answers. Together, they identified some quick remedies. As Mike probed, Sandy realized that while the Macdonald switch was at capacity in terms of cards in the racks, several cards were only partially utilized. In all, 32 ports were still available, though spread over several cards. By utilizing each card in the switch fully, two could be removed and line cards (which connect to external lines) could be substituted. This would give an immediate improvement in service labels as 16 external lines could be added (for a total of 32). As well, a long-distance call monitor could be attached to the Macdonald switch, allowing long-distance calls to go out over the local lines attached to that switch. (All long-distance calls from the residences had been routed through the tie trunk to the main switch, where a monitor recorded usage for later billing. The tie trunk between the Mac and main switches reached capacity every weeknight, blocking many incoming and outgoing calls.) While the solution meant that costs to the university would increase because of the additional lines, reduced use of the FX and WATS lines, and rental costs for the second monitor, service levels would increase significantly as there would be much less traffic on the tie trunk. This was the type of breakthrough that was needed, and everyone at the meeting was elated.

In fact, the next day Bell informed the university of a CRTC decision regarding external lines. Up to this point, Bell had to charge separately for local, FX, and WATS lines. As of December 1, Bell would be allowed to provide these separate services, but could also combine them into existing lines with an appropriate discounting pricing structure. For Laurier, this meant that instead of having external lines designated either local or long distance (FX or WATS), and paying higher tariffs for long-distance calls on local lines, any external line could be used for any purpose. So the decision to add 16 lines to the Macdonald switch and open them to outgoing long-distance calls would have less financial impact—there would only be the cost of the additional lines (about $65/line/month, including taxes) and the monitor rental (about $400/month). Given Laurier's volume of long-distance calls (in the range of $65,000 per month for the university and residences), there was a flat 55 percent discount.

Bell monitored the revamped residence system in mid-January, when students were back and the winter term was under way. The study showed the only problem remaining was with incoming calls, which had to come through the tie trunk from the main switch to the Macdonald switch. The midnight-to-1 A.M. period was the busiest, and then blockage was still common. On some weeknights it began around 11 P.M. To correct this "B channel" problem would require adding up to 28 trunks—which was impossible, as both the main and Macdonald switches were at capacity. But overall use of the phone system by residents was up, and most people were very pleased with the improvements (although some were still upset by the peak-time blockage and lack of voice mail). The number of outgoing lines at the Mac switch had been increased to 40, with one dedicated to 911 use as a safety consideration.

At the project team's November meeting, the possibility of returning the residences to an analog system had been discussed seri-

ously for the first time as well. This could be accomplished by installing analog/digital conversion cards in the switches. There was no possibility of delivering data over the current lines because of the capacity problem, so that potential benefit of the digital system was gone in any case. Even with an upgraded switch it would not be viable financially to carry data on the lines, so the idea of providing access to the university computer system from every residence room via the phone system would have to be dropped. Computing services had a few study rooms in residence wired for computer access, and this service could be extended to more rooms in the future. The investment in digital phones (586 at about $150 each) was a sunk cost, but many of these phones could be used in the final phase of the conversion for the rest of the campus. Residents had been told that voice mail would be available after November 1, but it had become apparent that the current system did not have the necessary capacity—in fact, it could accommodate only 200 users in total. About 15 residence floor dons had been given the service, but that was it. Back on an analog system, students would be able to use their own phones and answering machines, and disconnect their phones and move them without causing problems (as described in the Laurier Phone System A case, incoming residents had brought analog phones with them; every time the phones were plugged in, the line went down). By mid-February, the project team had agreed that whatever the chosen overall solution for the campus upgrade, the residence lines would be changed back to an analog system.

The team met several times during December, January, and February, and focused their discussions on the upgrade—defining "must-have" capabilities versus "nice-to-have" (see box below) and exploring options. Issues needing further consideration

Necessary Criteria:

1. Acceptable service level—less than 2 percent blockage at any time for any user.
2. Satisfy projected changes and demand increases for the next 10 years.

Desirable Criteria:

1. Minimize overall cost, based on revenues and expenses, both initial and ongoing.
2. Minimize initial capital outlay.
3. Minimize risk re changes to future revenues and expenses (implications of CRTC decisions).
4. Easier maintenance of the system.
5. Easier administration of the system.
6. Conversion ease—minimize disruption during conversion.

were identified and dealt with. Only solutions meeting all "necessary" criteria were considered further.

Alternatives Considered

Figure 3–2 shows in block diagram format the alternatives being considered for the upgrade. While all met the "necessary" criteria listed above, they varied significantly on the "desirable" criteria. An explanation of each, with additional cost information, follows.

Alternative 1: One Big Switch (Figure 3–3)

The first alternative suggested by the consultant was to install a Meridian Option 81 switch, using all possible equipment from the existing switches. This could be either an AC- or DC-powered system. Bell pricing incentives made the DC option preferable, even though it would not allow as much reuse of existing equipment as the AC option. Every campus user would be connected directly to this switch, as would all external lines. Capital costs would amount to $468,785.

Technically, the Meridian Option 81 would provide an elegant solution. There would be adequate capacity for both the short and long term, and the "B-channel" issue would be eliminated. One set of facilities would provide full phone and voice mail services, simplifying management and administration of the system.

Alternative 2: Original Bell Proposal (Figure 3–4)

This proposal was received from Bell in November, before the consultant was engaged. A four-stage process would be used to solve the immediate problems and complete the phone system upgrade across the entire campus. Rebalancing would move frequent users from a heavy-traffic switch to a lesser-used switch, and would involve both reprogramming the switch software (approximately 30 minutes per user moved) and wiring room jumper changes (approximately 10 minutes per user). Total costs

---

FIGURE 3–3   Alternative 1: Centralized Single Node Platform

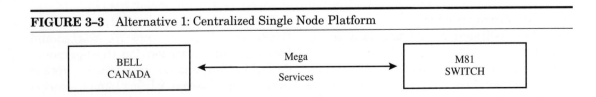

FIGURE 3–4　Alternative 2: Distributed Multinode Platform

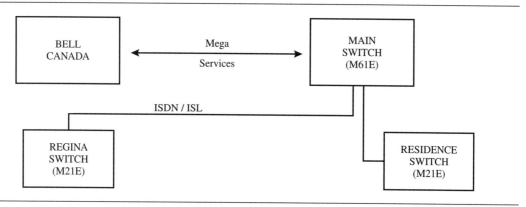

(including taxes and allowing for power protection) would be $259,609. The university would be responsible for all rebalancing. Bell's solution addressed operational and service problems in the short term, but would have growth limitations (the Option 61 switch has a port capacity of about 1,350, depending on the mixture of cards and features installed, while the M21 switch supports up to 600 users). From a system administration view this was a potentially "messy" solution as it required an evaluation of traffic and users each term, with possible subsequent rebalancing.

Alternative 3: Revised Bell Proposal (Figure 3–5)

Late in January, Bell presented a new plan, which would upgrade the central teaching switch to an Option 61 and return the residences to Bell (their "Student Residence Plan"). The current residence switch would be removed, and 90 percent of its parts used in upgrading elsewhere on campus. The total cost (including taxes and power protection) would be about $132,791. Each residence phone would have its own number and Bell would maintain the entire residence system. Bell would bill the university

monthly and provide an itemized list of costs. Laurier would bill students for their long-distance calls, and the monthly line-rental charge would be included in residence fees.

This solution addressed short-term service issues. While the capital cost was attractive, the consultant raised these considerations:

- The contractual agreements associated with this alternative would likely prevent the university from taking full advantage of revenue opportunities such as long-distance "affinity" programs with resellers such as ACC Corp.
- Bell indicated the service was a nonstandard offering (although the company had recently negotiated an agreement with the University of Waterloo); its availability in the longer term could be an issue.
- The plan appeared to be based on a "sharing group" of students, administered by the university. KPMG understands the sharing-group concept to be the subject of possible representations to the CRTC by Bell's competitors.

FIGURE 3–5   Alternative 3: Distributed (Residences Separate)

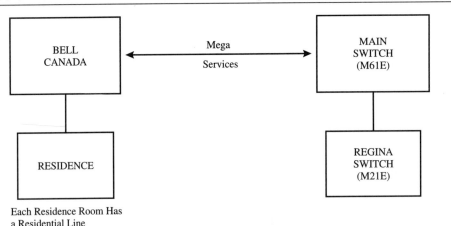

Each Residence Room Has
a Residential Line

- The cost/revenue analysis presented by Bell assumed a high level of participation by students. The level of participation might not be sustainable in the longer term as direct marketing of long-distance services becomes more intense. In fact, Laurier and Bell could be required to present students with alternatives as part of the introduction of equal access (automatic connection to the long-distance provider of your choice) this summer.

Alternative 4: Upgrade Both the CT and Mac Switches (Figure 3–6)

Last, the project team considered upgrading both the residence and the main campus switch. The Mac switch and residences would be converted into a stand-alone system, with full voice mail and trunking services. The capital costs, including a UPS (uninterruptible power supply) for both switches would be about $249,474. This alternative would address the capacity issues and allow the university to control revenue from student long-distance calling and voice mail.

Factors to Consider in Selecting a System

Ralph felt considerable pressure to stay within the $150,000 budget figure that had been suggested to him when he became Acting VP of finance and administration for the year. However, he wanted to consider all costs and benefits, both initial and ongoing. In addition, there was great uncertainty about the revenue side from student long-distance use. Ralph's preferred means of dealing with uncertainty was to do a sensitivity analysis, using optimistic, realistic, and pessimistic scenarios.

The project team worked with the consultant to identify all the costs, revenues, and risks. There were the initial capital costs. Then there were ongoing costs, including administration and trunking. Administration costs were estimated at $186,900 per year for alternatives 1 and 2 (providing for a technician, part of a manager's time, clerical

FIGURE 3–6   Alternative 4: Decentralized and Distributed

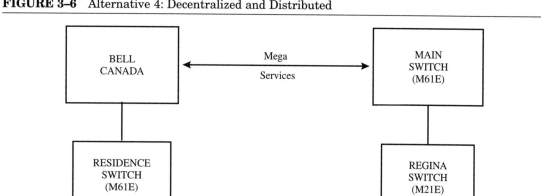

support, switchboard operators, and housing-office costs associated with preparing long-distance billing and managing residence phones). Alternatives 3 and 4 would eliminate one part-time switchboard position, saving $15,000. And alternative 3 would result in additional clerical savings of $6,000 per year.

While there was considerable uncertainty about growth in the next decade, Ralph was certain there would not be a decline in the number of students either on campus or living in residence. Government funding for universities was under review and the best guess was that it would change to encourage more growth. Historically, the university system in Ontario had grown at an annual rate of 3 percent, and Ralph saw this as an upper boundary. It was reasonable to assume that Laurier would experience growth somewhere within these limits, and that growth would lead to a corresponding increase in phone use.

One new building was being constructed on campus, and plans had been made to move some departments to the east end of campus (which would add more users to the

Regina switch). The Regina St. move would require an estimated $13,800 in upgrade costs for the switch there (alternatives 2, 3, and 4) and $7,500 for installation. The new science building would incur $15,000 in installation costs.

For alternatives 1, 2, and 4, annual revenue to the university from direct charges to residents was estimated to be $85,000 ($45,000 for line charges and $40,000 for administrative overhead). For alternative 3, Bell would pay the university $3/month/line during the academic year for administering the billing. All the alternatives would generate some revenue from long-distance services provided to students. For alternative 3, the potential revenue during the fall and winter terms (September through April) was estimated to be $10,000 per month and $0 during the summer (May through August). Alternatives 1, 2, and 4 would result in revenues of approximately $12,800 per month during the same period. While the university had considerable control of the overhead and administration charges included in residence fees, there would be far less control of long-distance revenue. For alternatives 1, 2, and 4 Laurier would still control all the phone lines and so could expect continued revenue from student use. However, there was uncertainty about the gross level of billings, as long-distance rates were expected to decrease. Using an optimistic estimate, net revenues would not be eroded over the next 10 years; using a pessimistic one, net revenues would decrease by 15 percent per year for two years, 5 percent the following year, and then hold steady. For alternative 3, there was the possibility that future CRTC rulings, or student pressure, could result in other carriers picking up some or all of the residence traffic. An optimistic estimate for this alternative was that net revenue would hold steady for 10 years, while a pessimistic one was that it would drop 15 percent next year, 5 percent the following year, and then be lost entirely.

Also under alternative 3, since Bell's Advantage discount was based on annual volume, the university would incur increased long-distance charges. Currently, Laurier received a 55 percent discount, and this would drop to 45 percent if the residence long distance was withdrawn. The financial impact would be about $3,000 per month.

Trunking costs would vary by alternative. For alternatives 1 and 2, 110 lines would be required to handle all university and resident phone needs adequately, at a cost of $65/month/line. For alternative 3, 70 lines would be sufficient to handle the university's needs. And under alternative 4, the economies of sharing lines between the university and the residences would be lost, resulting in a total of 160 lines required (again at the business rate of $65/line/month). Ralph also had concerns about a recent CRTC ruling regarding measured

costs,[2] which could have a significant effect on line costs. Bell estimated it would be mid-1996 before such a program would be introduced. While the CRTC had not addressed residential threshold pricing, it seemed reasonable to assume that this would follow.

General maintenance costs, including replacements parts and possible Bell maintenance work, was estimated at $10,000 per year for alternatives 1, 2, and 4 (approximately $15 per telephone), and $5,000 per year for alternative 3. All the new equipment would carry a one-year warranty, so maintenance costs would not commence until a year after the upgrade.

Decision

Place yourself in the role of the consultant. The project team is meeting again next week, and you are to make a recommendation at that meeting.

Assignment Questions

1. Recommend a plan of action to the project team. Justify your plan.
2. Compare the A and B cases. What lessons would you draw from Laurier's experiences?
3. Are there other factors Ralph has not considered that could affect costs or revenues?

---

[2]With computer communications making increasing use of telephone lines, Bell recognized that their pricing structure, based solely on people talking to each other, was no longer appropriate. Under threshold pricing, the monthly line rental fee would include network access (dial tone), unlimited incoming calls, and a fixed amount of outgoing local calls. Any outgoing local calls exceeding this amount would be charged on a usage basis.

4. Compare/contrast the spreadsheet analysis of the four alternatives with Bell's analysis. Do you have any concerns with either approach? Which alternative would you recommend? (This question requires that the instructor give Appendices 1 and 2 to the class.)

SOUTH DAKOTA WORKER'S COMPENSATION

Bruce White

Overview

The Department of Labor for the State of South Dakota is a state agency charged with handling labor-oriented issues for the state. One of the functions of the Department of Labor is to handle worker's compensation claims for workers who get injured on the job. This case study investigates bottlenecks in processing and explores a solution through automation.

Worker compensation claims arise from individuals who are injured on the job. In South Dakota, the Worker's Compensation Division under the Department of Labor is totally state-funded, and does not receive federal funding. In addition, it is not an income-generating division; that is, fees are not charged for services rendered, licenses, judgments, and no other revenue other than state-appropriated funds is received. The worker compensation function is to protect employees from not receiving appropriate compensation from employers when they are injured on the job.

This case was prepared by Bruce White, Dakota State University, as the basis for class presentation and discussion rather than to illustrate either effective or ineffective handling of an administrative situation.

Background

An individual who is injured on the job, has a file in the Worker's Compensation Division organized by a unique eight-digit claim number. Information for worker's compensation claim files is accepted from insurance companies representing the company where the individual is employed. Worker compensation claims must be filed within two weeks of an injury. All private companies within the state are required to file a statement of worker compensation insurance coverage. When the employee is first injured, a paper form called a first report of injury (FROI) must be filed within two weeks. The forms are organized sequentially by the eight-digit state claim number. An individual who is injured a second time in a separate occurrence receives a new claim number as all records are related to a particular injury, not to the individual as one individual could potentially have several different injury claims. All information is organized and filed by the claim number. No cases are filed by the worker's name, so if a worker calls and asks for the status on his/her claim without knowing the claim number, it must first be looked up in a notebook to find the correct claim number. The claim numbers start with a two-digit year, followed by a six-digit number, so 96002138 would be the 2,138th claim in the year 1996. Claims rarely go over 10,000 in any given year.

In addition to the first report of injury forms, the claimant's file may include (and generally does) a variety of additional information. Such information might be medical reports from physicians and other health practitioners, claims for payment from the individual or his/her insurance company, counterclaims from the employer's insurance company disputing the amount of the claim. For example, an individual may claim a 40 percent impairment for six months, while the insurance company for the employer may counter this claim with medical reports that support a 25 percent impairment for four months. Frequently there are disputes on the amount to be settled on which may result in legal hearings and judgments. The Worker's Compensation Division has three full-time attorneys that analyze disputed cases, hold hearings, and declare judgments.

Worker's compensation files are confidential. Information in a specific file can only be obtained by the claimant, the insurance company, the employer, or attorneys for any of the parties. Some cases are handled smoothly, with the claimant receiving appropriate reimbursement for the injury and treatment of the injury. Other cases are more difficult as there may be disagreement as to the extent of injury, on the type and expense of treatment, etc. These cases may be appealed to the attorneys for the Division of Worker's Compensation who can legally proclaim final judgment and settlement for the claim. Due to the type and severity of the injury, claims can be settled quickly or continue throughout the claimant's life with various settlement types ranging from temporary partial impairment to full permanent impairment.

Over the years, the workload has grown so that the current system of handling worker compensation claims has been stretched. The material is stored in file folders in sev-

eral rows of file cabinets. The worker's compensation file area takes up over 1,000 square feet of storage space. Some files are relatively large (300 to 500 pages of information) due to many medical reports and legal opinions. Other files may only hold the initial first report of injury if the injury was not serious and the claimant, the employer, and the insurance company did not follow through on the claim. Because this is not an income-generating area, there has been little growth in staff while there has been growth in the number of worker's compensation cases filed. The files are in large steel file cabinets in drawers large enough to store files of various thicknesses. When a specific file is desired, a clerk must find the right file cabinet, correct drawer, and the desired file.

Each new claim (FROI) starts a new file, which is stored in a large folding envelope in large filing cabinets in the worker's compensation area in a State of South Dakota office building in Pierre, South Dakota (the state capitol). As additional information relating to the claim comes available, it is filed in the existing folder. While there may be several items in the folder the four most common items are: (a) the first report of injury standard form (required in a folder); (b) medical statements from doctors and health practitioners relating to the claim (which are in no particular format); (c) form 110—agreement to settlement; and (d) form 111-request for a hearing. Form 110 is filed by the insurance company when they are ready to settle with the injured employee. The worker's compensation staff case workers review the form to see if (a) it is filled out correctly, and (b) that the amount of settlement is reasonable. Form 111 is filed if one of the sides involved in a claim disagree and want a hearing with attorneys for the worker's compensation office to review the case. Generally form 111 is filed by an insurance company who wants to close the case, but can't reach an agreeable settlement with the claimant. This can come about where the opinion of the claimant's medical professionals may differ from the opinions of the insurance company's medical professionals. Files in complicated cases can reach to 1,000 pages or more, with multiple medical opinions, legal opinions, and related materials.

Additional Information

In the 1993 legislative session, the Legislature of South Dakota directed the Department of Labor to increase the information base and enhance the record keeping associated with the worker's compensation function. As part of the legislature directive, the department was to develop a comprehensive project plan and study alternative methods of storing and retrieving the data. The Business and Education Institute at Dakota State University was asked to assist the Department of Labor in analyzing the worker's compensation function of the Division of Worker's Compensation. The analysis team consisted of Marla Anderson and Bruce White.

To conduct an analysis of the worker's compensation function, it was decided to analyze the work flow of the current system, through observation, interviews, and document sampling.

Employees[1] in the Division of Worker's Compensation staff (and their job functions) are:

Les Hanson—director of Worker's Compensation Division

Kathy Wysnicki—mail-opening function, some filing

Delores (Dee) Selleck—clerk, filing and organizing responsibilities

---

[1]Names have been changed for this case study.

Nancy Thoman—clerk, filing and organizing responsibilities

Maria Belenger—case worker (especially form 110)

Dan Williams—attorney, case worker

Connie Walsh—attorney, case worker

The normal work flow is displayed in Figure 3–7.

The normal flow of information starts with incoming mail. The mail is opened, date- and time-stamped, sorted, and separated by form and purpose. Some incoming mail is returned for more information (such as worker's Social Security number, description of injury, and more). The clerk who opens the incoming mail possesses a basic understanding of the types of forms and generally separates the material appropriately.

First report of injury (FROI) claims that have been properly submitted are routed to a clerk who starts a new file for the claim, enters the name and claim number onto a paper legal pad and also enters basic information into a mainframe application that is used to create reports for the federal government on worker injuries. This paper legal pad is the basic cross-reference source for matching names with the sequential claim number. The claim number assigned is the next unused number. If an interested party calls for information about a specific claim and does not know the claim number, it will be looked up on this legal pad.

Medical forms are directly filed into existing folders without additional staff intervention. These forms can be from one page to several pages long. Generally these are not in any specific format, and most frequently they arrive in the mail, although faxed medical forms are acceptable.

Form 110 (agreement to settlement) is generally routed to a specific case worker (in this case Maria Belenger), who will pull the entire file relating to this claim, perform

FIGURE 3–7   Flow Chart of Department of Labor Worker's Compensation Document and Work Flow

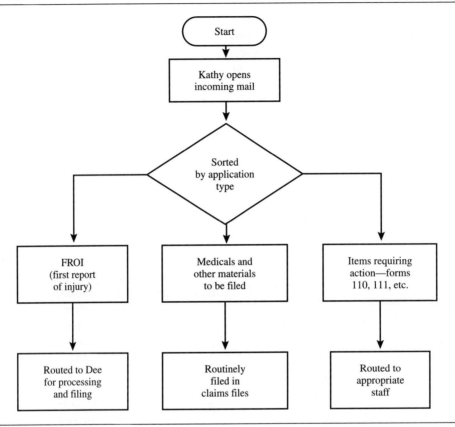

routine analysis, and generally decide on one of three options (a) accept the agreement to settlement (approximately 85 percent of the time); (b) reject the agreement to settlement (approximately 10 percent of the time); or (c) ask for additional information (approximately 5 percent of the time). Depending on the decision, a letter is sent to the parties notifying them of the decision. Many decisions will require insurance payments to the claimant over a period of time, so the file remains active. Quarterly reports are required to be filed for active accounts that have been settled.

Form 111 (request for a hearing) is routed to an attorney (generally on a rotating basis to balance workload), where one of three events happens. It is (a) accepted and a clerk will contact all parties involved to set up a hearing—in Pierre, in the claimant's city, or in select cases, via two-way interactive television; (b) rejected due to incomplete information either in the claimant's folder or on the request for hearing form; or (c) rejected if the attorney considers the request for a hearing to be a delaying tactic on the insurance company's part from arriving at a fair and equitable statement with the claimant;

the attorney may issue a settlement judgment at that time.

There are additional forms that may be filed, such as quarterly reports of compensation for cases that have been settled, but are still active as the employee is receiving compensation. Other incoming mail may include various requests for information, generally by attorneys representing one of the sides in a case.

Other information and requests come in by phone. Generally one specific person handles the phone calls. These are generally for information that may be released over the phone. In most cases, the staff person takes the name and number of the caller and returns the call after looking up the information in the files. It may take several minutes to find the correct file, get the information, and return the call.

Case workers handle cases only as action requests occur. As mentioned previously, a medical report is not acted upon until a request for action occurs (generally through form 110 or form 111).

Fortunately over the years, few items have been misfiled. When one of the attorneys or case workers are working on a particular case, a blue cardboard bookmark is inserted in the file at that point. Occasionally, someone may have to check various desks of case workers or attorneys to find a missing file. The average retrieval time to obtain the correct file folder from the file cabinets is approximately four to five minutes. The average time to retrieve an active file folder that is not in the file storage area is approximately 15 minutes. If a claimant or insurance company calls with a question about a case, the case workers or attorneys have to take the caller's phone number and call him/her back. Generally it takes 10 minutes to retrieve the information before the call is returned. Because of the demands on floor space and the size of files, files over

three years old are moved to a storage section three floors away in the same office complex. Since some of these files are still active, it takes considerable time to access them. Although generally these active files are only receiving quarterly reports, occasionally these files require action by the worker's compensation staff. There is a state program to microfilm documents over a certain age, but because of a backlog, files are not being microfilmed at a fast enough pace. For the few files that have been microfilmed, the worker's compensation staff has to go to the records archive area to get the files and use a microfilm reader.

Situation
With the increase in files and file size, retrieval times have increased. Thus, when the state legislature requested a study of the record keeping involved in keeping worker's compensation files, alternate methods were to be studied to store and retrieve the data.

Analysis

A Possible Solution to the Worker's Compensation Function
To facilitate quicker retrieval of documents, having multiple copies of files available (such as with both a case worker and an attorney), better management of documents and files, and faster response to phone calls, one alternative that was considered was an electronic document image-processing system in conjunction with an electronic data interchange (EDI) and fax system.

Document Image Processing
In document image processing, documents are scanned and converted into computer formats, similar to the way a fax machine transmits documents. The images are then stored as bit maps electronically. The

equipment to do document image processing are:

- A scanner (or scanners) to read the document. Scanners generally convert the document to a series of on-off bits like a fax machine. Some scanners (with appropriate software) can convert the document back into text with Optical Character Recognition. For some documents, like medical reports, it would take considerably less space for the material to be stored as text (like a word processing document) rather than be stored as an image or picture.
- A computer to process the images. For all staff members to access documents stored electronically, local area networks with access to shared storage devices are preferred.
- A large monitor to better see the scanned images.
- Storage:
  - Storage on disk units (hard drives) is generally faster for input and output, but documents can take up a large amount of space. Even when compressed (that is white spaces removed from the storage requirement), documents may take around 50K (or 50,000) bytes per page.
  - Storage on optical storage devices is generally a little slower for input and output, but can hold a large amount of data. Normally the storage is a compact disk (CD) device that can store billions or trillions of bytes of information. The storage can be compared to putting entire encyclopedias on CD-ROM disks. If optical storage is used, then appropriate hardware for writing and reading the optical device is needed. Generally legal experts prefer the use of WORM technology—"write once–read many"—where the document is written to the optical device, but cannot be altered or changed. Thus a document is guaranteed to be legally the same as the original.
- Software for scanning, storing, indexing, retrieving, displaying, and printing optical images.

In using a document image-processing system, a user would take incoming documents, scan them and store them as electronic images. The originals can then be stored off-site in less expensive storage, or in some cases, destroyed. The scanned images are indexed with different key fields, such as claim number, employee, employer, date of injury, insurance company, city, or other important fields. This allows for retrieval of the image by other than just the claim number.

A staff worker working with a worker compensation case, would be able to bring up the image of the various documents on his or her screen without having to search the file cabinets and bring a paper folder back to his or her work area. Comments can be added to the folder like adding Post-it Notes to a paper document and stored in the electronic folder. More than one person could potentially view the information on-line. If needed, the documents could be printed for a copy to take to hearings.

Because of the speed of the processing, staff workers receiving phone calls relating to a claim, can bring up the documents on-line while the caller waits, thus saving the expense and time for calling the individual back. If necessary, the documents could be faxed or sent by electronic means to one of the parties involved in a claim. Provided that the document was properly scanned and indexed originally, there is little or no possibility of misfiling a document.

A Document Image-Processing System Would Have the Following Features

- Documents would be scanned and saved as computer images.
- The scanned images would take up only a small fraction of the space the original documents require.
- The scanned images would be available electronically in a matter of seconds as compared to the several minutes it currently takes to retrieve paper folders.
- The originals could be stored someplace off site (generally in much cheaper storage) to meet legal requirements.
- The images could be retrieved at any computer within the division through multiple search keys, such as the claim number, the last name of the claimant, the company name where the claimant was working, or the insurance company handling the claim.
- Multiple copies of the same document could be viewed at the same time by two different individuals.
- Images could be printed in case a printed copy was desired.
- Images would be retrieved from disk storage within two seconds and from optical storage within five seconds.
- It might be possible for a case worker to electronically retrieve a document while on a phone call with a claimant.
- Multiple-page documents (such as long medical reports), would have the first page of the document retrieved in the time mentioned above, while the other pages would be loaded into memory for fast review.
- Images would be stored on disk storage for the first few months while claims tend to be more active, and then removed to optical storage (assuming that more retrieval would be made during the first months).
- Images would have the same legal aspects as documents where "best available" documents are required.
- Saving documents as images would free up a large amount of storage space.
- Saving documents as images could increase confidentiality (only authorized personnel would have access to the document image-processing system).

Electronic Data Interchange Features

Electronic data interchange (EDI) is where documents are electronically transmitted. The most common (and easiest understood format) is electronic mail. Instead of having a printed copy of a doctor's examination report of a claimant, the electronic (disk) version of the document would be saved (such as in the form of a Microsoft Word document, or WordPerfect document). When needed, the document could be loaded into any computer in the division to be viewed.

- Documents could be sent from the insurance companies to the Division of Worker's Compensation through electronic mail, the Internet, or using a modem.
- The insurance companies would not have to print and mail documents, but electronically send them.
- The Division of Worker's Compensation would not have to open the mail and file the documents in a paper file, but retrieve them from the electronic mail server and place them in the correct disk "file" folder or subdirectory.
- If needed, the documents could be printed out.
- Documents are received quicker than ordinary mail.
- Companies that send the electronic mail would save money on stamps, envelopes, paper, and more.

- Companies that receive the electronic mail can file the information quicker into an electronic file, as well as print it as needed.

Using Facsimile (Fax) Machines

Other documents might be faxed in (rather than electronically sent or sent via regular mail). For example, the legal requirements are that the originating form—the first report of injury (FROI) form—must have the signature of the claimant. A Microsoft Word or WordPerfect document would not have the signature, thus a paper copy like a fax would be needed. These forms could then be scanned into the computer. If it was necessary to verify a signature, the scanned image could be viewed on the screen or printed.

Summary

This case presents information about handling worker compensation claims for the State of South Dakota, and an alternative using electronic storage with document image processing, electronic data interchange, and fax technology.

Assignment Questions

1. Would a document image-processing system benefit the worker's compensation department?
2. How would a document image-processing system work at the Worker's Compensation Division of the Department of Labor?
3. How would a typical employee of the worker's compensation department react to electronic documents rather than paper files?
4. What would be some benefits of converting to a document image-processing system?
5. What would be some of the costs of converting to a document image-processing system?
6. What alternatives might there be other than a document image-processing system?
7. What security issues might arise?
8. How might the current process be streamlined other than with document image processing?
9. What additional analysis would need to be conducted before finishing the analysis phase? Would additional interviews of workers need to be conducted? If so, who and why?
10. Would it be necessary to find additional information about document image processing or electronic data interchange? If so, where would the research begin? What sources would need to be checked?
11. What concerns might a staff employee of the department of worker's compensation have about a system where all the information is stored electronically as compared to physical paper files?
12. How would electronic files make the job of a staff attorney easier?
13. The external users of such a system would generally be insurance companies representing one of the parties of a worker's compensation claim. What advantages would a document image-processing system and an EDI system give to such users?
14. What increased benefits (both tangible and intangible) would a document image-processing system and an electronic data interchange system give to worker compensation claimants?
15. What would be the expenses and costs (both tangible and intangible) associated with a document image-processing system and electronic data interchange system?

HOLLY HOTEL

Gordon C. Everest

Holly Hotel has grown rapidly over the past several years with happy holidayers and a bustling business clientele. They have been adding more rooms, more extension wings on existing buildings, and whole new buildings creating a large complex of facilities serving a wide variety of needs. They desperately need computer support to keep track of rooms, facilities, reservations, guests, the usage of allied services, and billings. Such computerization would enable them to better serve their customers and guests and make more efficient use of their facilities and staff.

The first step in computerizing is to prepare a *logical data model* of the information required to support the various functions and activities performed in the hotel.

Rooms and Other Facilities

There are several different kinds of rooms in the hotel complex. Most are set up for *sleeping* with one or two double beds (which may be regular size, extra long, queen size, or king size). Any given room could have two different types of beds. Some sleeping rooms have a minimal amount of extra space, some have an extra large open area with chairs and tables for meeting, etc., or for extra rollaway beds. All sleeping rooms have toilet and bath facilities, telephone, television, closets, and drawers. All sleeping rooms are designated as smoking or nonsmoking. A sleeping room is rated according to the number of sleeping guests it can accommodate (assuming adults, with adjustments made for small children).

A *suite* consists of a sleeping room with an additional, separated room for meeting or working. However, there is only a single hallway access door to the suite. If there are separate hallway access doors to adjacent rooms (whether sleeping rooms or meeting-only rooms), the rooms are considered two separate rooms and can be allocated separately.

Some rooms are *meeting rooms* only without sleeping facilities. Some meeting rooms have toilet facilities and some do not. Meeting rooms are rated according to their seating capacity assuming the guests would be seated around tables. Since an outside courtyard or a pool patio could also be the site of an event, they are treated as meeting rooms. A sleeping room may be adjacent to at most one meeting room. A meeting room may have one or two adjacent sleeping rooms. In addition, some sleeping rooms are adjacent to another sleeping room with a private-access door between them. Some meeting rooms are very large, such as a ballroom seating up to 10,000 persons. Some have large movable walls to divide them into multiple smaller rooms. All movable walls have a door. Each of the smaller rooms has a separate designation along with an indication of which rooms it is adjacent to. Two rooms are considered adjacent if there is a door between them.

Many of the rooms can serve *multiple functions*. For example, a suite could be assigned as a sleeping room or as a meeting room only. In a pinch, a meeting room could be used as a sleeping room (with rollaway beds), but only if it has toilet facilities. Some

---

This case was prepared by Gordon C. Everest, University of Minnesota, as the basis for class presentation and discussion rather than to illustrate either effective or ineffective handling of an administrative situation.

rooms also have a bed which folds up into the wall, turning it into a meeting room. A room with permanent beds cannot be assigned as a meeting room.

There are many more rooms in the hotel complex than is possible for any one person to remember. Moreover, at any given time a room may be undergoing renovation or reconstruction, or not be made up and cleaned. The computer must keep track of all room relationships and availabilities. Ideally and eventually, the computer system should enable the staff to see a graphical representation of the layout of a room and its facilities, and to zoom out to include adjacent rooms.

Each room has its own base *rental rate* per day. Sleeping rooms are allocated on a daily basis from 4 P.M. until 12 noon the next day. Earlier or later extensions are granted depending on when housekeeping gets the room ready or is available to get the room ready. Longer extensions entail a surcharge on the daily rate. Meeting rooms are scheduled on an hourly basis throughout the day and evening. The usage times are generally designated as: breakfast, morning, lunch, afternoon, supper, evening, and sometimes night. Each noneating usage is charged at the half-day rate with discounts for multiple noneating usages. One noneating usage slot is granted free of charge for each paid eating usage of the meeting room. A paid bar is considered an "eating" usage of the room. Meeting room charges may also be reduced or waived based on the number of guests staying in the hotel as a result of the event being held in the meeting room.

Designating the *location* of the various facilities follows some pattern. The hotel complex consists of multiple buildings, each with multiple floors and multiple wings. Room numbers are assigned uniquely only within wings which have a variety of alpha-numeric designations. Wings are designated uniquely within buildings, which are also named. A room number consists of one or two digits designating the floor or level, followed by two digits designating the room number on the floor. Wings differ by proximity to indoor or outdoor swimming pools, proximity to parking garage and loading dock, and handicapped access. Often a whole floor of a wing is designated as nonsmoking. These factors are often important to parties making reservations.

Customers: Guests, Hosts and Billing Parties

Customers of the hotel include: *guests,* who stay overnight in sleeping rooms, and *hosts,* organizations or individuals who host meetings or meals in meeting rooms. It is sometimes necessary to distinguish the *billing party* who is responsible for making payment, from the party using the facilities. For a meeting room there is only one party responsible for making payment. However, if multiple guests stay in a sleeping room, the billing can be split up any way the guests agree, as long as there is some responsible party. Furthermore, a guest may switch from one room to another during the visit, and still receive a single (composite) bill for the visit. In some cases of a split billing, the room may be separately charged to a billing party, while any phone calls and other usages are charged to the guest occupying the sleeping room.

Much of the information to be retained in the computer system surrounds *events.* An event is a meeting or other gathering of persons requiring the use of one or more rooms. Often guests are at the hotel to attend an event and are to be so affiliated. Each event will have a host who is either a guest or a billed party (or both). An event has a duration, and several facilities will be used in conjunction with the event. A scheduled event may also record estimated attendance and an estimated number of guests.

Reservations

Reservations are made up to two years in advance (or more for major functions) for meeting and sleeping rooms. When making a reservation, the customers express their needs and desires in terms of: bed type and size, number of guests, location, proximities, smoking or nonsmoking, etc. Different and additional information is gathered for events.

Specific room assignments may not be made until the date draws close in time. (This is necessary because of the unpredictability of specific room availability due to breakdown, repair, and renovation. Even then, last minute changes are necessary due to unexpected breakdowns and the desire to accommodate changes in guest plans). In making or changing reservations, the hotel staff must have accurate and current information on the actual and projected usage of all facilities.

Advance deposits are sometimes required depending on the *qualifications of the customer.* The qualifications are a function of their past history with the hotel, their cooperativeness, their flexibility in negotiating the usage of facilities, their promptness in making payment, etc. In an effort to be responsive to customer needs and demands, the hotel staff is given considerable latitude in making decisions and assessing charges. This must be done in the light of the *total* relationship the customer has with the hotel—including past visits or events, and the complete spectrum of usage on the current visit. For example, when a customer checks into one of the public restaurants or the health club with a couple of guests, it is desirable for the staff to know that they are responsible for renting the ballroom for three days and hosting 200 guests who are paying to stay at the Holly Hotel.

Transactions, Charges, and Billings

There must be a *responsible party to be billed* for all usage of facilities and services in the hotel. *Charged services* include sleeping room usage, meeting room usage, meals (or drinks) in meeting rooms or delivered to sleeping rooms or served in a public restaurant, telephone calls, general extra charges for room service (delivery, set up, equipment rental such as projectors and screens, installations such as phone lines or computer hookups), or business services (photocopying, computer time or equipment rental, printing, fax), charges from retail shops in the hotel complex or for services (such as a masseuse in the health club or racquetball court fees).

Each charged service is recorded on a *transaction* transmittal form (and eventually directly into the computer system). All charges must be recorded in a timely fashion so that an up-to-date rendering of a guest's total bill is always available. For example, if a guest ate in the restaurant and made a phone call just before leaving, those charges should be reflected on the final billing when they check out just a few minutes later. Billed charges must be recorded with sufficient detailed information to enable the responsible party to verify the charges. The hotel also records expected or authorized charges, and ordered services in an effort to anticipate the level of accumulated charges and avoid any surprises. This information may be gathered as part of the reservations process.

The billed party is generally a hotel guest staying in one of the sleeping rooms. A billed party may also be an outsider, a local host living at home, or some organization.

It is possible for a billed party to be responsible for the charges of multiple guests. Even if the responsible party is an organization, it is still necessary to have the name of an individual who is acting on behalf of (under the authority of) the organization.

Current Status of Guests and Facilities Usage

In making reservations and during actual usage, it is important to keep track of who is assigned where and who is using what facilities. At all times it is important for the hotel staff to know how to contact a guest or host at the hotel, at least to the extent possible with all the information which is available to or voluntarily given to the hotel. This means keeping track of the sleeping room they are currently assigned to (if any), the organizational event (meeting, conference, sponsor, etc.) they are attending (if any), their own organizational affiliation, that is, the organization which they work for. When the computerized system is in place, each guest will receive a plastic card. As they move about within the hotel, they have the option of running the card through readers indicating their current location. The card is used to gain access to sleeping and meeting rooms (along with an optional PIN). As such, the hotel always knows when someone uses the card to gain access to a room. Readers are placed in various facilities such as every meeting room, restaurants, and health clubs. In this way, the guest may, at their discretion, use the card to inform the computer of their current location. Each card reader has two slots coming (entering) and going (leaving the facility). Cleaning and repair personnel also have magnetic cards to record when a particular room becomes available.

When it is important to guests that they can be contacted, the hotel can be kept informed through several facilities. Guests can leave outgoing messages on their telephones (as with a home answering machine) informing callers and the hotel of their whereabouts or when they will be available. At their option, a guest may request that information concerning their whereabouts be kept confidential—not to be revealed to any callers. Of course, hotel staff can always take a message and relay it to the guest, who can then decide whether or not to respond to the call.

Basic Business Operations and Related Information Systems

In developing the logical data model, think about the basic activities which take place as part of the operation of the hotel:

- A person calls to schedule an event and make reservations for usage of facilities.
- A guest calls to reserve a sleeping room for some number of nights.
- A customer comes up to the front desk to check in, which involves assigning her or him to a particular sleeping room.
- A guest comes up to the front desk to check out, in which case she or he must be presented with an up-to-date bill.
- At any of the above times, the hotel staff should be able to display a profile of the customer showing past visits and usages.

Related computerized information systems (not part of this assignment) include:

- Food services—specific orders and details of charges.
- Housekeeping services—supplies, inventories, and ordering.
- Financial accounting, general ledger, and reports.
- Accounts payable, purchasing, and vendor/supplier information.

A Successful Team Effort

The success of Holly Hotel is due in large measure to the team effort felt by all employees. They are collectively motivated by a desire to best serve the customer. However, as the operation grows this objective becomes threatened. The staff need rapid access to complete, and current information to adequately serve, the needs of their guests and hosts, and fairly respond to their demands. Computerization offers the promise of keeping the staff in touch with their customers.

Assignment Questions

1. Propose a database structure that models the real world and satisfies the stated (and assumed) information requirements.
2. Prepare a brief narrative describing the context, purpose, objectives, and major organizational processes to be supported by the designed database; an overall description of the database and its major entity types; and any assumptions made, problems of interpretation, etc., in doing this assignment. You may wish to include a legend explaining your notation, particularly if you use something different than presented in class or in the text. Include here problems related to the application domain (see question 3).
3. Prepare a memo giving feedback on this assignment, any suggestions for improvement, and helpful hints for the next class. In a separate memo (optional), discuss your use of any computerized database design support tool—whether it was worthwhile, what you felt you learned, and difficulties and frustrations encountered.

SYSTEMS ANALYSIS AND DESIGN AT TRUNDLES

Len Fertuck, Yolande E. Chan, and Richard J. Simm

Part A

It was a crisp fall day when Sinjin Smythe reviewed his day planner. He was the owner and manager of Trundles—a fashionable and elite restaurant in the north end of Washington. Tonight would be a typical evening at Trundles. Exclusive dishes would be served to

---

This case was presented by Len Fertuck, University of Toronto, Yolande E. Chan, Queen's University, and Richard J. Simm, Deloitte and Touche, as the basis for class presentation and discussion rather than to illustrate either effective or ineffective handling of an administrative situation.

many of Washington's power brokers—politicians, diplomats, and business leaders. Many of the other Washington establishments envied Sinjin's savvy and his ability to attract and maintain this network of influential people.

Equipped with his MBA from a northeastern U.S. business school, Sinjin had learned the importance of customer service and had subsequently carved out a very lucrative niche in the Washington restaurant business. A typical evening at Trundles with four or five guests, including drinks and gratuity, would run about $400. Trundles had received a five star rating only one year after opening its doors.

Trundles was a small and very eccentric restaurant. The interior was predominantly neoclassical in style, accentuated with traces of art deco in the furniture. It sat 100 patrons and had a full service bar. The kitchen staff was comprised of an executive chef, five sous-chefs, a pastry chef, and four washing staff. The serving staff was comprised of 20 wait staff, eight bussing staff, two bartenders, and three maître d's. Sinjin was present most evenings, overseeing the dinner events and interacting with the guests. Trundles served only the most fresh, high-quality food. Purchases from suppliers were frequent and in small portions. While Sinjin made it a policy of sourcing most food items regionally, several in fact were sourced internationally. Sinjin had negotiated a contract with a local supplier which could provide two-hour turnaround on most food orders.

With the restaurant only open to serve dinner, Sinjin spent most of his days planning the evening meals for his discriminating clientele and developing relationships. This strategy had proved very successful; many of the patrons attended Trundles at least once a month.

While Sinjin's client development accounted for the major part of Trundles strategy, two other forces were often at play. First, Trundles had the benefit of their existing client base. Many patrons, more than pleased with the level of service from Trundles, would, through their own networks, promote Trundles and its "club-like" atmosphere. Second, Sinjin had the benefit of a well-connected family. Sinjin's father was a partner in a prestigious Washington law firm—primarily involved in lobbying—while his mother was involved in one of the more influential political action committees. As such, Sinjin had personal access to many of Washington's power brokers. Consequently, Sinjin was often inundated with calls and inquiries regarding the restaurant, its dinner events, and the process by which you could "make" the guest list.

The Trundles Experience

Unlike many restaurants, Trundles was an innovator and had redefined the term *customer service*. Rather than have the guest make the reservation, Sinjin would arrange an *invitation* to the restaurant and plan the meal for the evening. This forced Sinjin to plan his dinner events at least a month in advance.

Each meal would have a *theme*—the individual dishes would complement one another and contribute to the creation of a pleasing ambiance. Furthermore live entertainment was often present to add to the evening. This ranged from a concert pianist, a flautist, or a jazz ensemble, to a string quartet for baroque themes.

Each meal would typically include an appetizer, soup, main entrée, various vegetable dishes, a dessert, and beverages. While Sinjin had the flexibility and autonomy he needed to develop whichever menus he chose, his patrons appreciated receiving the invitation well in advance of the planned evening. If a potential invitee did not RSVP positively, Sinjin would invite another guest to the dinner event. In essence, Trundles provided a personalized, carefully planned, small group dinner experience.

The Next Step

Still a small operation, Trundles had grown significantly since its inception five years ago. Although Sinjin enjoyed the challenge associated with planning the meals, these events had lately become almost unmanageable as there were too many administrative details to remember. Sinjin thought that if he were tied too closely to administrative detail, he would lose his effectiveness as a manager. Sinjin also felt the need to expand the restaurant's repertoire. However, keeping track of all the individual ingredients, recipes, cookbooks, menus, themes, and guest information for dinner events was becoming too difficult and too time consuming. Sinjin was seriously considering having a computerized database system developed to help organize all the information. Moreover, Sinjin had already envisioned integrating this new system with his accounting and spreadsheet packages on his Pentium personal computer and his point-of-sale terminals. With all this in mind, he was unsure how to proceed.

The Information Requirements

The following afternoon, Sinjin sat down with his executive chef, Neil, over a cup of espresso. After discussing the plans for the evening, Sinjin introduced to Neil the concept of a database management system for Trundles. Sinjin felt that if he couldn't sell Neil on the idea, the project wouldn't get off the ground. Neil concurred with Sinjin that both were chasing too much administrative detail and losing focus on their primary responsibilities. As the discussion progressed, both considered the information that the database would manage. Neil began with the recipes:

> Each recipe[1] has a unique name, such as *Chicken Breasts Stuffed with Goat Cheese and Pecans in Leek Sauce.* It is important to know the number of servings that the recipe will make, and to classify it to indicate whether it is a soup, appetizer, main course, vegetable, dessert, or beverage. The ingredients could be

---

[1]Note that, technically, the *recipe* is the set of instructions to prepare a *dish*. However, as each individual dish has only one set of instructions, and each individual set of instructions will prepare only one dish, Sinjin often uses the terms interchangeably. His automated system will consider *dish* and *recipe* as synonyms.

multiplied to serve more people if required. Each recipe has a list of ingredients with an associated quantity and measuring unit, for example, half a cup of pecans.

Neil continued:

> A recipe is located on a particular page in a recipe book. It has become difficult to locate particular recipes, though, as different books often have recipes with the same name but with different ingredients or different quantities of the same ingredient. However, each recipe book has a unique name, like Anton Mosimann's *Fish Cuisine.*
>
> Regardless of the recipe, tracking the ingredients, quantities and units does not suffice. There are also general comments and instructions with every recipe, and these must also be stored.

Sinjin considered the dining events:

> A meal is a collection of recipes that work well together. For instance, *Amish Dutch Dinner* consists of *Chicken Corn Soup, Scalloped Oysters, Sauerbraten, Potato Dumplings, Pepper Slaw, Cucumbers in Cream Dressing,* and *Pineapple Bavarian Cream.* However, some of these dishes might also appear in other meals.
>
> A dinner event is a meal served on a particular date to a particular group of guests. It is important to keep track of which dishes have been served to which patrons and on which evenings the patrons have attended Trundles. I also record the ingredients that individual patrons dislike, or are allergic to. Ultimately, I would like to track the date of their last invitation, the date of the last attended dinner event, the number of negative RSVPs, the total dollar amounts spent when they attended, and some brief comments about each patron. I feel that with this information, we will better understand our guests and can better tailor our service. In sum, it will allow us to be more effective in planning the dinner events.

Sinjin did not want to serve a guest the same meal twice. Nor did he always invite guests to return to the restaurant. He also maintained the current address and contact numbers, whether a home or office telephone number or even a facsimile number, of each patron so invitations could be prepared and sent once the meal and guest list had been finalized.

Finally, Sinjin considered the possibility of the database system being used to manage Trundles' food and beverage inventory. However, he believed that this function was beyond the scope of the objectives of the core system. Moreover, he felt that this module could be integrated at a later date with both the database system and the point-of-sale terminals.

Sinjin and Neil finished their espressos as they reviewed their brief notes. Both were confident that a computerized database management system, that would meet their needs, could be developed. Neil looked forward to concentrating on finding new, exciting recipes and Sinjin anticipated channeling his efforts once more into coordinating and planning future dinner events.

As Sinjin left the table, he felt assured that they had accurately identified the information requirements for the system and that the database design phase could commence.

Assignment 1: Entity–Relationship Diagrams

Project Assignment Guidelines
Assignments may be completed by groups. It is recommended that all project submissions include the following standard items:

- A *cover page* with the project title, each team member name, the course identification, and the date of submission.
- A *table of contents* that lists the items being submitted.

- A *cover letter* or *memo* to explain the purpose of each component and any special features of the components that are not obvious from the submitted material.
- A *completed peer evaluation form* or *memo* that indicates relative *individual* project assignment contributions.

All assignments are of an incremental nature. Thus, it is important that all project assignment material is available when assignments are being reviewed and graded. It is recommended that groups prepare a project binder to contain all submitted assignments. This binder can be kept by your professor in a secure area. Creation of a similar binder or file that contains copies of submitted assignments and working documents is recommended for use by the project team.

It is expected that all project submissions will adhere to project standards to promote consistency throughout the systems analysis and design process and within the project deliverables. Although teams are not required to submit documented project standards, as the term progresses, teams may wish to create project standards (e.g., naming conventions, report formats) for use within the team.

Deliverables
Your consulting team has been selected to manage the systems analysis and design project at Trundles. Assume that a detailed system design must be completed in 10 weeks.

If you are asked to prepare a written design, use the information available in the Systems Analysis and Design at Trundles case, part A, to prepare:

1. An *entity–relationship diagram* of the entities which will need to be tracked in the Trundles database.

2. A *table of detailed attributes for each entity* identifying the primary key, any foreign keys, and the attributes, and specifying whether null values are allowed. All tables should be in third normal form.

If you are asked to implement a design using a database package, such as Microsoft Access, use the information available in the Systems Analysis and Design at Trundles case, part A, to define:

1. A *table of detailed attributes for each entity* identifying the primary key(s), any foreign keys, and the attributes, and specifying whether null values are allowed. Ensure that these tables are in third normal form. Include any attribute properties supported by the database package, such as format, default values, indexes, etc.
2. An *entity–relationship diagram* to link the defined tables.
3. *Integrity rules* that enforce update and deletion of related records, if supported by the software.

Part B

Obtaining and Storing the Information

Now that the database structure was designed, Sinjin was eager to begin storing information in the new system. Over the years, Trundles had collected volumes of recipe books, and hundreds, if not thousands, of recipes that needed to be entered. Sinjin and Neil started to organize and list the books, recipes, ingredients, meals, and events. Sinjin gathered guest information as this would also have to be entered into the system. In addition, there would need to be a process to enter new information Sinjin acquired after he transferred his files to the newly automated system. Usually, whenever Sinjin or Neil bought a new recipe book, they browsed through it and selected recipes which they thought would be appropriate for use in the restaurant. Many times, Neil would experiment and catalog his own recipes.

Neil also wanted to be able to find recipes that used a particular ingredient. For instance, last week he had acquired some smoked Scottish salmon and needed a recipe that would do it justice. At other times, he needed lists of possible recipes in a category that used an ingredient, such as soups that used calamary.

Planning the Meals

After deciding the "theme" and creating the dinner event, Sinjin first selected a set of recipes. Some of the recipes might exist in the file and some might be newly added ones. Having a list of recipes that used a particular ingredient was helpful. Sinjin wanted to be able to identify quickly recipes that would be appropriate for the event. However, this was not an easy task. It required close consultation with Neil to identify which dishes worked well together and which dishes fit with certain themes. Finally, Sinjin thought it would be helpful to have a complete list of food items and ingredients once the menu items were finalized, to help with the preparation of food purchase orders for the coming month.

Planning the Dinner Events

Sinjin felt his biggest challenge (and most time-consuming task) was producing the guest list for his soirées. Sinjin started with a preliminary list. He identified select patrons by examining food dislikes, allergies, and meals previously served. Appetizers, desserts, and drinks, unlike entrées, could be served to the same patron more than once.

Sinjin needed a process that identified all guests who had not yet had the entrée in the planned dinner event. Ideally, the process would provide a list of allowable guests that Sinjin could select from. The selected guests would be automatically placed on a mailing list and mailing labels would be generated for their invitations. He would then mail, fax, or call the invitation to the potential guest. (Sinjin found that different guests preferred one or more of the three contact methods.) If the guest did not RSVP positively, Sinjin continued the process until a minimum number of patrons filled the restaurant, permitting the restaurant to achieve its profit targets. Sinjin left a few empty seats to allow for last minute walk-in guests. However, walk-in guests could not always be seated and served.

Sinjin was anxious to have the new system implemented and fully operable shortly. Trundles had recently been selected to feature in a future edition of *Architectural Digest* and Sinjin looked at this as an opportunity to showcase not only the architectural design of the restaurant, its menus and atmosphere, but also the new database management system.

Assignment 2: Data Flow Diagrams

Deliverables
Using the information in parts A and B of the Trundles Restaurant case, describe the required system processes. Include the following:

1. A *statement of purpose* for the Trundles information management system (TIMS).
2. An *event list* to identify each event that will trigger a response from the system being designed.
3. An *event diagram* to correspond to the event list. The event diagram should identify the terminators that trigger each event, the data flow initiated by each terminator, the process that will respond to the event, the output(s) produced by that process, and the terminator that will receive the output.
4. *Leveled data flow diagrams* for the process of creating a guest list.
5. *Amended database definitions* if any new data requirements are discovered during your analysis. If no new data requirements are discovered, include a copy of the existing entity–relationship diagram to provide the context for your analysis.
6. If you are using a CASE tool for your design, include reports generated by the CASE tool which verify the integrity of your design.

Assignment 3: User Interfaces— Windows and Reports

Deliverables
Using the information in parts A and B of the Trundles Restaurant case, submit the following:

1. *List all the screens* that will be required in the Trundles information management system. If there is a hierarchical relationship between them, draw a tree diagram or a dialogue design diagram to show the order in which the screens will be accessed.
2. *List the screens that will be needed to respond to each event* in the event list of the previous assignment.
3. Design the *main menu* that will be used to select application screens in the Trundles information management system.
4. Design *screens* to enter data about recipes, events, and patrons.
5. Design a *report* listing possible patrons for a dinner event, and information that can be used by Sinjin to narrow the guest list further manually.

6. *Attach amended documents* from previous systems analysis stages if you discover new data or processing requirements.

Assignment 4: Project Implementation and Evaluation

Deliverables
Prepare a brief report to address either question 1 or 2:

1. Assume that you have completed the design of the TIMS, the newly designed automated system for Trundles. Describe how you would go about implementing this new system. Discuss

objectives, tasks, and a tentative timetable. Highlight the strengths and limitations of your plan.

2. Conduct a brief postimplementation review to describe your experience with this systems analysis and design project. Address the following:
   a. The particular strengths/benefits and weaknesses/limitations of your design for TIMS.
   b. Key lessons learned in the analysis and design process. What might you do differently in your next systems project?
   c. A summary of the knowledge and skills you have gained.

MS. EHREE HOSPITAL

Len Fertuck, Yolande E. Chan, and Sherry L. Jack

Part A

Management Information Systems at Ms. Ehree Hospital

Jerry Michelson was pleased to give Michelle Forester a tour of the information systems (IS) department. As a seven-year veteran of the department, Jerry knew the hardware, software, and applications like the back of his hand. His on-the-job experience had enabled him to successfully implement a number of systems at Ms. Ehree Hospital. Michelle, too, was pleased to have the resident expert in the department give her the "grand tour." This was her first day

on the job as a systems analyst at Ms. Ehree Hospital. She enthusiastically listened as Jerry showed off the latest acquisitions.

> We have just installed a new IBM AS/400 minicomputer. It has 4 gigabytes of memory, 16 gigabytes of disk space, 20 printers, and 128 networked PCs connected to every desk and nursing station in the hospital.

Jerry explained that the hospital directors had recently approved a major plan to update and enhance the information technology in the hospital. This plan incorporated a shift from COBOL flat file systems to an integrated relational database management system. The new AS/400 will act as a data server with a DB/2 database that communicates via the industry standard database query language (SQL). Applications will be developed using Microsoft Visual Basic for some applications and

---

This case was prepared by Len Fertuck, University of Toronto, Yolande E. Chan, Queen's University, and Sherry L. Jack, Alberta, as the basis for class presentation and discussion rather than to illustrate either effective or ineffective handling of an administrative situation.

Microsoft Access as a database client to connect to the DB/2 database. Access provides facilities for query-by-example, screen design, and report design.

Although the department personnel were enthused about the new equipment and software, they also expressed apprehension. While the tools were supposed to be easy to learn and use, they represented a significant shift from the current mode of operations for the department.

A Meeting with the Director of Systems Development

After her tour of the IS department, Michelle Forester met with her immediate supervisor, Doug Warren, the director of systems development at Ms. Ehree Hospital to discuss objectives for the next quarter.

To develop the information technology plan that the board of directors had recently approved, Doug had met with hospital departmental management to discuss information needs. The plan included short- and long-term plans for the IS department. The first project on the list was the development of the hospital patient care data system. This system would develop and manage the central hospital patient database. The database would in turn be accessed by various department applications. The hospital patient care data system would be Michelle's first assignment. Her initial contact would be Samuel Peterson, the director of administration at Ms. Ehree Hospital.

During Michelle's meeting with Doug, he provided her with a list of his expectations:

- Design a new hospital patient care data system.
- Write a complete high-level specifications for the system.
- Specify the tables required and the attributes for each table so that the standard database query language SQL

could be used to implement the database.
- Specify the reports generated by the system and the contents of each report.
- Specify the required screens.

Before Michelle left to gather information on the system, Doug suggested other factors Michelle should consider when working on the project:

- The hospital patient care data system would be coded, tested, and implemented by the IS department in Ms. Ehree Hospital.
- Evaluations would be based on how well the system satisfied the user needs, the completeness and clarity of the design, and the efficiency of the database structure.

Doug also reminded Michelle that she had only 10 weeks to complete the system design.

An Introduction to the Hospital Patient Care Data System

Michelle Forester decided that her next step was to meet with Samuel Peterson, the director of administration. Samuel was responsible for, among other things, all personnel promotions, equipment acquisitions, and the operations of the admissions department. Although he had been preparing for a two-week convention in Europe, he agreed to meet briefly with her later that afternoon.

When she arrived, Samuel gave Michelle a stack of forms used by the hospital. He indicated that only five forms were used consistently by the staff: hospital admission form, hospital discharge report, hospital emergency report, hospital patient chart, and a health department patient report. (See Exhibits 3–3 through 3–7.) Years of changes and revisions had made all other forms obsolete. Samuel had to cut short

EXHIBIT 3–3　Ms. Ehree Hospital Admission Form

Patient's Last Name		First Name			Middle Name	
Street Address		City			State	Postal Code
Birthdate	Religion	Admission Date	Sex	Age	Insurance Number	
Have You Been in Miss Ehree Before? ☐ Yes　　☐ No		Home Phone	Bus. Phone		Relationship to Insured	
In Emergency Notify Name						
Address						
Relationship		Home Phone	Bus. Phone			
Family Physician		Referring Physician			Attending Physician	
List Allergies						
Requested Accommodation ☐ Private　☐ Semiprivate　☐ Ward		Floor	Wing		Room Number	Rate
Clergyman		Address			Phone	
Current Medications						

Insurer Name	Address	Policy Number
Hospitalization		
Employer's Accident		
Disability		
Automobile Accident		
Other Third Party		

Signature of Person Filling Form	Relationship to Patient	Date

EXHIBIT 3–4 Ms. Ehree Hospital Discharge Report

<table>
<tr><td rowspan="10" style="writing-mode:vertical">PATIENT</td><td>Patient's Last Name</td><td>First Name</td><td colspan="2">Middle Name</td></tr>
<tr><td>Street Address</td><td>City</td><td>State</td><td>Postal Code</td></tr>
<tr><td>Birthdate   Religion</td><td>Admission Date   Sex   Age</td><td colspan="2">Insurance Number</td></tr>
<tr><td>Have You Been Admitted Before?
☐ Yes   ☐ No</td><td>Home Phone   Bus. Phone</td><td colspan="2">Relationship to Insured</td></tr>
<tr><td colspan="4">Insurance Company or Billing Address</td></tr>
<tr><td>Family Physician</td><td colspan="3">Consultants</td></tr>
</table>

PATIENT

Patient's Last Name	First Name	Middle Name	
Street Address	City	State	Postal Code
Birthdate / Religion	Admission Date / Sex / Age	Insurance Number	
Have You Been Admitted Before? ☐ Yes ☐ No	Home Phone / Bus. Phone	Relationship to Insured	
Insurance Company or Billing Address			
Family Physician	Consultants		

DIAGNOSIS

Initial Diagnosis

Final Diagnosis

Complications and Infections

Procedures Performed

DISCHARGE

Medication

Follow-Up

Condition on Discharge
☐ Better   ☐ Same   ☐ Worse   ☐ Expired

Coroner's Office Notified
☐ Yes   ☐ No

Disposition
☐ Discharged   ☐ Transferred   ☐ Discharged Against Advice

Physician's Signature   Time

Nurse's Signature   Time

☐ Patient Notified of Required Follow-Up

EXHIBIT 3–5   Ms. Ehree Hospital Emergency Report

REGISTRATION	Patient's Last Name / First Name / Middle Name Street Address / City / State / Postal Code Birthdate / Religion / Admission Date / Sex / Age / Insurance Number Have You Been Admitted Before? ☐ Yes ☐ No / Home Phone / Bus. Phone / Relationship to Insured Admitted By Relationship / Home Phone / Bus. Phone / Triage ☐ Emergency ☐ Urgent ☐ Deferable ☐ Elective ☐ Transfer Family Physician / Attending Emergency Physician List Allergies / Current Medications Present Complaint
NURSING	Temp / Pulse / Blood Pr / Weight / Respiration / Time Treatment
PHYSICIAN	Diagnosis / X-Rays / Tests Ordered Treatment Physician Signature / Time
DISCHARGE	Discharge Diagnosis Medication Condition on Discharge ☐ Improved ☐ Unchanged ☐ Deteriorated ☐ Deceased / Coroner's Office Notified ☐ Yes ☐ No Disposition ☐ Discharged ☐ Transferred ☐ Discharged Against Advice / Physician's Signature / Time Patient Notified of Required Follow-up / Nurse's Signature / Time

EXHIBIT 3–6   Ms. Ehree Hospital Patient Chart

<table>
<tr><td rowspan="6">PATIENT</td><td colspan="5">Patient's Name</td><td colspan="2">Identification Number</td></tr>
<tr><td>Birthdate</td><td colspan="2">Religion</td><td colspan="2">Admission Date</td><td colspan="2">Current Date</td></tr>
<tr><td>Floor</td><td colspan="2"></td><td colspan="2">Wing</td><td colspan="2">Room</td></tr>
<tr><td colspan="7">Allergies</td></tr>
<tr><td>Temp</td><td colspan="2">Pulse</td><td>Blood Pr</td><td>Weight</td><td>Time</td><td>Signature</td></tr>
</table>

<table>
<tr><td rowspan="5">NURSING</td><td>Treatment</td><td>Time</td><td>Signature</td></tr>
<tr><td></td><td></td><td></td></tr>
<tr><td></td><td></td><td></td></tr>
<tr><td></td><td></td><td></td></tr>
<tr><td></td><td></td><td></td></tr>
</table>

<table>
<tr><td rowspan="6">LABORATORY</td><td>X-Rays</td><td>Billing Code</td><td>Test Name</td><td>Billing Code</td></tr>
<tr><td>1</td><td></td><td>1</td><td></td></tr>
<tr><td>2</td><td></td><td>2</td><td></td></tr>
<tr><td>3</td><td></td><td>3</td><td></td></tr>
<tr><td>4</td><td></td><td>4</td><td></td></tr>
<tr><td>5</td><td></td><td>5</td><td></td></tr>
</table>

<table>
<tr><td rowspan="3">PHYSICIAN</td><td colspan="3">Instructions</td></tr>
<tr><td colspan="3"></td></tr>
<tr><td>Diagnosis</td><td>Signature</td><td>Time</td></tr>
</table>

EXHIBIT 3–7   Health Department Patient Report

Hospital				
<div align="center">**Ms. EHREE HOSPITAL**</div>				
Patient's Surname	First Name		Initial	
Street	City		State	Postal Code
Religion	Sex ☐ Male ☐ Female	Age	Admission Date	Discharge Date
Insurance Company Paying for Care, If Any				
Family Physician	Attending Physician		Consultant	
Diagnosis				
Condition on Discharge ☐ Better ☐ Same ☐ Worse ☐ Deceased		Disposition ☐ Discharged ☐ Transferred		
Communicable Diseases				

their meeting as the board of directors had telephoned with an emergency. He suggested she review the forms and then contact the head nurse in admissions, Wendy Morrison.

After a quick examination of the forms, Michelle knew that if these forms were accurate, she would have enough information to draft some initial specifications. An entity–relationship diagram and a table of detailed attributes for each of the entities would be useful for her discussion with Wendy Morrison. She could also identify primary and foreign keys, specify the type and width of the attributes, and decide whether null values should be allowed. The database tools are flexible so she could make revisions later if required.

The Hospital Patient Care Data System Process

Michelle and Wendy met later that same week. Wendy, who had worked in a number of departments and used many of the hospital forms, proved to be a valuable resource for Michelle. Wendy explained the process:

There is no such thing as a typical patient. They are all different. However, each goes through three basic stages: admission, treatment, and release.

In the admissions process, patients are normally admitted at the front admissions desk. They may arrive with a completed hospital admission form that they receive when their doctor schedules them into the hospital. If they have not filled it in, the admission desk helps them to complete it. The other way that patients get into the hospital is through the emergency room. Patients there arrive unexpectedly, so the emergency admitting desk always has to prepare the form for them.

Also, some patients "spontaneously" arrive in the maternity ward. When a baby is born, one of the nurses uses a regular admitting form to register the new patient. The patient usually does not have a name yet, so "Baby" is generally used as a first name.

This process happens every time a patient comes to the hospital. Even though we save all the forms, currently it is easier to get the information from the patients than to get it from the files.

Wendy also commented on the differences between the emergency admissions form and the regular admission form:

The emergency report is designed to cover admission, treatment, and discharge. The form follows the patient through the emergency department. Most emergency patients are discharged right after minor treatment, such as setting a broken bone or stitching a cut. On the other hand, an accident victim may go straight into surgery with a nurse trying to get the information along the way.

Most admissions are more complex than the emergency patients. They require many tests and treatments. That is why we fill out a daily patient chart for each patient. The different reports and charts act as a permanent record of the treatment that the patient has received. In case of complications, the doctors and nurses can find out what treatments have been given previously. In some cases, we need records of treatment from many years ago. We also use the treatment record for patient billing purposes.

Similarly, the discharge of regular patients is more complex than the discharge of emergency patients. The discharge report expands on the information in the discharge section of the emergency report. With the regular patient, there are usually several

treatments that must be described and more information than is required for the emergency patient. In addition, the health department requires a patient report for patients that have been in the hospital for more than 24 hours. Furthermore, if the patient dies, there are special reports for the coroner's office and a government death certificate to fill out. These contain some of the same information, but go to different users.

The hospital appeared to operate on a complex series of forms and reports:

In fact, there are dozens of forms and reports that go to different users in the hospital. Every department has its own forms. Depending on the treatment, there will be drug orders from the pharmacy, tests from the laboratory, preparations from the operating room, meal plans from the dietician, exercises from the physiotherapists, and x-rays from the radiologist, for example.

Michelle knew that she would have additional opportunities to learn more about these other forms and reports in future phases of the IS project.

A Review of the Hospital Patient Care Data System Design Requirements
After her meeting with Wendy Morrison, Michelle stopped by Jerry Michelson's office for a brief review of the technical requirements of the hospital patient care data system. She knew that Jerry would know about the existing files and data structures used in the current systems. Michelle also knew that she needed some direction as to the scope of the hospital patient care data system.

Jerry suggested that Michelle concentrate on the admissions, emergency room, and discharge procedures to begin with. He reminded her that the hospital patient care data system maintained all the information for those patients who currently were, or ever had been, admitted to the Ms. Ehree Hospital. The hospital patient care data system would extend beyond the admissions process and would include the processes that Wendy had discussed (treatment and discharge, for example). The files for these processes would be linked to the personnel files. Although procedures for billing and other departments would be incorporated into the project at a later date, detailed designs for database, forms, and screens for these additional procedures were not yet

required. However, Jerry advised that Michelle should review a sample COBOL data description for the rehabilitation unit (see Exhibit 3–8). This, apparently, was a typical example of the data collected from most forms: the forms usually had some identifying information, tables of lists of medications or treatments, several fields to check off or describe specific diagnostics used by specialists, and several text lines to describe the patient's condition or proposed treatment. Each specialty department,

---

EXHIBIT 3–8 COBOL Data Division for Rehab File

```
01 REHAB
02 PATIENT
   03 LASTNAME                      PIC X(15).
   03 FIRSTNAME                     PIC X(15).
   03 MIDDLENAME                    PIC X(15).
02 MEDICATION OCCURS N TIMES
   03 MEDICINE                      PIC X(15).
   03 DOSE                          PIC X(10).
   03 FREQUENCY                     PIC X(5).
   03 STARTDATE                     PIC X(6).
   03 ENDDATE                       PIC X(6).
02 PROBLEMS
   03 IMPAIRED SPEECH               PIC X(1).
   03 IMPAIRED COMPREHENSION        PIC X(1).
   03 IMPAIRED MEMORY               PIC X(1).
   03 IMPAIRED LEARNING             PIC X(1).
   03 INAPPROPRIATE BEHAVIOR        PIC X(1).
   03 DISORIENTED                   PIC X(1).
   03 LOW MOTIVATION                PIC X(1).
02 HOME SITUATION                   PIC X(80).
02 DISCHARGE PLAN                   PIC X(80).
02 GOALS OCCURS N TIMES
   03 GOALSLINE                     PIC X(80).
02 PHYSICIAN                        PIC X(15).
02 THERAPIES OCCURS N TIMES
   03 THERAPY                       PIC X(40).
   03 FREQUENCY                     PIC X(5).
   03 STARTDATE                     PIC X(6).
   03 ENDDATE                       PIC X(6).
   03 THERAPIST                     PIC X(15).
```

however, had its own required information and some needed to add new information as various treatments progressed.

Michelle also learned that at Ms. Ehree Hospital, personnel were classified into doctors, nurses, and staff. Each person had a five-digit personnel number and three 15-character fields for last, first, and middle name. Although the hospital recognized that many individuals have more than one middle name, the hospital had found that only one middle name was required to adequately meet their information needs.

With this new information that Jerry had provided, Michelle was determined to complete an entity–relationship model with identification keys. She knew that once she understood how the rehabilitation unit data fit into the data model, she could add other departments and specialties as needed. The standard approaches taken to handling lists, descriptive fields, and lines of unstructured text, could be applied to the other hospital areas.

Assignment 1: Entity–Relationship Diagrams

Project Assignment Guidelines
Assignments may be completed by individuals or teams. It is recommended that all project submissions should include the following standard items:

- A *cover page* wilth the project title, student names, the course identification, and the date of submission.
- A *table of contents* that lists the items being submitted.
- A *cover letter* to explain the purpose of each component and any special features of the components that are not obvious from the submitted material.

Note that all assignments are of an incremental nature. Thus, it is important that all

project assignment material is available when assignments are being reviewed and graded. Preparation of a project binder to contain all submitted assignments is suggested. This binder can be kept by your professor in a secure area. Creation of a similar binder or file that contains copies of submitted assignments and working documents is recommended for use by the project team.

Project Standards and Procedures
It is expected that all project submissions will adhere to project standards to promote consistency throughout the system analysis and design process and within the project deliverables. Although teams are not required to submit documented project standards, as the term progresses, teams may wish to document project standards for use within the team. Some areas to consider include:

- Procedures for making revisions to project documents.
- Standard formats for reports.
- Standard formats for screens.
- Standard identification for project documents.
- Standard naming conventions for entities, tables, data elements, and other components of the project design.

Assignment
If you are asked to prepare a written design, use the information available in the Ms. Ehree Hospital Case, part A, to prepare:

a. An *entity–relationship diagram* of the entities revealed by the forms, reports, data file, and case discussion.
b. A *table of detailed attributes for each entity* identifying the primary key and any foreign keys. Ensure that these tables are in third normal form.

If you are asked to implement a design using a database package, such as Microsoft

Access, use the information available in the Ms. Ehree Hospital Case, part A, to define:

a. A *table of detailed attributes for each entity* identifying the primary key(s). Ensure that these tables are in third normal form. Include any attribute properties supported by the database package, such as format, default values, indexes, etc.
b. An *entity–relationship diagram* to link the defined tables.
c. *Integrity rules* that enforce update and deletion of related records, if supported by the software.

Part B

The Pharmacy Labeling Application

Work was progressing quickly on the hospital patient care data system. Michelle had completed the database design and was looking forward to developing screens and reports. An opportunity quickly presented itself when Doug Warren provided Michelle with an additional assignment—the pharmacy was having problems preparing all the labels for its prescriptions and wanted the IS department to develop a labeling system. Michelle would have an opportunity to learn more about an individual department in the hospital sooner than she expected. Further, the pharmacy labeling application would become the first departmental application to use the new database designed for the hospital patient care data system.

Phil Stevenson, the head pharmacist, was enthusiastic when Michelle asked him to describe his concerns about the labeling process and what was expected from an automated system. Phil was a knowledgeable resource as he had worked at Ms. Ehree Hospital for 15 years and had seen numerous changes.

Ms. Ehree Hospital operated an individual unit dosage system. Each dose of each prescription was prepared separately and sent to the nursing stations daily. This method of preparing medications had reduced the waste of drugs and also reduced the chance that an overdose or wrong medication might be given to a patient. It did require more paperwork, though. As each dose was prepared in a central location, each dose required a label that specified the name of the patient, the room, the name of the medication, the size of the dose, the time it was to be administered, and the doctor who prescribed it. This averaged 4,000 labels a day as each of the 500 patients in the hospital received an average of eight doses of medication daily.

During each shift, a nurse from each nursing station brought all the prescriptions for the patients served by the station. The pharmacy then prepared the doses for the following shift and placed them on a tray to be sent to the nursing station. The nurses administered the medications to patients in their wing during hourly rounds through the rooms.

Phil explained that the pharmacy received prescriptions in one of two ways. First, doctors used a standard form to list prescriptions (see Exhibit 3–9) which was then brought to the pharmacy by the nurses. Second, sometimes the pharmacy received rush orders that were needed immediately. In those cases, individuals waited for the medication to be prepared so they could take it with them.

Phil provided detailed information on the sections of the prescription form:

All patients are identified by their name. The floor, wing, and room tell us where to send the medication. All rooms for the same floor and wing are sent together. We try to arrange the medication in order of room number to make it easier for the nurses to find the medications. They usually go around the ward from room to room administering all

EXHIBIT 3–9   Ms. Ehree Hospital Prescription Order

<table>
<tr><td rowspan="6" style="writing-mode: vertical">PATIENT</td><td colspan="2">Patient's Last Name</td><td colspan="2">First Name</td><td colspan="3">Middle Name</td></tr>
<tr><td colspan="2">Floor</td><td colspan="2">Wing</td><td colspan="3">Room</td></tr>
<tr><td colspan="4">Status

☐ Transferred   ☐ Discharged</td><td colspan="3">Date</td></tr>
</table>

	Cancel	Drug	Form	Dose	First Time	Last Name	Times Per Day
PRESCRIPTION	☐						
	☐						
	☐						
	☐						
	☐						
	☐						
	☐						
	☐						
	☐						
	☐						
	☐						
	☐						
	☐						
	☐						
	☐						
	☐						

Doctor's Authorization   _____

medications scheduled for the same time. The drug column has the name of the medication to be provided. The form distinguishes different forms of the same drug, such as oral, topical, or injectable. The dose is the amount of active ingredient administered at a time, such as 250 mg or 10 cc. The first time, last time, and times per day tell when to prepare the doses. For instance, if the first time is Jan/20/9A.M., the last time is Jan/24/9A.M., and times per day is four, then the drug is administered every six hours at 9A.M., 3P.M., 9P.M., and 3A.M. On each calendar day, two doses are prepared for the day shift and one for each of the other two shifts. This is repeated until the afternoon shift on January 24. The cancel box on each line is used to communicate that an order is to be canceled before the last time has expired. The pharmacist will not fill a prescription without a doctor's signature. Some drugs are controlled by law. In addition, it is important that the doctor is aware of all medications the patient receives.

During the discussion, Michelle learned more about how the pharmacy operated. The prescriptions were sorted by room number, wing, and floor. Then prescriptions were matched with any that were already on file for the same patient. A patient at Ms. Ehree Hospital might have prescriptions for a dozen different medications at the same time. Some might be standing orders, like a sedative, that were prepared each day. Some might be new medications ordered to treat a new condition. Some might be cancellations or changes of existing standing orders. For example, a dosage might be reduced or an oral form might be substituted for an injectable form.

When the discharged box was checked to show that a patient had been released, all standing orders for the patient were canceled. The transferred box was checked to indicate when a patient was transferred to another hospital room. All standing orders for the patient were then moved to the new room number. If the cancel box for a drug was checked, then the standing order for that drug would be canceled by changing the last time to the end of the previous shift. If the dose had been prepared, the cancel box was checked and the last time changed so that the dose would not be prepared again. If a new prescription was for a drug that was already on the standing order, then the standing order was canceled and the new order would be filled with the other orders for the patient. The new order usually represented a change of dose, form, or time.

Phil also explained to Michelle that one of the responsibilities of the pharmacist was to be aware of potentially harmful combinations of drugs. Every new prescription was compared against the existing patient medications to determine if dangerous "cocktails" could result. Pharmacists used special catalogs to conduct this check and to identify lists of drugs that might react unfavorably. If a dangerous combination was found, the pharmacist would call to ensure that the prescribing physician knew about the potential problem. Sometimes the physician would prescribe the combination anyway because the complications would be less serious than the problem being treated.

Phil pointed out that at a pharmacists conference he had heard of a program, called *Cocktail,* that could automatically identify these interactions if provided with the list of drugs being prescribed. He was not sure where it could be obtained, but would look for literature on it in his files. When Michelle learned about this, she quickly made a note to herself.

Phil had provided a comprehensive review of the activities in the department and Michelle believed she had enough information to start the system design. She knew that the new hospital patient care data system database would simplify the development of the pharmacy labeling application.

An Update from Wendy Morrison

When Wendy became aware that Michelle was working on the pharmacy labeling application, she immediately contacted Michelle. The nurses had some suggestions for improving the way the medications were delivered and thought the new application could help.

Wendy told Michelle that the nurses would prefer to receive medications arranged by time and by room number. Apparently, with the existing system, nurses had to sort through all the medications to find the dosages that were to be administered at any particular time. She believed that sorting by time, and then by room number, would simplify their jobs. The nurses also believed that the new approach would reduce the chance of an individual dose not being located until after it should have been administered.

Consultation with the Pharmacy

Suspecting that a change in which labels were printed (sorted by time and room number instead of just by room number) might affect how the pharmacists conducted their activities, Michelle contacted Phil and discussed Wendy's suggestion. While receptive, Phil was concerned that if all the doses for a drug for a particular patient were not prepared at once, then the pharmacists could waste time unnecessarily traveling back and forth to the supply cabinets. He could foresee situations in which a pharmacist would prepare a dose and return the drug to the supply shelf, only to have to retrieve it again to prepare subsequent dosages. After much deliberation, Phil agreed that a new line on the label indicating dose number of total dosages for the shift (for example, 1 of 3 to

show that this was the first of three dosages) would solve the problem. Michelle also said she could develop a report that would list all the medications needed for a single shift at a nursing station. Phil felt that this would save time as many patients on the same ward required the same medicine.

With the knowledge that the deadline for the design of the hospital patient care data system and the pharmacy labeling application was quickly arriving, Michelle set to work. She thought it was time to review the purpose of the entire hospital patient care data system. Michelle believed that providing a list of events and data flow diagrams would be the best place to start. The pharmacy labeling application needed to be put into the context of the overall hospital patient care data system.

Assignment

Using the information in parts A and B of the Ms. Ehree Hospital case, provide:

a. A *statement of purpose* for the hospital patient care data system. Include reference to the pharmacy labeling application.

b. An *event list* to identify each event that will trigger a response from the system being designed.

c. An *event diagram* to correspond to the event list. The event diagram should identify the terminators that trigger each event, the data flow initiated by each terminator, the process that will respond to the event, the output(s) produced by that process, and the terminator that will receive the output.

d. *Leveled data flow diagrams* to describe the pharmacy labeling application that is intended to print labels for the pharmacy. Assume that Michelle has obtained the *Cocktail* program to check for interacting medications.

e. *Amended entity–relationship diagrams* and database definitions if new data requirements are discovered during the analysis. These will provide an up-to-date context for your analysis.

Assignment 3

Using the information in parts A and B of the Ms. Ehree Hospital case:

a. *List all the screens* that will be required in the hospital patient care data system. If there is a hierarchical relationship between them, draw a tree diagram or a dialogue design diagram to show the order in which the screens will be accessed.

b. *List the screens that will be needed to respond to each event* in the event list of the previous assignment.

c. *Design the main menu* that will be used to select application screens in the hospital patient care data system.

d. *Design an input screen* to gather the data required when a patient is admitted. Show the position and formats of any additional panels that may appear during the use of these screens. Identify any validation that needs to be performed on each of the data fields.

e. *Design a nursing station report* that lists daily all the patients at a nursing station showing the floor and wing of the station and lists the room, name, admission date, and age of each patient.

f. *Design a pharmacy report* that lists all the medications needed for a single shift at a nursing station.

g. *Include amended documents* from previous stages of your analysis if you discover new requirements. Include a copy of the data definitions for each file used in the screens and reports you design.

If you are asked to implement a design using a database package, such as Microsoft Access, you can use it to implement c, d, e, and f.

Part C

The Progress of the Hospital Patient Care Data System and the Pharmacy Labeling Application

The development of the requirements for the hospital patient care data system provided Michelle with a comprehensive overview of the data at Ms. Ehree Hospital. A common user interface, which had been approved, was one result of her efforts. Michelle knew it was important that continuity was maintained throughout the applications that used the data managed by the hospital patient care data system. These standards had easily been applied to the pharmacy labeling application which was progressing well.

Michelle used data flow diagrams to document the results of her meetings with Phil and Wendy. They provided Michelle with useful feedback and comments which she incorporated into her design. Then, working closely with Phil and Wendy, Michelle produced and received approval for a number of screens and reports for the application. She was now prepared to progress to the next design step which involved creating detailed design specifications for the pharmacy labeling application. Structure charts and program modules descriptions would be needed by the IS programmers who were working with Michelle. Michelle looked forward to the completion of the design of the pharmacy labeling system, her appraisal, and the selection of her next assignment.

Assignment 4

This assignment is based on the data flow diagram of the pharmacy labeling application produced at the end of Assignment 3 and any changes to that diagram suggested by your professor. Complete the following tasks:

a. *Convert the pharmacy labeling data flow diagram to a structure chart.* Include utility modules to perform standard tasks such as sorting, accessing files, and accessing output devices. Assume COBOL is the 3GL to be used to implement the system.

b. *Provide brief descriptions of the program modules* specified in the structure chart.

c. *Update the data flow diagram,* if necessary, to reflect any changes that result from the design of the structure chart. Include a copy of the revised data flow diagram.

Assignment 5: Project Implementation and Evaluation

Prepare a brief report to address either question 1 or 2:

1. *Describe how you would implement this new system,* assuming that you have completed the design of the hospital patient care data system. Discuss objectives, tasks, and a tentative timetable. Highlight the strengths and limitations of your implementation plan.

2. *Conduct a brief project review.* Describe your experiences with the design of the hospital patient care data system and the pharmacy labeling application. Address

a. Particular strengths and weaknesses of your design (including the databases, high-level processes, screens, reports, and detailed structure charts).

b. Key lessons learned in the analysis and design process. What might you do differently in your next systems project?

c. A summary of the knowledge and skills you have gained.

Chapter 4

Construction

This chapter describes the stage in the SDLC that deals with the construction of the information system and ensures that the information system performs as required.

HARDWARE AND SOFTWARE SELECTION

Sometimes during the construction of an information system it may be necessary to acquire either hardware or software. In all cases, what is acquired should be evaluated against a preestablished list of requirements. When involving external suppliers, a formal selection process should be implemented and followed consistently.

SOFTWARE ENGINEERING

Software engineering is defined as structured with an automated support approach to information systems development. Of a number of important concepts involved in software engineering, the following four are highlighted. First, documentation is produced as a direct result of an activity and is not a separate task in itself. Second, a modular approach is taken; that is, each function is factored into a low-level process. It then becomes possible to reuse modules as building blocks in the development of an information system. Third, the concept of cohesion is applied to evaluating a module. Cohesion measures how unified a module is and the objective is to develop a highly cohesive module to accomplish one and only one individual task. Fourth, coupling is another concept applied to the evaluation of modules. Coupling is a measure of the relationship between two modules. The objective here is for loose coupling which means the modules are independent of each other.

CASE

Computer-aided software engineering (CASE) is the automated step-by-step methods for software and information systems development to reduce the amount of repetitive work on the part of the developer.

4GL

A fourth-generation language (4GL) is a programming language that can be employed directly by end users to quickly develop information systems. 4GLs are nonprocedural and are parameter-driven.

Prototyping

This is a process of building a preliminary working version of an information system quickly and inexpensively for demonstration and evaluation so that users can better determine their information requirements.

PRODUCTIVITY

If the decision is made to develop the information system within the corporation then it becomes important to ensure a productive approach to the task. Various software metrics are available to assist in the evaluation of the productivity of the information systems development activity. These metrics may include some of the following: lines of code (LOC), executable lines of code (ELOC), decision counts, function points. Further, a number of productivity tools are available, such as application generators, reusable modules, report generators, and all the concepts associated with structured programming and software engineering.

QUALITY ASSURANCE

Quality may be defined as the degree of excellence inherent in the information system. Quality must be built into the information system from the beginning, and cannot be inspected into the final product. Although it may not necessarily be obvious that an information system is of good quality, a system with poor quality will command attention through failures and the constant need for modification. Each company, and perhaps each project, should adopt and use consistently some form of quality standards.

TESTING

The objective of testing is to demonstrate that specific requirements have been met. Testing strategies may involve either code testing, where the detailed logic of a program is examined, or specification testing, where the results of the program are evaluated based on specific inputs. The levels of testing relate to units (a module or a program), the system (interaction of modules or programs), and special tests such as peak volume or year-end. The test data used may be either live or artificial.

THE CASES

EMC Accounting Software

Ron Craig

This case deals with the replacement of an accounting system for a small church. The major decision here revolves around three options: (1) revise the existing system, (2) buy a standard accounting package, or (3) buy a DBMS and develop a customized system. An interesting complication in this case is the fact that everyone involved is a volunteer.

When the Software Selection Process Doesn't Go by the Book

Susan F. Schwab and Ernest A. Kallman

This case focuses on the processes involved in selecting hardware and software for performing the administrative functions of a medium-sized private college. Such applications are analogous to the accounting and financial functions of a commercial business. The case is particularly useful in demonstrating the difficulty of making hardware and software decisions. It is clear from this real-life project that the textbook approach (gathering some standard information about vendors and evaluating that information against a set of general criteria to arrive at a winning vendor) does not work. The information received is not "standard," the criteria are not "general," and the process does not result in a clear "winner."

Party Hardy

Karen S. Nantz

This case provides the opportunity to design and develop an order-taking and accounts receivable database for a small party supplies company. Experience is gained in the development of an entity–relationship diagram, the normalization of data, and the design of data flow diagrams.

Systems Development in the Federal Judiciary

R. Ryan Nelson

> This case discusses the alternatives to systems development available to a senior management committee consisting of users of a rather large government organization. The case highlights the important role that both organizational structure and readiness (in the form of methodology, technology, and people) play in making systems development decisions. The committee of 14 federal judges had just listened to several opposing arguments on how to best develop information systems, and were now prepared to render judgment on an issue that was clearly outside their field of expertise.

EMC ACCOUNTING SOFTWARE

Ron Craig

Roger was concerned, even anxious. For the past five years he had been treasurer at EMC, and was now looking forward to stepping down from this volunteer position. But he knew the problems he had faced each year when he tried to update the accounts in the church's accounting software package. Even after working with the system for almost five years, he knew how to use it, but not how it worked. He wanted to have a better accounting system in place before he turned responsibilities over to someone else.

Because Roger knew little about computer hardware or software, he asked another member of the congregation to investigate options and recommend a replacement package. But that person, Susan, was very busy. The weeks were slipping by and it was now November: in less than two months Roger would be finished and someone new would take over (and that someone had not yet been found). Year-end would be the natural time to convert to a new system. Roger hoped he wouldn't have to learn it or be involved in the conversion; he hoped the new software would be so easy to learn that the incoming treasurer could handle everything.

Introduction

EMC is a church in Elmira, Ontario. Donations of over $200,000 were received during 1991 from a membership of more than 200. In many respects the church is like a small business. Revenues (donations) are received regularly during the year (but there are no accounts receivable). Most expenses are paid by check, with accounts payable batched a couple of times a month. A small petty cash fund is used for incidental expenses. There are two full-time and three part-time employees on staff, so the usual employee remittances are made to Revenue Canada for personal taxes and other deductions. EMC owns two buildings—the church itself and a house next door.

Unlike a small business, churches pay no federal or provincial income taxes or municipal property taxes. There is no inventory to track, nor is project management or budgeting a concern.

As with any organization, budgeting and cash flow control are important. An annual budget is set in December, which projects annual revenues and expenses; these are then evenly divided over the coming year on a monthly basis. Then actual monthly revenues and expenses are tracked. There are seasonal expenses (such as heating), and periodic lump sum payments (such as an annual pension plan contribution). Revenues vary monthly (summer is poor, December is always highest) which creates unevenness in the monthly cash flow. While it would be possible to have better estimates of actual monthly revenues and expenses, this has not been done in the past, and there have not been any problems.

Computing History

EMC has a DTK AT-clone that has been in use since 1986. It has a 40M hard drive, and both 5 1/4-inch and 3 1/2-inch floppies. DOS 3.01 is in use as the operating system. A Panasonic KX-P1124 dot matrix printer is attached.

At the time this computer was purchased, Roger had just taken over the treasurer's position. The previous treasurer had maintained the church books on his personal computer system. A computer science graduate, whose full-time job was with NCR as a software engineer, he had written his own accounting program to use with the apartment buildings he owned. In fact, he and his wife maintained the books for several small businesses.

The current accounting package had been transferred to the church's computer in 1986. It provided an income statement and balance sheet (see Exhibits 4–1 and 4–2 for samples).

Unfortunately, all knowledge of this accounting software resided in the head of its originator (Bill), who no longer attended the church. There was no documentation whatsoever. An extended batch language controlled the various programs and files. The specific programs had been written in PL/1, then compiled.

At the beginning of each calendar year, Roger would want to make changes to the various church accounts. Some previously defined accounts would no longer be required, as there was no activity, and new accounts would need to be set up to reflect new activity.

So Roger would get together with a member of the congregation who knew something about computers. This person would go into the various files and find the one that contained the list of accounts.

Bill had set up a menu system on the church's micro, which he had written himself. When the machine was booted, a list of options would be displayed, and the accounting package was one of these options. Bill had partitioned the hard drive into three logical drives, with parts of the menu system on drives C and E. The accounting package resided on drive C and comprised several files. The file-naming convention was not descriptive, so it was necessary to investigate several files before finding the particular one that required updating. But once they had found the correct file, it was a simple operation to use EDLIN to modify a few lines. No time was spent to document how the changes were made or which files were involved.

EXHIBIT 4–1   Income Statement Format

	Expenses Month to Date	*Expenses Year to Date*	*Budget Year to Date*
General fund:			
Revenue			
Expenses			
Income over (under) expenses			
Missions fund:			
Revenue			
Expenses			
Income over (under) expenses			
Building fund:			
Revenue			
Expenses			
Income over (under) expenses			
Total income over (under) expenses			

EXHIBIT 4–2   Balance Sheet Format

Assets

Current assets:
Bank account
Petty cash
Total
Noncurrent assets:
Building
Total Equipment and furnishings
Total
Land
Total
  Total assets

Liabilities and Equity

Current liabilities:
Notes payable
Total
Equity:
Church capital account
Total
  Total liabilities and equity

Accounting Needs

Susan had arranged a meeting with Roger to learn more about the requirements of the proposed accounting package.

Susan: Tell me about your current accounting system.

Roger: I use the computer program to generate the monthly statements. It doesn't take much time—I enter everything in a single batch. There are usually 40–50 entries to be made.

Susan: And what does your computer program do for you?

Roger: I get a monthly report of revenues and expenses, and a balance sheet. Here's a sample.

Roger shows Susan two reports (these are outlined in Exhibits 4–1 and 4–2). The income statement has three columns: expenses current month, expenses year to date, and budget year to date. The balance sheet lists assets, liabilities, and equity.

Susan: What are the things you like about this software package?

Roger: It goes pretty quickly, and prints out the reports that the executive board wants. I have to give the board a monthly report, and post it on the bulletin board so anyone in the congregation can see it.

Susan: What problems have you had with the current package, and what features are lacking?

Roger: Well, it's always a problem at year-end when I want to change some of the accounts. Sometimes I want to delete accounts, and other times I want to add new accounts. And sometimes I just want to change the account name. There's no documentation on how to do this, so I have to get someone else to do it for me.

The whole system is not very user friendly. While I know what to do, I don't know why I'm doing it. I would have a hard time training someone else to use it.

Since I'm finishing off my term as treasurer, I want to get a better system in place for the new person.

Susan: Your computer program only does part of the bookkeeping. What do you do by hand?

Roger: There's the monthly bank reconciliation. I can use the computer program to some extent, but it looks for checks by amount rather than number. So if there are two checks for the same amount, it assumes the earlier check was processed by the bank.

There's also the payroll. We have two people paid biweekly and three paid monthly. Only three people have deductions.

I also do the accounts payable by hand. Sometimes I prepare checks weekly, and sometimes I let this go for a couple of weeks. It depends on how many invoices we have to pay, and how much money we have in the bank.

Deposits are made weekly, at the bank drop-off box. A record is kept in the deposit books.

Susan: What about GST? The church gets back half of what it pays out, doesn't it? How have you been tracking this?

Roger: I've just been charging it along with whatever we were billed for. Since this is the first year we've had to pay it, I haven't got around to sending in a claim. The computer program has no way to handle it.

Susan: Do you operate on a cash or accrual basis—do you record expenses as you are invoiced for them or as you pay for them?

Roger: We record expenses after we issue the checks.

Susan: So the new accounting package will need to generate an income statement and a balance sheet, and handle the month-end bank reconciliation. The monthly income statement printout needs to include budget figures. And the package's accounts payable module needs to consider GST. It could do the payroll, but that is optional. Are there any other things you would like to see?

Roger: Not in terms of what it can do. But we need a package that is easy to use. I want to see a manual explaining how to use the package, and how to change account names. Just having some documentation would make for a much better system.

Investigation of Options

During the interview Roger had mentioned the 4Cs (Canadian Council of Christian Charities) as a possible contact, so Susan began with a call to their office. Talking with the office manager, she found that they were using Bedford, and were pleased with it. The office manager didn't know if Bedford could handle a monthly budget comparison, but did give Susan the name of a local consultant who knew all about Bedford, along with the name of someone in Barrie who distributed an American accounting package called Money Counts.

Susan phoned the person in Barrie, and was sent sample printouts. This person had set up a business to develop and sell accounting systems for churches. The basic package cost $35, and could handle budget comparisons with actual expenses and provide multiple print formats. However, it could not handle GST directly (users could get around this by setting up a special account).

Susan also phoned several churches to find out what they were using. No two were using the same package. Several had custom applications that had been developed using database packages (one had even been developed by programmers at The Mutual Group). One suggested using Quicken (though they did not use it themselves, someone had sug-

gested it to them). And another one was using NewViews, a sophisticated accounting package suitable for medium-sized firms (the treasurer at this church was a CA who was familiar with the software and had developed a custom application).

There were a few integrated packages on the market that included accounting, church membership, and other applications. These were all from the United States, so the accounting package did not include GST consideration.

Conclusion

It was now almost the end of November, and Roger wanted to have the new system in place by year-end. A new treasurer had not yet been found. But Roger felt that it would be easier to find someone to take over if the new system were in place. It would be ideal, he felt, if he could finish off the year on the old system and have the new person start in January with the new one. That way, he would not have to learn it. He was waiting for Susan's recommendation.

Assignment Questions

1. What are the essential accounting needs of EMC?
2. In what ways are the accounting software requirements of a church the same as, or different from, a small business?
3. What are the business and information system issues in this case?
4. What factors should EMC take into account in choosing a software product?
5. Recommend an accounting software package for EMC. Should they consider buying a package, or custom designing their own software? Is there another option open to them?
6. What other considerations, besides the choice of software, should Roger be aware of?

WHEN THE SOFTWARE SELECTION PROCESS DOESN'T GO BY THE BOOK

Susan F. Schwab and Ernest A. Kallman

Background

This case focuses on the processes involved in selecting software and hardware for performing the administrative functions of a medium-sized private college. Such applications are analogous to the accounting and financial functions of a commercial business. The college is an independent institution serving about 7,300 students in undergraduate, graduate, and continuing education programs. Courses and degree programs are concentrated in business-related disciplines, and the college describes its mission as the education of business professionals who have strong grounding in the liberal arts and sciences.

The administration is organized into six divisions: academic affairs, student affairs, business and finance, institutional advancement, institutional planning/human resources, and information services. Typical functions in the first five divisions are: recruiting, admissions and student records; dormitory and student activity records; tuition billing, general accounting and financial functions; fund raising and alumni records; and government reports and personnel records.

Defining the Need

The information services (IS) division is trying to evaluate and plan the IS support

needed for the college's administrative functions. The goal of the project is to create an IS environment that will meet the college's needs for day-to-day operations, management decision making, and planning activities over the next decade. [Note: Though the information services division is also responsible for supporting academic computing, the "classroom" computing requirement is accommodated through a separate planning effort.]

The project began with a collegewide evaluation of current and projected information requirements. Next, existing systems were evaluated in order to determine how well they met those requirements. The college's applications software had been purchased five years before; the vendor went bankrupt soon thereafter, and the college began at that point to maintain the applications with its own internal staff.

The major findings from this evaluation were that the college's existing systems functioned reasonably well, and that they provided adequate support for most areas. The planning team noted, however, that while no crisis existed, the existing information systems did have some major functional and technical deficiencies. Specific problems were:

1. There was no support or very poor support for some major functional areas such as human resources, fixed assets management, financial aid, budgeting and financial reporting, and physical plant management.
2. There was little support for compliance with external reporting and processing requirements. These included the

---

This case was prepared by Susan F. Schwab and Ernest A. Kallman, Bentley College, as the basis for class presentation and discussion rather than to illustrate either effective or ineffective handling of an administrative situation.

requirement for depreciation of fixed assets, promulgated by the financial accounting standards board; certain federally mandated requirements for employee fringe benefits; and the use of a federally mandated algorithm for awarding financial aid to students.

3. In addition to the deficiencies noted above, there was a documented multiyear backlog of programming requests.

4. In some key areas, the administrative database needed to be redesigned to accommodate application requirements. In addition, the database required a clean-up effort: it contained some fields that were unused, some whose use was unknown, and some that contained erroneous data.

5. The existing systems were becoming more difficult to maintain. At the time of the evaluation, there were about 4,000 application program modules, many of which were poorly structured and documented, and which had been patched and modified frequently.

6. The existing systems did not support certain strategic activities, such as enrolling planning, marketing, fund raising, and strategic decision making.

It was estimated that it would require 36 person-years, over four calendar years, at a cost of about $3 million, to fix the existing systems. This effort would address all of the known database problems, improve the quality of software and documentation, and address all documented backlog items. This price tag did not, however, address the major functions that were completely lacking (such as human resources), nor did it provide for the strategic activities in number six above. The planning team concluded that the existing systems were "fixable," but at great expense in both time and money.

Gaining Management Approval

The next phase of the planning project was conducted by a consultant. The use of consultants for this phase of the project was considered important by the IS management staff because they wanted to get an opinion on the state of administrative IS that was both competent and unbiased. In addition, they felt that the consultant's opinion would lend credibility to the project, especially on the critical question of keeping or replacing existing systems. The consultant's assignment consisted of an evaluation of the findings of the planning study thus far, and the analysis of alternatives for addressing the needs that had been identified. These alternatives included making major investments in enhancing existing systems, or replacing and augmenting them with new applications software, either purchased or custom-developed. The consultants did identify several commercially available applications packages that seemed to be a reasonable fit with the college's requirements. This led them to recommend replacement of the current administrative systems. Like the planning team, they noted that, although no immediate crisis existed, the college should enhance its applications in order to position itself for the future.

An examination of the commercially available packages identified one that was based upon the same software and database technology as the college's existing systems, and that shared the same underlying functional and technical design. This package performed the same functions as the college's in-house systems, and would be relatively easy to enhance to provide the additional capabilities that the college had custom-developed. It had two further advantages: (1) it supported external reporting and processing requirements, such as the depreciation, fringe benefits, and financial aid award requirements noted earlier and (2) it was supported by a strong vendor. Even before a detailed evaluation of all of the alternatives began, it appeared that employing this vendor's software was superior to staying with the existing systems, and so it became the "fallback" choice should no other alternative be acceptable.

The findings and recommendations were presented to the college's Information Services Steering and Planning Committee (ISSPC). ISSPC members include all six college vice presidents, a faculty representative and one person from a committee representing administrative users. The ISSPC endorsed the recommendations and agreed to multiple-year funding for replacing the existing systems. Next, the recommendations were presented to appropriate committees of the college's board of trustees. (The board of trustees is analogous to the board of directors in a business firm.) These committees included the one for information services (which had to approve the project's direction), the Business and Finance Subcommittee (which had to approve the budget), and the Executive Committee, composed of key trustees (which had to endorse both). The college's trustees approved the recommendation to replace the existing systems, and allocated funds for the conversion project to begin in the following fiscal year. By the time all of these approvals had been obtained, nine months had elapsed since the beginning of the planning project.

Selling the Approach to the College Community

Once management approval was secured, it was time to be back to the user community to update them on the project and to present the recommendation to replace the existing system. This was done in a meeting of the college's 50 senior administrators. The reactions of the user community were mostly positive. They felt as if their needs had been heard and acknowledged. There were, however, some concerns: first, that the cheapest alternative, and not the best alternative, would be selected; and second, that a purchased package would limit flexibility in terms of getting specific modifications. They felt this way because in the preceding five years administrators had gotten used to receiving the personalized service and custom programming support traditionally available from an in-house systems staff. It was impossible for the project team to completely reassure the user community on these issues, but an important promise was made: users would be fully involved in all decision making about the new administrative systems. The project team could not guarantee that everyone's wish list would be fulfilled, but it could at least assure that the interests of the user community would be represented. The users seemed to be willing to keep an open mind about the project, and to lend their support.

The information systems staff was not as easily convinced of the desirability of replacing the existing systems. This group had spent the preceding five years supporting these systems; they had a major investment in them, and didn't like seeing their work "thrown away." They also tended to view the recommendation to replace the existing systems as the "hidden agenda" of the VP for information services and the director of administrative systems, both of whom were new to the college. There was also some uncertainty as to what would happen to people's jobs if the college changed systems. Would their skills still be needed, or would they be replaced with people having the technical skills needed in the new systems environment? Both the VP for information services and the director of administrative systems met with the staff to address these concerns. They made several commitments:

no one would lose his/her job as a result of the conversion to new systems; all staff would receive whatever technical training was needed to support the new environment; the IS staff would also be fully involved in the selection of the new systems. In addition to these commitments, the director of administrative systems had an additional conversation with key members of her staff in which she reviewed their resumes, and showed them how they would broaden their skills and experience by participating in the replacement effort.

Thus, all major campus constituencies, trustees, officers, managers, users, and IS staff, were willing to move forward on the evaluation and selection of new administrative systems.

Staffing the System Evaluation and Selection Process

IS management was now faced with determining a process to evaluate the various alternatives and make system recommendations. They had three major goals for the process: (1) to identify appropriate solutions, (2) to make the right choices, and (3) to get all major campus constituencies to support the choices. Getting and keeping the support of the administrative user community and the college officers was especially important because the acquisition of new systems was proposed at a time of significant financial constraint at the college. There was stiff competition for scarce budget dollars, and if expectations for the new system waned, the budget allocations might be reduced or withdrawn altogether.

In designing the evaluation process, IS management began by articulating two strongly held beliefs: first, functionality (i.e., results for the user) is the single most important criterion in the selection of new systems. Thus, the evaluation process would be software-driven, and not hardware-driven. Second, they believed that users should have a major role in the process. Users should specify requirements for new systems, participate fully in the evaluation of alternatives, and be a major force in making final decisions. Based upon the earlier phases of the planning study, the IS organization found the college user community to be knowledgeable and articulate about system requirements, to possess the necessary analytic skills to be able to evaluate alternatives and understand technical issues, and to be willing to devote large amounts of time to the process.

Given these beliefs, and given their goal of ensuring broad support for the project, IS management organized a fairly large cast of characters to be involved in the system selection process. Project teams were organized on three levels: (1) a management team, (2) three work groups representing functional, technical, and academic computing constituencies, and (3) user evaluators.

The project's management team was charged with directing the progress of the project, reviewing and approving requirements and specifications, resolving disputes between user divisions, and taking the institutional viewpoint on all major decision issues. This group was the project's decision-making body, and it was responsible for making the final selections and recommendations for the acquisition of new systems. Its decisions needed to be approved by the ISSPC.

The management team was chaired by the VP for information services. It included a key representative from each division of the college, a faculty representative, the director of administrative systems, the director of computer and network services, and the managers of the three work groups. The user representatives for each division were nominated by their vice presidents. While this nomination ensured that the chosen representative had the support of his or her vice president, it did leave some campus constituencies feeling underrepresented in the process. The academic affairs division, for example, was represented on the management team by the assistant undergraduate dean. Although he was quite familiar with information requirements in all parts of his division, the graduate school felt that its needs would be better served if it had its own representative.

The three work groups were responsible for developing and documenting the system requirements and for representing the interests of a particular constituency. These included a "functional work group," responsible for generating functional application requirements; a "technical work group," responsible for determining technical and vendor requirements; and an "academic work group," responsible for representing the interests of the academic computing community.

The "functional work group" was chaired by the college's internal auditor, a system user with a broad, campuswide perspective. This group also included three programming project leaders from the administrative systems department, and four key users. The "technical work group" was chaired by the manager of data administration, and included a representative from systems programming and computer operations, and two key users who had strong technical skills and who were concerned about support for end-user computing. The "academic computing" work group was chaired by a faculty member and included an IS staff member. In addition to their responsibility for articulating system requirements, these groups participated in the system evaluation process.

Finally, there were a large number of users involved in the process. Key users from all departments would eventually attend demonstrations of administrative

packages, file written evaluations, make recommendations of "semifinalist" packages, conduct on-site package evaluations at vendor and customer sites, again file written evaluations and recommend finalist vendors to the management team.

Defining Detailed System Requirements

Once project staffing had been accomplished, the process of finding and evaluating new administrative systems began in earnest. The first step in the process was the issuance of a request for information (RFI). The RFI was sent to the known major vendors of software packages specifically designed to support college and university administration, 13 vendors in all. Two other vendors independently learned of the RFI, and also supplied information. The vendors were asked to supply information describing their companies, the functional capabilities of their product, the hardware and software environment in which it ran, and the size and nature of their customer base.

While awaiting the RFI responses, the work groups began to develop and document application and system requirements. They interviewed system users and managers in every department, and generated high-level application requirements for each of 48 business or system functions. This included 17 business and finance functions; 11 in academic affairs; five in student affairs; nine in institutional advancement; and six general institutional functions. A "function" in this context is analogous to "accounts payable" or "grade reporting."

The application requirements document included a general description of the function, the business importance of the function, including comments on why this function should be automated, the specific features that are desired in a system to support the function, an indication of whether these features are "wants" or "needs," an indication of how well these features are provided by existing systems, and a general description of data flows and interfaces to other system modules (see Exhibit 4–3).

The functional requirements were reviewed and approved by signature, by three different groups: (1) the manager responsible for the business function, (2) the managers of departments whose systems are connected to this function, and (3) the project's management team. The approval process, particularly the requirement that users sign their requirements document, served to reinforce cooperation and commitment to the project and to assure users that their specific interests were represented accurately. The inclusion of the management team in the review process not only served as a valuable check but also provided assurance to top management and the trustees that the specified requirements were reasonable and justified.

In addition to application functional requirements, a set of technical and vendor requirements and evaluation issues were drafted by the technical team. These included issues related to the vendor's software package, its history, growth path, and vendor support; characteristics of the database management system; system software and hardware issues; application development tools provided by the hardware platform on which the package is based; availability of end user computing tools on that platform; and the nature of support for office automation. Like the application functional requirements, these requirements were reviewed and approved by the project's management team.

By the time the requirements process was complete, the work groups had developed many hundreds of requirements and desirable features for the new systems. While

these requirements were not of equal importance, it was felt to be impossible to come to agreement on a ranking or weighting of so many factors. This feeling was ultimately borne out by the experience of the work groups and management team. As they learned more about the different alternatives, their assessment of the relative importance of different factors kept changing. It was also felt to be an impossible task (and a waste of time) to attempt to evaluate all of these factors simultaneously, for all vendors. The management team developed an evaluation strategy that provided for successive evaluations and culling of vendors, with increasingly detailed package evaluations only for those vendors who "stayed in" until the very end of the process.

The Evaluation and Selection Process

The "first cut" of the vendors was made by the management team who developed some rules of thumb for identifying vendors worthy of further consideration. The criteria included: (1) that the package appear to provide good functionality, (2) that the vendor have a customer base that included other colleges equivalent to or greater in size than this one, and similar in organizational structure and program offerings, and (3) that the vendor show a sustained history of doing business in this market. Basically, the management team was looking for the appearance of a "good fit" with the college, from a vendor who was strong enough to stay in business and support its product. The industry leaders were automatically included in the group of vendors to receive further evaluation. The other vendors were evaluated more closely by sending members of the work groups to attend a demonstration of the product to evaluate how well it fit the college's requirements. In general, the vendors who were culled were those whose only markets were very different from

---

EXHIBIT 4–3 Applications Requirements Document

Administrative Systems Requirements Business and Finance

Function: *Accounts payable*

Providing timely processing and payment of college liabilities.

This function needs to be automated for timely processing of approximately 1,800 checks each month. This includes vouchering, printing of checks, and reconciling bank accounts.

Features	*Need/* *Want*	*Present* *System*
Vouchering	N	Yes
Purchase order acceptance	N	Yes
Automatic relieving of encumbrances	N	Yes
Printing checks	N	Yes
Audit controls (checks over $10,000 need approval of two vice presidents)	N	No
Student refunds	N	Yes
Bank reconciliations	N	Yes
Travel advances/expenses for faculty and staff	W	No
Vendor maintenance/inquiry	N	Yes
Reports	N	Yes

Data Flows

Input:	Invoices
	Student refund requests
	Employee deductions
Output:	Postings to general ledger
	Update purchase orders
	Checks
	Reports

Interfaces	*Input*	*Output*	*Contact*
Purchasing	X	X	Barney
Receiving	X		Barney
General ledger		X	Jones
Accounts receivable	X	X	Jones
Human resources	X		Smith

the college, i.e., small, two- or four-year undergraduate-only colleges, or public institutions. These vendors' products were consistently found to have design limitations that would preclude their successful use at the college. Some packages, for example, were unable to support adequately the different degree programs the college offers. Eight of the original group of fifteen vendors were dropped from further consideration.

Each of the seven remaining vendors was invited to respond to a request for proposal (RFP). The RFP included the functional and technical requirements that had been identified by the working groups. The vendors were asked to respond to the requirements, as well as to provide a price proposal, a recommended hardware configuration, company and financial information, and a complete list of clients.

While the management team believed that important information would be obtained through the RFP process, it was convinced that the written information provided by the vendors would not be adequate to evaluate the packages. It reasoned that the vendor proposals would identify what capabilities their products provided, but not how well those capabilities were implemented, how well they fit the college's needs, or how easy the packages were to use. These issues could only be evaluated by seeing the package in use. Therefore the seven vendors were invited to conduct on-campus demonstrations of their products so that college users and systems staff could see how the package worked, "kick the tires," ask questions, and form their own judgments.

Before the demonstrations began, one of the work groups devised a specific evaluation form to be used for each of the 48 major functions desired in the new system (see Exhibit 4–4). The evaluation forms were based upon the application requirements document. For each requirement in a speci-

fied functional module, users were asked whether or not the package supported it, how well the package met that particular requirement, and how easy the package was to use. Space was also provided for comments. The forms were to be filled out by every person attending a demonstration, for every function they were qualified to evaluate.

The on-campus demonstrations were scheduled over a seven-week period, with one demonstration each week. A typical demonstration lasted for three full days, with one day devoted to academic affairs and student affairs functions, one day to business and finance and human resources functions, and one half-day to the institutional advancement functions, with the second half of that day focused on end user computing and general technical issues.

The demonstrations were open to the entire administrative user community and to the information systems staff. About 60 users, vice presidents, department heads, and administrative staff attended, along with about 20 members of the IS staff. The attendees included all of the most knowledgeable users on campus.

The demonstrations were not a perfect evaluation tool, but they were largely successful. On the negative side, users found the evaluation forms difficult to fill out. Not all items on the forms were covered during the demos, and the order of presentation of the demos did not match the order of items on the forms. Also, it was sometimes difficult to separate the quality of a vendor's product from the quality of the presentation. Despite the limitations of the demos, the college users quickly became very adept at evaluating the products. They learned to adopt a "show me" attitude, and not to believe claims about a product's capabilities unless those capabilities could be demonstrated. During the demos, striking differences between the products became apparent. The

---

EXHIBIT 4–4   Systems Evaluation Form

Administrative Systems Evaluation Guide

Function: Accounts payable   *Vendor:* _____
Reviewer: _____   *Date:* _____

For each of the listed features respond to the following:
(Each feature is designated as being either needed or wanted.)
  1. Is the feature in the vendor package?
  2. Does the feature meet your needs?
  3. What are its exceptionally good characteristics?
  4. What are its exceptionally bad characteristics?

Features:
  1. Vouchering (need)
  2. Purchase order acceptance (need)
  3. Automatic relieving of encumbrance (need)
  4. Printing checks (need)
  5. Audit controls—checks over $10,000 need OK of two VPs (need)
  6. Student refunds (need)
  7. Bank reconciliations (need)
  8. Travel advances/expenses for faculty and staff (want)
  9. Vendor maintenance/inquiry (need)
  10. Reports (need)
  11. Controls on payments for services (want)
  12. Ability to authorize (automatically) payments for services, e.g., leases (want)
  13. 1099 for personal services (want)

Overall evaluation:
  Ease of use: _____   Good   _____   Bad
  Meets your needs: _____   Yes   _____   No

Other comments:

_____

_____

_____

(Use additional sheets, if necessary)

_____

college users were able to identify those packages that seemed to be a good fit with their requirements, and those that clearly did not meet them.

The product demonstrations also provided some unanticipated benefits. Prior to the demos, it had been rumored that the system selection process was "wired," implying that the new system had already been selected by the IS staff and that user input was only being sought to give the appearance of user participation. The rumor mill had decided that the college had selected the vendor who happened to be a market leader. The demos themselves completely dispelled this rumor, for two reasons. First, the demonstration conducted by the so-called selected vendor was of very poor quality, and it was clear to everyone that this vendor's product did not meet the college's requirements. Second, the planning group nagged users to fill out their evaluation forms, constantly stressing that their input was important. As a result, users came to believe that the system selection had not already been made, and that they really did have a voice and a vote. The credibility of the project was greatly increased.

The demonstrations also enhanced the relationship between the information systems staff and the user community. During the seven weeks of demonstrations, users and IS staff suffered through long days in a darkened classroom with uncomfortable chairs, poor climate control, and lousy lunches. The experience of going through the demos together (and maybe even of shared suffering) generated a lot of camaraderie, and those who participated came to know each other much better than they ever had before. In addition, the IS staff came to be seen as advocates for the user community. During the demos, the IS staff were very persistent in their questioning of vendors to make sure the vendors adequately demonstrated the product capabilities required by the users.

After the demonstrations were over, the written evaluations were compiled and summarized. The usefulness of the written evaluations was mixed. The number of items completed on the evaluation forms tended to be low. The principal problem encountered by users was that not all items addressed by the forms were adequately addressed during the product demonstrations. Users therefore found it difficult to complete many of the items. In addition, a particular item on an evaluation form was meaningful to only a small number of college staff. [Staff members were instructed to evaluate only those features that they themselves used and were qualified to judge.] Thus, the evaluative data

tended to be sparse, and it was impossible to compute statistically significant results.

The written commentary provided by the user–evaluators proved to be more useful. All of the evaluators' comments were compiled on a single form for each product of each vendor, and a general qualitative assessment of each package emerged. While all parties agreed that further evaluation was required, the demonstrations and the comments they generated were quite revealing of the differences among the packages.

At this stage of the process the management team sought to further cull the available options, eliminating any package that, in the view of college users, did not provide adequate functional support. The management team convened a meeting of each group of users who had attended the demonstrations to discuss the alternatives and eliminate those options that were judged to be inadequate.

The meetings were organized by functional area, e.g., the business and finance users met as a group, as did human resources users, academic affairs users, and so on. Each meeting was "facilitated" by outside consultants knowledgeable about administrative computing in colleges and universities and each of the alternatives being evaluated. The consultants led the users through a discussion of the strengths and weaknesses of each alternative, supported by the written evaluations and comments summaries. The consultants then conducted a vote among the users to determine which packages deserved further evaluation, and which should be culled. Each functional group was instructed to vote for those packages that would best meet their needs, not taking into account the needs of any other division of the college. Similarly, the votes of other user divisions were not revealed before users cast their own votes. Any differences of opinion between divisions would be resolved later, by the project's management team.

It should be noted that the consultants, while knowledgeable, were disinterested parties, and never expressed their own opinions on the packages. The administrative programming staff attended each meeting and expressed opinions on the strengths and weaknesses of each package. The programming staff did not, however, cast any votes.

The meeting-and-voting procedure was designed with two purposes in mind. First, the management team sought to identify those alternatives that seemed to be the best fit for the requirements of each division of the college. The process was therefore designed so that critical distinctions among the packages would be highlighted. This was the reason that discussions were led by consultants who were knowledgeable about the alternatives, and who could therefore point out key features and differences in each vendor's offering. Second, and equally important, the management team sought to ensure that users would support the selection process and the decisions that came from it. For this reason, discussions were led by disinterested consultants (and not by the planning team or the IS staff), and the IS staff refrained from voting. The voting procedure was also an important mechanism for convincing users that they had a meaningful role in the evaluation, and for increasing their support for the process.

Like the user groups, the IS staff met as a separate group, and they too discussed the packages, basing their evaluations on the software technology and support implications of each alternative. The IS staff meetings were conducted using the same methodology as the user meetings, with the same consultant facilitators and voting procedures. Here, too, the goal was to highlight key distinctions among the alternatives, and to get the IS staff invested in the decision process.

The results of this process (the on-campus demonstrations, user evaluations, and consensus-generating meetings to identify the "short list" of good alternatives) were very positive, and in some ways surprising. First, each group proved to be very perceptive in its ability to discriminate among the packages. Users recognized that all of the packages they viewed would provide a reasonable level of support for day-to-day operations. The real distinctions among the packages were in how well they supported planning, management, decision making, and certain activities that had strategic importance to the college (recruitment, enrollment management, financial management, etc.). In each division, users rejected those alternatives that provided poor support for the college's strategic initiatives.

Second, the user–evaluators also demonstrated fairly deep understanding of the technical issues related to the various packages. They understood that certain database management systems and programming languages and tools were more flexible than others, and that some packages would therefore be easier to support and enhance. They also appreciated differences in user interfaces, and understood that some packages would be easier to use than others. Finally, they appreciated that certain technical environments provided a great variety of tools for *ad hoc* reporting and analysis and other forms of end user computing, and that these environments were more desirable than those which provided more limited tools.

A pleasant surprise to the management team was the fact that, in making their recommendations for "finalists," each division independently arrived at similar conclusions. Two alternative vendors emerged from the user evaluation meetings, in addition to the "fallback" vendor identified earlier in the process. There was no need for the management team to resolve disputes or to weigh the priorities of one division against those of the others.

The management team endorsed the recommendations of the user groups, and forwarded them to the Information Services Steering and Planning Committee (ISSPC) and the Information Services Committee (ISC) of the board of trustees which added their approvals. The management team also made a series of presentations to the College Budget Committee, and to the Business and Finance and the Executive Committees of the board of trustees, to bring them up to date on the project status, and to reaffirm the allocation of a budget for the system replacement project for the next fiscal year. The project was budgeted, subject to approval of the final system recommendation by the ISC.

With approvals in hand, the management team then turned to the task of completing the evaluation process. Up to this point, the evaluation process had focused primarily on functionality. It was acknowledged, however, that more detailed functional analysis was required; both the on-campus demos and the vendor proposals were not sufficiently detailed for an in-depth functional evaluation, and provided no real "hands-on" experience with the products. In addition, there were many other important issues to address. These issues included, among others, the strength of the vendor's business; an assessment of their marketing and product strategy; the quality of support from the vendor; an assessment of each package's underlying database and software technology, and the implications of this technology for the college; and an evaluation of the hardware environments in which the packages functioned.

The management team felt that these issues were best addressed in person, by spending time with the vendors in order to go through each package in depth, get a feel for the vendor's business, discuss future directions, etc. Evaluation teams of key users and systems staff were created who would evaluate each system module and the vendor's business and technical qualifications. These evaluation teams spent several days visiting each vendor's office. They also visited client reference sites for each vendor. Upon the completion of their visits, evaluators were required to write a "trip report." The evaluation visits took several months to complete and involved extensive travel by both users and IS staff. While the evaluators also used less time-consuming and less expensive methods (Dun & Bradstreet reports, requesting financial statements, conducting telephone reference checks), the in-person visits provided the most useful information.

When the visits were complete, the trip reports were summarized in a large table, many pages in length. Through the table it was possible to compare the three alternatives on all of the important issues at a glance. This summary was presented to the evaluators (those who had taken the trips) in one large meeting, for the purpose of verifying that their findings had been captured accurately. With just a few corrections, it was agreed that the document accurately reflected the evaluators' assessment of the various alternatives.

At this point in the process, the project's management team had sufficient information to complete their evaluation and make final recommendations. It had already been established that each of the options provided good functional capability, and that from a functional viewpoint, no option was clearly superior to the others. The decision factors that proved to be most important were vendor-related business issues, the expected growth path for the application packages, and differences in the database and software technology employed by each package. For example, one application vendor appeared to be strong both financially and organizationally; their package, however, relied on a database management system supplied by another vendor whose long-term viability was questionable. A second vendor was planning to completely redevelop their applications using fourth-generation software and a relational database. In this case, the management team felt that this vendor's current package would be supported for only a few more years, since the vendor's R&D funds were being shifted to support the migration to new technology. One vendor, however, was viewed as having a strong advantage because their package was designed for maximum tailorability to customer needs, was based upon very powerful software and database technology, and, since it was at the very beginning of its life cycle, was expected to have a long useful life. The management team felt that this vendor's option would support both the immediate processing requirements of the college as well as ill-defined future requirements.

In its discussions, the management team gave added weight to these issues. It felt that these factors provided advantages for the college from a long-term, strategic viewpoint. Issues considered less important, particularly over the 10-year expected life of the system, were ease of conversion and price. (There were not significant price differences in the options.)

The vice president for information services (and chair of the management team) conducted a roll call vote to select the final option. Of the 12 members of the team, 10 voted for the package perceived to have the greatest flexibility, power, and useful life expectancy; 1 member voted for the lowest-priced option; and 1 member voted for the option that was the best functional fit for the users he represented. The group had previously agreed that the will of the major-

ity would be the recommendation passed on to ISSPC and the Information Services Committee. The group also realized that it would be necessary to explain this choice to the dissenters carefully, and to assure them that their concerns and needs would be addressed.

The management team's recommendations were endorsed by both the ISSPC and the Information Services Committee. The trustees instructed the team to proceed with an evaluation and recommendation of new hardware to support the recommended package. Upon approval of the hardware selection and the final project budget, the trustees would then authorize the IS staff to proceed with the purchase of both new software and new hardware, and to begin the implementation of the new systems.

Summary

This project, although more than 30 months in progress, is only partially completed. There remains the hardware selection process, the implementation plan and the actual conversion. Although to some extent the hardware selection is strongly influenced by technical considerations, there is a significant political and human element to be accommodated. The implementation plan, too, has many variables to be weighed, such as the college calendar, the dependencies between application areas, the availability of people for training, and the like. Finally, in spite of the thoroughness of the plan, the conversion to actual operation is bound to force new problems to the surface that may require rethinking some previous decisions.

But the most important phase is done. The sequence of events is correct. The software decision was needed in order to drive the appropriate hardware decision. User support had to come through the software decision process, since the software is primarily responsible for giving them the results they seek. This user support is a prerequisite for a successful conversion and efficient system operation. The software decision process was essential, too, for garnering the support of management and the trustees. Only by experiencing such a deliberate and controlled process would they commit such a large amount of funds and be willing to expose the college to the other risks involved in such a major systems change.

Assignment Questions

1. What are the major risks for the college in the approach it has chosen, i.e., converting to an entirely new system through package software purchases, rather than rewriting in-house?
2. Do you think it was really time to replace the existing systems or should the college have waited until the need was more critical?
3. Examine the applications requirements document (Exhibit 4–3). Does it do the job? Is it clear and understandable? How would you modify it?
4. Examine the systems evaluation form (Exhibit 4–4) and comment on its usability. Do you think the committee dealt with its shortcomings well? If not, how did problems with the form bias the process? What would you have done differently?
5. Do you agree with the criteria used to select the final vendor? Could you justify this methodology and logic to the other two?
6. Was this process only practical and worthwhile because this was a college environment or could the same approach be used in a business or government organization? What might need to be changed? What would stay the same?

PARTY HARDY

Karen S. Nantz

Introduction

You have just taken on a new client—Party Hardy. This small business provides party equipment and supplies to the Anytown area. To date, it has kept all of its records in a manual system. The owners, Pat and Marsha Hardy, have contracted with you to automate their equipment rental and supplies purchasing system.

This case was prepared by Karen S. Nantz, Eastern Illinois University, as the basis for class presentation and discussion rather than to illustrate either effective or ineffective handling of an administrative situation.

Background Information

Party Hardy started in 1990 as an in-home business for Marsha Hardy. She started a balloon delivery business after she and her husband moved to Anytown from Lafayette, Indiana. Mrs. Hardy worked in a balloon business there while she and her husband attended college. The original business took orders for balloons and delivered them on a cash-only basis.

In 1993, Mrs. Hardy expanded her business to include items related to balloons. She started carrying greeting cards, crepe paper streamers, plastic cups and plates for special occasions, confetti, and party favors.

She also started renting helium cylinders for persons purchasing balloons.

In 1995, Mrs. Hardy again expanded her business to include the rental of wedding-related items—candelabra, wicker flower baskets, punch bowls, glass plates and cups, silverware, cake stands, etc. She moved into a building at 903 Pine St. that she rents for $400.00 per month.

Currently Mrs. Hardy employs two full-time workers to consult with customers and take orders. She also employs four students who work part-time filling and delivering orders. Her business is still mostly cash and carry, but she does have some credit customers whom she bills each month on an invoice system.

At the present time all orders are taken manually and billed manually. Mrs. Hardy is finding that not all items are being marked off as returned, causing her embarrassment and loss of customers when she improperly bills customers for returned items.

The Future of Party Hardy

Mrs. Hardy said, "My goal is to be the premiere balloon and party rental service in Adams County. I would like to see our employee base expanded by 1999 to include five additional full-time employees with two delivery vans. I could see the need for 10–15 additional student workers. At the moment, I do not see expanding the range of services, only the number of parties/events that we handle. I would eventually like to automate all functions— payroll, employee records, tax information, and accounts payable. At the moment, however, I just want to automate the order taking and accounts receivable.

I can also foresee an employee incentive program so that employees receive a percentage of the sales they take and deliver. I would also like to be able to find out more about the orders and the customers—which products are selling best, in what months are certain products selling best, who are our best customers, etc."

To aid you in developing this system, see copies of her order form, invoice form, and partial product list (Exhibits 4–5 through 4–7).

Assignment Questions

1. What additional fields does Mrs. Hardy need to add to her list of products? Would you recommend changes in the product codes? Why or why not?
2. Write a proposal to Mrs. Hardy that addresses her concerns, outlines the steps you will take to complete the project, and proposes a solution based on your current information. Be sure to address technical, organizational, and financial feasibility.
3. Develop an entity–relationship diagram (ERD) that shows the relationship and cardinality among entities. State any assumptions you are making.
4. Develop normalized relations from your ERD into at least third normal form. For each relation, identify the primary key, foreign keys, and other attributes needed to complete this design. State any assumptions you are making.
5. Create context and level O data flow diagrams for Party Hardy. Create additional levels of data flow diagrams as you are directed by your instructor.
6. Develop this system using a database management system. Create the tables, input the product codes, develop a small customer table, and create some orders.
7. In consultation with your instructor, develop input and output forms using good design techniques.

EXHIBIT 4–5 Order Form

Party Hardy
903 Pine St.
Charleston, IL 61920
Phone/FAX: 217-BAL-LOON

Bill # _____

Date _____

Customer # _____   Deliver to: _____
Name   _____   _____
Address   _____   _____
City,State,Zip _____   _____
Phone   _____   _____

Occasion: _____   Date: _____

Quantity	Item #	Description	Unit Price	Delivery Cost	Total
SUBTOTAL					
TOTAL					

Notes:

EXHIBIT 4–6 Invoice Form

Party Hardy
903 Pine St.
Charleston, IL 61920
Phone/FAX: 217-BAL-LOON

Date: _____

Customer# _____

_____

_____

_____

Bill Number	Description	Total

TOTAL AMOUNT DUE _____

The total amount is payable on or before the 15th day of the current month. Any bills not paid by the 15th will incur a $10.00 late payment charge.

EXHIBIT 4–7 Partial Product List

List of Products for Party Hardy

Product Code	Product Description	Cash/Carry Cost or Rental Cost	Delivery Charge
	Cash and Carry Items		
B-100	Latex balloon	1.00	.50
B-101	Mylar balloon	2.00	.50
B-101	Specialty balloon	3.00	.50
B-102	Mixed latex bouquet (1 dz.) with streamers	15.00	3.00
B-103	Mixed mylar bouquet (1 dz.) with streamers	25.00	3.00
B-104	Mixed specialty bouquet (1 dz.) with streamers	40.00	3.00
B-105	Crepe paper streamer (100 ft. roll)	4.00	
B-106	Plastic cups (1 dz.)	1.50	
B-107	Plastic plates (1 dz.)	2.40	
B-108	Confetti (1 oz. pkg.)	1.00	
B-109	Party favors (each)	1.00	
B-110	Bulk balloons (1 gross)—not inflated	100.00	
B-111	Helium cylinder—disposable	15.00	
	Rental Items		
R-100	Candelabra—holds 7 candles, not included	25.00	5.00
R-101	Spiral candelabra—holds 25 candles, not included	40.00	5.00
R-102	Dripless candle	2.00	
R-103	Wicker flower basket	15.00	3.00
R-104	25-cup punch bowl	10.00	3.00
R-105	50-cup punch bowl	20.00	3.00
R-106	Glass plate	1.00	.10
R-107	Glass punch cup	1.00	.10
R-108	Silverware (place setting)	1.00	.10
R-109	Crystal cake stand	5.00	1.00
R-110	Tablecloth (covers 2' × 8' table)—includes laundering fee	10.00	1.00
R-111	Table skirt (covers 2' × 8' table)—includes laundering fee	10.00	1.00
R-112	Brass arch	50.00	10.00
R-113	Brass pew candleholders	20.00	5.00

SYSTEMS DEVELOPMENT IN THE FEDERAL JUDICIARY

R. Ryan Nelson

Introduction

On June 20, 1995, in their biannual meeting, the Committee on Automation and Technology (CAT) was faced with a decision that would likely determine the future course of automation in the federal judiciary. The committee of 14 federal judges had just listened to several opposing arguments on how to best develop information systems, and were now prepared to render judgment on the issue of systems development. At 8:00 A.M. the meeting came to order and the chair of the CAT committee, Judge Owen Forrester, called for the adoption of one of the following six resolutions:

1. That to the maximum extent feasible, all new applications or major enhancements be outsourced.
2. That to the maximum extent possible, all new applications be developed by the Office of Automation and Technology (OAT) within the Administrative Office of the U.S. courts.
3. That to the maximum extent possible, all new applications be developed within the courts.
4. That all three strategies be utilized
   a. Equally.
   b. But that _____ (or _____ and _____) be utilized primarily.

5. That all three strategies be used and the allocation be made project by project based on the best proposal.
6. That all three strategies be used, but that case management systems and probation systems should continue to be done by OAT in the Administrative Office.

With the exception of option 2, each of these resolutions represented a significant departure from past practice and if adopted could potentially bring about dramatic change in organizational size, structure, and resource allocation. After reading position papers and listening to oral presentations from OAT staff, court personnel, and external consultants, the judges felt that they had "heard enough"—it was time to make a decision.

Background Information

The judiciary is an independent branch of the federal government. It does not lie under the jurisdiction of the president, and it is not subject to the control of the Office of Management and Budget. It has its own hierarchy, administrative structure, and decision-making mechanisms. Of course, the judiciary does not enjoy total independence from the other branches of the government. It is subject to a host of federal statutes, and the courts must obtain their funding from the Congress each year through the appropriations process. Moreover, the judiciary's space and facilities program is subject to the control of the General Services Administration.

Article III, section 1, of the Constitution of the United States provides that "the judicial power of the United States, shall be vested in one supreme Court, and in such inferior

---

This case was prepared by R. Ryan Nelson, University of Virginia, as the basis for class presentation and discussion rather than to illustrate either effective of ineffective handling of an administrative situation.

Courts as the Congress may from time to time ordain and establish." Over the last 100 years three types of inferior or lower courts have been established as follows:

United States Courts of Appeals
The courts of appeals are intermediate appellate courts created to relieve the Supreme Court of considering all appeals in cases originally decided by the federal trial courts. The United States is divided up into 12 regional judicial circuits, each with a United States court of appeals. At present each U.S. court of appeals has from 6 to 28 permanent circuit judgeships (167 in all).

United States District Courts
The district courts are the trial courts with general federal jurisdiction. Each state has at least one district court, while some of the larger states have as many as four. There is also a U.S. district court in the District of Columbia. Altogether there are 94 district courts located throughout the United States. At present, each district court has from 1 to 27 federal district judgeships (649 in all), depending upon the amount of judicial work within its territory.

United States Bankruptcy Courts
In 1978, Congress responded to the growing number of bankruptcy cases being filed by modifying the law of bankruptcy to establish a bankruptcy court as an adjunct to the United States district court. Altogether there are 91 bankruptcy courts with between one and 21 judgeships each (326 in all).

The Administrative Office (AO) of the United States Courts, under the direction of the Judicial Conference, provides support to the judiciary. The mission of the AO continues to evolve in response to the changing needs and priorities of the federal judiciary. At its creation in 1939, the AO was a simple organization which provided classic administrative support such as purchasing, personnel, budget, and financial control services. Today, in addition to these basic functions, the Admin-istrative Office also provides support to the Judicial Conference and its committees, facilitates effective communication among the three branches of government, works to obtain needed resources from the Congress, and provides automation support, program and policy advice, and assistance to the courts.

A recent organization chart for the AO is depicted in Figure 4–1. In total, approximately 800 AO personnel in Washington, D.C., support over 26,000 court personnel and judges located throughout the country. AO budget authority for FY 1995 was approximately $47 million of the $2.9 billion earmarked for the entire judiciary.

Three Primary Options

At the time of the June 1995 meeting of the CAT committee, three basic options for developing information systems had emerged: insourcing, outsourcing, or court-based. Each option came with its own set of pros and cons as well as its own set of champions.

Insourcing

Given its primary emphasis on OAT-developed systems, this option comes the closest to maintaining the status quo from an organizational mission, size, structure, and resource allocation point of view. The principal champions of insourcing are OAT personnel led by the assistant director of OAT (a.k.a. the chief information officer).

Yet, based upon a recent assessment of their systems development environment, OAT is not prepared to singularly meet the future development needs of the judiciary. More specifically, a significant amount of investment would be required in the following areas:

• *Methodology.* The cornerstone of OAT's SDE is a six-phase waterfall SDLC process.

FIGURE 4–1   Abbreviated Organization Chart for the Administrative Office of the U.S. Courts

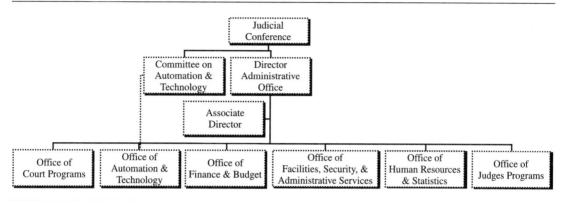

- *Technology.* This includes both development tools (e.g., PowerBuilder and VisualBasic) and computer-aided software engineering (CASE) tools (e.g., IEF).
- *People.* Any changes in methodology and/or technology require an investment in people.

Outsourcing

Although the judiciary has relied heavily on external vendors and consultants over the years, most of these contracts have focused on tasks other than the development of information systems (e.g., planning and requirements analysis). One notable exception is the five-year, $75 million, Data Communications Network (DCN) installation contract, which as one person stated ". . . is an example of the type of development project that should be outsourced. Unfortunately, the DCN project is also a prime example of what can go wrong with an outsourcing project (i.e., contractual, modification, and communication problems)." Nevertheless, OAT managed to get over 60 percent of the network installed within budget over the first five years and is proceeding to complete the project.

In an interesting parallel to many private-sector organizations, this option seems to be favored by the top two administrative offices of the AO, the director and the associate director, when outsourcing would be cost effective and when one or more of the following situations occur:

- The judiciary lacks the necessary (application-related, technological, and/or methodological) expertise in-house;
- A suitable system already exists in the marketplace; and/or
- The judiciary decides not to devote resources to development within a given area.

Court-Based Development

Information systems have been developed in the field by court-based personnel since at least 1981 when the budget management (BUDMAN) system was developed in the fifth circuit court in New Orleans. Since that time, dozens, perhaps even hundreds, of systems have been developed for local and in some cases, multicourt use. Table 4–1 cites seven case examples of court-developed systems, including some of the key issues associated with their development.

TABLE 4–1   Case Examples of Systems Developed in the Field

System (Yr. Devel.)	Application	Software	Key Development Issues
ASAP (1994)	Finance	FoxPro	• AO spent approximately 8 months modifying court-developed system for "national" deployment • Excellent AO-field relationship • Multiple court units (seven members of CFS user's group) involved in modifying system
BUDMAN (1981)	Finance	C language and FoxPro	• Rapid, iterative development (3 months) • Adopted by over 100 courts • Poor AO-field relationship (re support)
ESP (1995)	Bankruptcy calendaring	VisualBasic + Access	• Four courts involved in developing national system • Use of JAD technique • Applying life-cycle management process • Need to integrate with other systems (e.g., CHASER) • Support unresolved
FINSYS (1989)	Finance	Clipper	• Tenuous AO-field relationship • Support unresolved
JAMS (1988)	District case management	FoxPro	• Rapid development (6 months) • High level of support from chief judge • Limited resources inhibited progress
M'PASS (1990)	Probation	FoxPro	• Rapid development (12 months) • Flexibility of system • Limited resources • used by three other courts
NIBS (1986)	Bankruptcy	FoxPro	• Rapid development (3 months) • Use of JAD technique • Pilot tested in three courts over 2 months • Distributed to 2/3 of bankruptcy courts within 1 year • Court-based support

Although the number of locally developed systems seems to be increasing at an exponential rate in recent years, with only a few exceptions (e.g., ASAP and ESP) they remain virtually ignored by the Administrative Office. That is, local developers are not required to follow rigid guidelines for development, fill in the right forms, and go through the right channels. This practice can be a mixed blessing. While the lack of controls can foster speed and creativity, it can also result in errors, reinventing of the wheel, and lack of integration with other systems. As might be expected, the primary champions of this option reside in the field.

Assignment Questions

1. Summarize and critique the three basic options for developing information systems in the federal judiciary.
2. Choose one of the six resolutions and prepare a memorandum to management defending your choice and making recommendations for implementation.

Chapter 5

Installation

The implementation stage of the SDLC is where the new information system is transferred into a working environment. The activities involved in this stage include planning, site preparation, acquisition of new equipment if necessary, training, and, finally, changeover.

PLANNING

A plan should be developed which describes all the activities that must occur in order to put the new information system into operation. Special conversion procedures may be required that will not continue after this stage. The timing of this stage may be difficult because of aspects such as the arrival and installation of new equipment and supplies, and seasonal factors regarding vacations and the availability of staff.

SITE PREPARATION

With the implementation of a new information system comes many other changes. New equipment may require modifications to the environment. If the process of conducting business is to be modified infrastructure changes will be necessary. This may lead to alterations in office layout and locations.

EQUIPMENT

Based on the requirements of the new information system it may be necessary to acquire and install new hardware or telecommunications services.

TRAINING

In all cases of the implementation of a new information system, training of the personnel must be carried out. It is important to note that without staff commitment it is possible for personnel to prevent the implementation of an information system. So training should involve both the provision of knowledge about the operation of the information system and the development of commitment to ensure that the system will operate as planned.

The aim of user training is to teach specific job skills. Although most user training deals with the normal operation of the system, it is important to also instruct personnel in the various processes involved in troubleshooting.

CHANGEOVER

Before the actual start-up of the new information system, it may be necessary to carry out data conversion. This activity involves setting up the new master files and any supporting files necessary for the new information system. It is important to ensure that all records have either been entered from source data or converted from an existing information system. It is mandatory to establish a cutoff date whereby the old and new data will be the same or at least comparable.

There are four approaches to procedure conversion. Direct conversion is where the new information system replaces the old system at a certain period of time. This approach may be used when the two systems are so different that no comparison of results is possible. Parallel conversion related to operating both information systems over a period of time. Operating both systems concurrently allows for cross-checking of results to ensure the accuracy of the new information system. Further, pilot conversion suggests that an information system may be implemented in various parts of the organization; that is, the new information system migrates across the organization with small implementation projects within different departments. Finally, phased conversions may be employed where parts of the new information system may be implemented at different periods of time.

THE CASES

Training End Users at the Internal Revenue Service

R. Ryan Nelson and Ellen Whitener

This case reviews the process of developing and conducting end user training for a new information system.

Apparelmaster

Bruce Johnson

This case presents a situation that has developed during a parallel conversion. A system, which centrally processed data submitted from throughout the United States and Canada, was sold to a vendor over 800 miles away. The programs and operating procedures were transferred to the new vendor's site and unit tested in the new environment. Then, because processing varied according to a weekly cycle, a week of parallel processing was performed with the results being distributed from the original location. Because all the programs ran and produced output in the correct format, the parallel was declared a success and the master files were transferred to the new location over the weekend and, starting the following Monday, production processing was distributed from the new location.

Production processing appeared to go according to plan at the new location until about Thursday when miscellaneous customer complaints began to occur. On the following Monday a significant number of postings were not processed and showed up on the error list. It was quickly determined that the weekly Wednesday realignment run had failed the preceding week. Thus new data sheets were not produced and when the customer tried, starting on the subsequent Monday, to use the new account identifiers, mismatches were encountered. The problem was fixed and several days of processing were rerun and distributed at significant cost.

An output check from the prior Wednesday verified that the realignment run also failed at the new location during the parallel run. When the personnel involved with checking the output were asked why they did not report the alignment errors, they said, "We did, and were told to ignore them."

GCSC/Raymond Bag

Bruce Johnson

This case presents a situation during conversion with the old and new payroll systems running in parallel. It seems to be impossible to reconcile the new system with the old system. One by one the discrepancies were identified and they all turned out to be errors in the original process. Because the users had been depending on the original system for years they had come to believe in its output and it was hard to convince them of its errors. Each error had to be detected and then the users had to be convinced.

TRAINING END USERS AT THE INTERNAL REVENUE SERVICE

R. Ryan Nelson and Ellen Whitener

From the early 1960s until the early 1990s the Internal Revenue Service (IRS)[1] functioned primarily as a batch-processing operation. That is, when end user personnel working on the front line needed information to perform their jobs they were forced to submit a request for that information to the IS department. Such a request initiated a lengthy process of running extracts from several different tape files, eventually producing a printout that was sent to the end user.

After 30 years of operating in such an inefficient manner, the solution for achieving dramatic improvements and modernizing the tax systems seemed straightforward—put the information on-line. Expectations were high for great improvements—faster response time, lower cycle time, and more accurate information. However, these expectations were not fully realized. Investigation suggested one major reason—although the information technology had been improved, the overall process had not been redesigned and personnel had not been retrained. Job manuals and process charts that dictated the way end users performed their jobs reflected the old paper-based processes and had not been changed to reflect the new system.

This case was prepared by R. Ryan Nelson and Ellen Whitener, University of Virginia, as the basis for class presentation and discussion rather than to illustrate either effective or ineffective handling of an administrative situation.

[1]As described in Exhibit 5–1, the IRS is a large bureau of the United States Department of the Treasury that increasingly relies on sophisticated information technology to accomplish its mission.

In retrospect, despite having taken a great deal of care in developing a successful system, no one had thought to redesign the work processes and train the end users how to perform those new work processes. To prevent similar practices in the future, Hank Philcox, the chief information officer (CIO), decided to embark on two major initiatives. First Philcox introduced a new six-phase process entitled the "training development quality assurance system (TDQAS)." Second, he created a "corporate education" department responsible for making training more coordinated and centralized. Each of these initiatives are described below.

A More Systematic Approach to Training, TDQAS

Prior to redesign, the old process for developing IS projects deemphasized systematic approaches to training. However, following the experience described above, project managers were charged with systematically incorporating a training plan, including a needs assessment, into the development and implementation of any new system. Figure 5–1 depicts each of the phases and subcomponents of the TDQAS. The first two phases, assessment and analysis, establish the foundation for end user training and consist of seven subcomponents:

1. *Identify training needs.* The goal is to identify problem areas that prevent an employee from performing his/her job successfully. In addition, an attempt is made to identify new training needs caused by changes in the way a job is performed (e.g., the introduction of IT).

EXHIBIT 5–1   The Internal Revenue Service (http://www.irs.ustreas.gov/)

Mission:	To collect the proper amount of tax revenue at the least cost; serve the public by continually improving the quality of our products and services; and perform in a manner warranting the highest degree of public confidence in our integrity, efficiency, and fairness.
FY 1993 budget:	$7.1 billion (IS budget = $1.5 billion; including $572 million for tax systems modernization projects)
Number of returns:	207,423,469
Number of employees:	113,352 (9,320 in the national office and 104,032 in the field offices)
Number of IS personnel:	8,868 (3,100 in the national office; 3,462 in the field offices; and 2,300 in the three computing centers)
Number of end users:	104,484 (6,220 in the national office and 98,264 in the field offices)

---

2. *Determine the focus of training development efforts.* The goal is to ensure the efficient use of resources by prioritizing training and development activities.
3. *Describe the trainee population.* The characteristics of the learner audience (trainees) are identified, including demographics (e.g., age, education, and reading levels) and knowledge, skills, and abilities.
4. *Inventory the job tasks.* An attempt is made to specify all of the tasks which are components of a job, thereby representing all of the possible "targets" upon which training programs could focus.
5. *Select the tasks for training.* A list is prepared that represents those tasks which are essential to job performance and require either formal training, on-the-job training, or the use of job aids.
6. *Analyze the tasks.* Each task selected for training is examined to identify the circumstances under which it is to be performed. A key objective of task analysis is to coordinate training development efforts by identifying the common training needs of a given occupation.
7. *Conduct a learning analysis.* The specific training objectives are written, the requisite knowledge and skills are determined, and the job-aid candidates are confirmed.

The Corporate Education Department

In 1993, Philcox created the "IRS University" (renamed Corporate Education) an entity designed to function as a "comprehensive educational system," paralleling similar efforts of corporations like General Electric and Ford Motor Company and consulting companies like Andersen Consulting and EDS. Headquartered in Washington, D.C., Corporate Education consists of three schools, each led by an executive dean:

- *The School of Taxation* provides technical training for service professional and paraprofessional employees to help them deal effectively with knowledgeable practitioners and taxpayers.
- *The School of Information Technology* provides IT-related training for both IS

FIGURE 5–1   The TDQAS Training Process

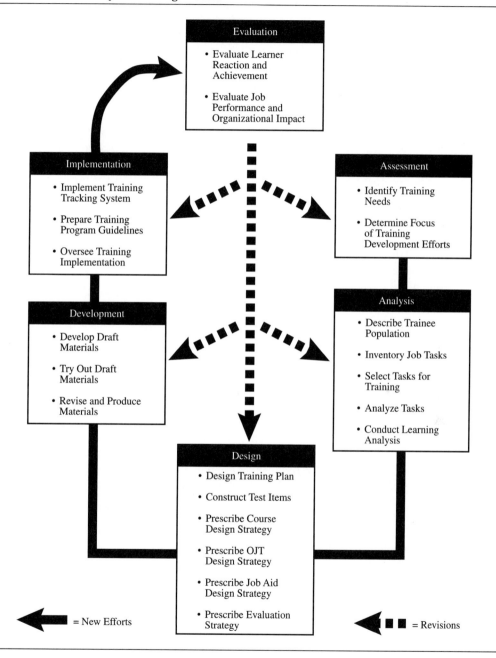

and end user personnel who increasingly rely on information technology to successfully perform their jobs.

- *The School of Professional Development* offers courses in personal leadership and general business. The leadership curriculum is designed to engage both current and future leaders in a process of continuously increasing their knowledge and skills associated with predefined attributes of an executive-level employee. The general business curriculum provides education in basic job skills and technical nontax areas, e.g., public affairs, procurement, labor management relations, etc.

One year after its initiation, a total of 107 employees worked in Corporate Education, distributed across the three schools as follows: Taxation (60), IT (8), and Professional Development (39). In addition, Corporate Education attempts to leverage their human capital by making extensive use of training technologies such as CBT and interactive television.

A Prototype Project

One of the first projects to benefit from the two training initiatives was the automated underreporter (AUR) project, one piece of the IRS's much publicized tax systems modernization (TSM) program.[2] The underreporting

subunit identifies potential discrepancies, such as taxpayers who may have underreported their income, by comparing the income they list on their tax returns with the earned and unearned income information provided by their employers, banks, stockbrokers, and other financial entities. Prior to the AUR, the batch approach required case workers to order copies of income tax returns and supporting documents and to calculate and compare reported income. If they found that discrepancies were sufficiently large, case workers would open a file to attempt to reconcile the reports or to calculate and collect taxes on the underreported income. The AUR project focused on designing and implementing an information system to accomplish much of the information gathering, income comparison, and discrepancy-calculation activities electronically.

From the initial stages of the project, IS professionals, end users, and trainers recognized their interdependence and worked cooperatively to design and implement the AUR system, thereby creating a cross-functional project team. They realized from previous experiences that their system would be more effective if all affected constituents were engaged in the project at an earlier point and to a deeper level. They worked together to both develop the system and design the training.

The activities of the cross-functional project team included developing a training plan. As they conducted their needs assessment and particularly the "audience analysis," they recognized that different constituents had different training needs to be addressed in the plan. Although the system would ultimately present the same core work processes and technologies, individuals and work groups had different interactions with the system. Information system designers, for example, knew how to write

[2]Tax systems modernization (TSM) is a 10-year multibillion dollar project to reinvent the IRS with more modern information systems. The effort is one of the president's priority projects. The modernization will bring far-reaching change that will dramatically improve the quality of the IRS's products and services and significantly increase employee productivity and professionalism servicewide. Rather than trying to update or develop a grand design information system for the whole organization at once, the goal of TSM is to phase in new information systems a subunit at a time and tie them together when they are complete (targeted for 2003).

the software, but they didn't know the basic work processes for evaluating underreporting. They needed training early in the process on the work flow. Incumbent end users (employees who had worked in underreporting under the batch system) knew the basic work flow but didn't know how it had been modified by the system or how the system worked. They needed training when the system was operational on both changes to the work design and on the system itself. Newly hired end users who had no experience with estimating underreporting would need training in the work processes and in the system. Finally, managers needed to know both how the new system worked and how to manage end user performance in light of the new system.

The team also recognized two other important training issues. First, end users had a wide range of comfort and experience with computers and information systems. At one end of the range, employees had no experience with computer-based information systems beyond those encountered in occasional daily life (i.e., automated teller machines or gas pumps). Unless addressed directly and early in the training process, their anxiety associated with the move to computerization could seriously hamper their motivation to learn and use the system. At the other end were employees with extensive experience with computers at home or in school who anticipated the implementation of the system with great enthusiasm. However, too much training on the mundane and basic aspects of computers would dampen their interest in the system as well. Similarly, employees varied in their keyboard skills. Some not only would need training in the system but in "typing" or keyboard skills.

Second, the developers recognized that demographic and educational backgrounds of end users differed by geographic location.

For example, work groups at more urban sites around the country tended to have higher education levels and more experience with computers and information technology than those at remote or rural sites.

The AUR project team incorporated these issues into the overall training strategy by developing a self-paced training approach and plan. The plan started with setting up computer work stations and inviting employees with no computer experience to pound on the keyboard and play with a variety of standard software packages. When they felt comfortable with the computer, trainees would start a series of modules on the system. They would work through each module at their own pace, and sit down with a manager who tested their mastery of that module before allowing them to go on to the next one. The modules and accompanying user guides were designed to be as realistic as possible—reflecting simulated cases and situations on-line.

More to Be Done!

Despite his success with his two end-user training initiatives and projects such as AUR, Philcox knew that there was a lot more to be done. For example, by 1994 there were approximately 50 tax system modernization (TSM) projects on the drawing board and over 30 active projects were in different stages of completion. Except in the most general sense, TSM projects operate independently when it comes to end user training, considering themselves unique entities with their own set of unique EUT requirements. Although the new systematic process of end user training goes a long way toward achieving the goals of an individual project, the higher-level goals of TSM and ultimately the organization as a whole would be improved with greater integration.

Furthermore, despite efforts to the contrary, implementation often deviates from the original plans. In the case of TSM projects, there is a tendency to deviate from training plans due to pressures to get the projects up and running, functional and operational, in a timely and efficient manner. This pressure often results in compromise, such as taking shortcuts with the TDQAS needs-assessment process. As one trainer explained, "time is a very important problem because most of the time when we are asked to do this [e.g., design training for an IS project] we are not given enough time to do it properly. I must tell you in the history of all the years I have been here, I have never actually done that [training] process from beginning to end."

The pressure has also driven system development toward implementation without coordinating with supporting functions. Although the project plan calls for integration, such as including trainers in on system development from the beginning so they can develop a training plan as the system evolves, the drive to write the software quickly pushes trainers away from the development process. Trainers are then required to wait until the system is complete to gain access to it to write the training materials. However, because the system is completed, implementation is planned immediately and no time is left to develop training materials. The dilemma was lamented by a Corporate Education specialist: "We've got to have the software developed before we can actually start developing any kind of training. And we don't get that until the end of the project and then they just want us to do it and get it out to them. . . . The project managers will tell you we are going to implement on this day

and training will tell you 'no, we have got to have the finished software product' and they are going to say, 'no, we can't do that, we'll develop our own training.'"

Besides time constraints, budget concerns also create pressures that move implementation activities away from plans. As in most organizations, the IRS has also had to rein in the budget on occasion; and support functions, such as training, frequently get their budgets reduced: "So you cut travel, you cut awards, and you cut training. Historically that has been the nature of the beast," stated a member of the School of Information Technology.

Signifying the progress that the IRS has made toward improving end user training, a manager on one of the TSM projects commented: "We've come a long way. . . . As an organization we never used to communicate together," implying that now they are communicating much more effectively. As satisfying as that statement is for Hank Philcox to hear, he realizes that his organization still has a long way to go before end user training is being given the respect and attention it deserves. The challenge will be to figure out what steps to take next.

Assignment Questions

1. Why didn't early tax systems modernization (TSM) projects achieve the results they desired?
2. What strategies did the IRS initiate to prevent disappointing results in future TSM projects? How were these strategies designed to improve results?
3. How can the IRS achieve greater effectiveness with its training efforts for TSM projects?

APPARELMASTER

Bruce Johnson

It was Tuesday afternoon; Pete Darning, Comserv's operations manager was inundated by phone calls from clients of the Apparelmaster (APM) system. Clients were calling from all over the United States and Canada complaining that they were unable to post transactions to their customer accounts (route stops). His control clerks also indicated what appeared to be an excessive number of errors in yesterday's (Monday, week 3, see Exhibit 5–2[1]) run of the APM system. Some of the clients were downright angry. Pete was really puzzled as to what could be amiss. His data center had begun production processing of the APM system last Monday (week 2) and, as best he could determine, all had gone well. The week before that (week 1) they ran parallel (see Exhibit 5–3 for definition) with the production system at Automated Data Systems (ADS). The parallel had been declared a success, thus the cut over last week (week 2). Why such massive problems all of a sudden—in this the third week of processing?

Apparelmaster was a nationwide (and Canadian) franchiser of service routes for commercial uniform rental. The individual franchisees were Comserv's clients. Comserv's processing was included in the franchise fee. The APM system centrally processed data submitted from throughout the United States and Canada. This processing had originally been done by ADS in Cincinnati. The transfer to Comserv in Mendota Heights was necessitated because ADS was going out of the service bureau business and being liquidated.

Comserv in Mendota Heights, Minnesota, had agreed to purchase the APM system and its processing rights from ADS in Cincinnati. Apparelmaster was not happy with the change but, given the pending liquidation of ADS, they agreed, with some stipulations, to the transfer. The APM system consisted of some 30 COBOL programs and sorts which ran on IBM mainframe hardware. The system did all the processing necessary to handle delivery routes for commercial uniforms to service establishments such as auto repair shops, cleaning services, and retail establishments. Data was submitted for each customer (called a route stop). This data concerned the uniforms to be delivered and picked up and the associated billing and accounts receivable.

The conversion appeared to be minor because both ADS and Comserv ran IBM-compatible hardware. The programs and operating procedures were transferred to Comserv in Mendota Heights and unit tested in their new environment. Bruce Johnson, a consultant to ADS, spent several weeks at Comserv performing the system conversion by compiling the programs, describing the sorts, programming and checking the job control instructions, and setting up operating procedures for the new environment. Testing, due to time and budget constraints, was limited to seeing if the programs ran on Comserv's hardware. This limited testing was consistent with ADS's culture, which dictated that things be done

---

This case was prepared by Bruce Johnson, Xavier University, Cincinnati, OH, as the basis for class presentation and discussion rather than to illustrate either effective or ineffective handling of an administrative situation.

[1]All week numbers refer to week number in Exhibit 5–2.

EXHIBIT 5–2 Processing Time Line

Week 1	Week 2	Week 3
M T W H F	M T W H F	M T W H F

X   Z'   Y   Z
Parallel   Production ——————————————▶ @ Comserv
Production   No processing . . . . @ ADS

EXHIBIT 5–3 SDLC Definition of Parallel

Parallel: In SDLC terms, to run two (the "old" and the "new") computer systems "side by side" in their entirety. The object is to get the "new" system, which is being groomed to replace the "old" to reproduce, often exactly, the results that are being and have been produced by the "old." To run parallel requires that the complete resources used by both systems be available.

in the simplest and cheapest way possible. After all appeared to run at this level, a parallel was conducted. Since processing varied according to a weekly cycle, a week of parallel processing was performed. During this time (week 2) the APM system was run separately in both locations with the results being distributed by ADS in Cincinnati. The data was first sent to Cincinnati for production processing, from there the results were distributed to the APM clients by mail and direct data transmission. Then the data was sent to Mendota Heights and processed again. The output from the parallel was checked by the operations personnel at Comserv, but was not sent to the APM clients. Instead it was placed in separate boxes by processing day and stored at Comserv. Since all the programs ran and produced output in the correct format, the parallel was declared to be a success. Thus the master files were transferred to Comserv in Mendota Heights over the weekend (end of week 1). Starting the following Monday (week 2) production processing was distributed from the new location.

Pete immediately called for Bruce Johnson and Phil Dent, the systems and programming manager to come to his office. He began to inform Bruce and Phil of the recent occurrences relative to the APM system. But he soon found out that Bruce and Phil were painfully aware that something was amiss with APM processing. They were already trying to determine what was happening so that the system could be fixed. In fact, Bruce had already instructed the data center control clerks to bring the boxes with the output from both the parallel (week 1) and last week's (week 2) runs to the second floor conference room where he and Phil were setting up a "war room." During last week's (week 2) production all output that was not distributed to clients was also stored in boxes labeled by day—as was done during the parallel run (week 1).

As soon as Bruce and Phil left Pete's office they went to the conference room and began going through the output from the first week of production at Comserv (week 2). Monday had a spattering of reported errors, which when checked turned out to be normal input errors from the clients. Tuesday was much the same. But when they came to Wednesday something was different! Ideas as to the likely source of the problem began to form in their heads as they studied the output. Wednesday is route stop realignments processing day (see Exhibit 5–4). There were several pages of error messages from the realignment run indicating that the realignment requests had not been processed. As soon as they observed this, Bruce and Phil wondered why such an occurrence had not been detected during the parallel the previous week, if indeed it had happened. And if it had not happened what was different?

A quick check of the box from Wednesday's (week 2) parallel verified that the realignment run also failed during the parallel (week 1). When Bruce asked the personnel involved with checking the output why they did not report the realignment errors during the parallel they said, "We did, and we were told to ignore them. Jim, the shift supervisor, said that we just don't have time or people here to handle such occurrences during the parallel. Besides this does not count, the output is not being distributed from here—but from Cincinnati. We must keep going—so don't worry about it."

Jim and the control clerks had made a very serious mistake as it subsequently turned out. The errors that they glossed over during the parallel turned out to be the very ones that Pete's operation faced here early in week 3. As Bruce and Pete continued their investigation the events leading up to the problem unfolded. Y in week 2 (Exhibit 5–2) is when the route stop changes (realignments) should have been processed to be effective the following Monday Z. But they "dropped out" and were not processed. Thus the transactions submitted for Monday's (week 3) processing did not take for the "new" route stop numbers or,

even worse, were processed under the wrong customer. That is, if 1107 was meant to be the new route stop for last week's 1106, since the realignment did not occur, it would be processed to the old 1107 (which should have been changed to 1108). See Exhibit 5–4.

The immediate problem was in the control settings which indicate that the processing of route stop changes was to take place during Wednesday's (Y) run. When the control instructions were not done properly in the parallel (X), the errors that indicated that the changes were not processed were not handled properly. Since it was a one-week parallel, processing problems at Z' did not occur—since the master files from ADS's processing the prior week (week 2) had been loaded before beginning production at Comserv (week 2). Thus when the realignment requests dropped out during the production run (week 2), everything seemed fine to the staff at Comserv—because the output looked the same as during the parallel (week 1), when they had been erroneously told by Jim, the shift supervisor, that it was OK.

Phil determined that control instructions permitting route stop changes were filled out incorrectly and thus the weekly Wednesday realignment run had failed both during the parallel (week 1) and during the first week of production processing at Comserv (week 2). Therefore new data sheets were not produced and when the customers tried, starting on the subsequent Monday (week 3), to use the new account identifiers mismatches were encountered. The problem was fixed and several days of processing were rerun and distributed at a significant extra cost and with much client dissatisfaction.

When this was all over and the shop was back to normal at last, Pete asked himself, "What exactly went wrong? And how do I prevent such occurrences in the future?

EXHIBIT 5–4   Identifier Used in the Apparelmaster System

RRSS: Where RR is the route and SS is the sequential stop within the route. Thus identifier 1112 means the 12th stop along the 11th route.

Paper work is produced in route stop (RRSS) sequence. The driver drives the route servicing each customer (route stop) according to the instructions on the paper work. Changes encountered while servicing the route are noted and the paper work is returned at the end of the shift for computer processing.

Implications

Over time, as shown below, the same route stop identifier can be used for multiple customers and a given customer may have multiple route stop identifiers. This is because the route stop identifier has multiple purposes.

Adding a customer within an existing sequence

If stops 01 through 12 for route 11 are already assigned and another customer is to be added between stops 05 and 06, then route stop identifiers 1106 through 1112 (and beyond until there is a break in sequence or the end of the route occurs) would have to be reassigned (moved up one) and all their records realigned. Thus stop 06 would become stop 07 and stop 06 would apply to one customer this week and another customer next week.

Splitting a route that becomes too large

Frequently routes become too large for one driver to service in the allotted time and routes are split. This means a new RR and possibly new SS within the route. Again route stop identifier varies with time.

Combing two or more (small) routes

From time to time, one or more routes become too small to service efficiently and thus some form of combination is made. At least some of the customers require new RR and possibly new SS to keep them in order. Again route stop identifier varies with time.

Because, in each of the cases described above, the route stop identifier is serving two purposes, route stops must be realigned. The two purposes are (1) that of sequencing stops within a route and (2) that of identifying a customer for service, billing, etc. Route stop is not a single-purpose identifier; therefore it is not stable. A single customer may, over time, have multiple route stop identifiers. This is not unique. Over time, a single route stop identifier may apply to multiple customers.

Assignment Questions

1. Describe the sequence of events that lead to the phone calls to Pete Darning.
2. There was a significant delay between cause and effect in this case.

Describe the reason for the delay and its effect.

3. Should Johnson have seen the problem before all the trouble happened?

GCSC/RAYMOND BAG

Bruce Johnson

Bruce and Fred had just spent the night reloading year-to-date data, making and testing minor changes, and running a "parallel" of the Raymond Bag (Bag) payroll system. This was the third week in a row that they had done this. They felt sure that this time they could make the results from their system match the system that Bag was currently using to pay their employees. If so, next week they could at last cut over, be the official system, and use their results to make the actual payroll checks that would be distributed. Then their company, General Computer Services Corporation (GCSC), could rely upon the data clerks and computer operators to do the processing. But since Bag had been depending on their existing payroll system for many years, they had come to believe that its output was correct. It was difficult to convince them that, in reality, their payroll output did contain processing errors. Each error had to be detected and shown to Ray Compton, "Bag's" comptroller, in order to convince them.

What could they do? Bruce Johnson was the executive vice president of GCSC and the project director for the entire Raymond Bag project which consisted of, in addition to the payroll, a cost system, sales reports, sales history, and general ledger. Fred Howard was GCSC's lead programmer for data center systems. Raymond Bag was a full-line bag manufacturer in a nearby town. They provided bags and related packing materials to grocery stores, moving companies, and manufac-

turers such as Procter & Gamble in Cincinnati, who was their biggest customer.

GCSC was a three-year-old software house and service bureau located in Middletown, Ohio. They had a dozen employees but they were grossly undercapitalized and their business was one of feast or famine. They were extremely strong technically and in their ability to manage projects. But they were weak in sales and had difficulty stabilizing their workload. They called it their zero mass/infinite velocity problem. They were hoping that ongoing work in their data center would stabilize their income and offset the peaks and valleys of consulting and contract programming.

As a part of this stabilization plan, GCSC agreed to develop and operate the systems listed above for Bag. The requirements for these systems were based on GCSC's prior experience with and knowledge of such systems, some sketchy memos supplied by Ray Compton and others at Bag about specific features that were not in their existing systems, and from studying the output from Bag's existing systems. Given GCSC's advanced productivity tools and talented staff they produced the systems on time and on budget which was remarkable given the short timetable and the tight budget. However, relying on the traditional SDLC approach, the comptroller and officers of Bag insisted on each system being run parallel to their satisfaction before the system was cut over to run on GCSC software and hardware. Generally this meant that the GCSC system should produce the same results as Bag's original system which was being run at another service bureau until GCSC could take over the processing of the systems. The payroll system was the first system planned for cut over. Johnson had become painfully aware that if

This case was prepared by Bruce Johnson, Xavier University, Cincinnati, OH, as the basis for class presentation and discussion rather than to illustrate either effective or ineffective handling of an administrative situation.

there were similar errors—accidents of history—in the other systems Bag was using, GCSC was in for some very hard times.

Who would have thought that a payroll system could be so hard to develop? But for the last three weeks Bruce and Fred's results had not matched the results from the existing system that was actually used to pay Bag's employees. All but one of the discrepancies were due to errors—accidents of history, Bruce called them—in the existing system, not in the payroll programs developed by GCSC. These errors were minor and tended to be self-adjusting over the course of the year, but since they were reflected in the year-to-date data, the erroneous results were "official." First they encountered an error in the cutoff levels for state tax calculations. The next week it was an error in calculating federal tax when a weekly pay period spanned a quarter—this Bruce found hard to believe but after hours of tracking down the discrepancy, this is what Fred found it to be. Last week they had encountered a simple-to-fix bug in GCSC's program that calculated city tax but, more importantly, an error in the original union health care deduction threw the results off. Thus Ray Compton would not authorize the check to be distributed from GCSC's system without at least another week of parallel operation.

The problem was not really in the nature of the payroll system, complex as payroll systems are. The real problem was that GCSC, desperate for the business, had agreed to do a parallel and match the results from the existing system. This forced GCSC to match exactly the results from the prior system—even though some of the results were wrong. This match is particularly important for payroll systems because of the significance of year-to-date data which is essentially a legal document. Once the pay checks have been issued, the data based

thereon is official—be it right or wrong. So even if Bag's prior system's results were wrong and GCSC's were right, GCSC had to align their system with Bag's, by reloading the underlying year-to-date data, paralleling again, and trying to match the outputs.

As the end of processing summary report came off of the printer, Bruce and Fred tore it off and hurriedly compared the run totals from their system to the one Bag had used the day before to pay their employees. One-by-one the figures checked till they came to FICA. GCSC's total was off by less than $2 for almost 400 employees. They were devastated!

As they investigated further, Bruce and Fred discovered that about half of the employees were getting a penny more deducted in FICA in GCSC's system when compared to Bag's existing system. Further investigation convinced them that while GCSC was rounding after calculating year-to-date FICA, the existing system was truncating year-to-date data. Again GCSC was right, but the existing system was official—since paychecks had been issued.

Even as tired and worried as he was, Johnson's thoughts took two directions at this point. First how could he convince Ray Compton to use GCSC's payroll system without precise agreement—which might never come? In fact, given the errors in Bag's existing payroll system, should never come! And how could he assure that neither GCSC nor he was ever again caught trying to match the results from an existing (computer) system?

Assignment Questions

1. How could errors occur in a system that had been used so extensively for so long?
2. Who were the decision maker(s)? What are his/her/their roles?
3. What were the constraints? Alternatives?

Chapter 6

Operation / Maintenance

This chapter describes the SDLC stage relating to that period of time when the information system is said to be in production. The user is responsible for the daily operation of the information system. The average life of an information system is about five years. Any changes to the system during this time will be conducted as maintenance.

TYPES OF MAINTENANCE

Maintenance activities may be categorized into three different types. Emergency maintenance will be carried out when the system fails. This is usually the result of either not meeting all the initial requirements or not detecting errors when the information system is tested. Enhancements are generated by the user identifying new or altered requirements after implementation. This is the result of users obtaining experience with the information system and determining what they consider a better way for the information system to function. Environment maintenance refers to changes that result from some entity external to the functioning of the information system. The computer environment may change with the implementation of new hardware or software. Further, the business environment may change because of new company processes resulting from product changes, organization changes, or revised government regulations.

THE CASE

Billboard Cost Accounting System

Bruce Johnson

Although this case relates, on the surface, to the maintenance stage, there are also some other considerations relating to initial requirements determination and ethics. Obviously, something has to be done to the current system because of performance degradation. This is a classic example of system mismanagement and misunderstanding.

BILLBOARD COST ACCOUNTING SYSTEM

Bruce Johnson

Johnson had just finished rewriting Billboard's cost accounting system—and no one but he knew. His client thought that he was just tweaking the cost system, maintaining and debugging it so that it would meet their unstated needs. And for this he was getting consulting rates. This was a far cry from last spring when he was fired from his position as manager of systems and programming (S&P) for Billboard Publications[1] for protesting activities of Billboard management (such as the cost system acquisition and subsequent events) that made it impossible for him to do the job for which he had been hired. As he smugly viewed his handy work he thought back on the events leading up to his unauthorized rewrite.

Cost accounting for Billboard's numerous publications was a tedious job involving large amounts of data for a wide variety of publication types and formats. While automation was called for and in spite of continued recommendations—actually insistence by Bruce Johnson, who was S&P manager—no project was established to look into the requirements and to specify such a system. One day it was just announced to Johnson and his S&P staff, that the company had

acquired a cost accounting system that was "compatible" with Billboard's hardware and software. Its installation was dropped into the lap of Johnson and his S&P staff without any regard to existing priorities or that there were no programming resources available without severely crippling other projects that were desperately needed and long awaited by company managers and workers.

The cost accounting system that was acquired did appear, at least to management and the cost accountants to be compatible—after all it was written in COBOL. However, major "incompatibility" problems were encountered immediately after the installation began. First in systems and programming and then, more importantly, in operations. The COBOL was for another computer line. Extensive testing and "debugging" were required to detect, analyze, and correct "minor" incompatibilities such as inconsistencies in the program code and incompatible file structures between the two COBOLs. This effort diverted time from new installations, etc., planned to improve the overall performance of the organization. And to Johnson was just one more example of how he and his organization were whipsawed from project to project, instead of working toward an orderly solution to Billboard's computing problems—much less opportunities. Once the cost system was "operational," however, the real problems surfaced. The acquired cost system was written for a single-user machine and Billboard operated

This case was prepared by Bruce Johnson, Xavier University, Cincinnati, OH, as the basis for class presentation and discussion rather than to illustrate either effective or ineffective handling of an administrative situation.

[1]See the Billboard Charts case for background information on Billboard Publications.

a multiuser machine which effectively juggled many on-line users as well as batch jobs. All the cost system programs ran on-line at high priority, most hogged the CPU, and some caused other jobs within the system to come to a halt for the duration of the cost system run. This severely irritated the other users of the system who came down on Johnson and his staff to do something— yesterday. Once again a major effort was undertaken to "patch" the cost system so that it would better integrate into the overall processing environment. And again effort was diverted from planned activities.

Even as the inconsistencies were encountered in the initial installation, the cost accounts were developing a laundry list of changes necessary to make the cost system do what they needed or wanted. As the operational problems were addressed this list grew even longer and more urgent. So even after this monumental effort and disruption, Billboard did not have the cost accounting system that they needed or wanted. How could they have had? They never determined what it was they wanted beyond a "cost accounting system."

Finally Johnson protested loudly about the cost system and other indiscriminate priority juggling, lack of long-range planning, and being whipsawed as each squeaky wheel got its grease in a never-ending cycle. He protested too loudly, in fact, and was fired. This left both Billboard and Johnson in the lurch. But an interesting solution to both of their situations was found. Johnson was engaged as an independent contractor almost immediately after he was fired. One of his assignments as an independent was to make modifications to the cost system in areas where it did not meet the perceived needs of the cost accountants. His task in this assignment was ostensibly to work off the cost accountants laundry list of changes, one by one, in "priority order." Without Billboard's knowledge and against their wishes, he used his knowledge of systems, Billboard's operation, cost accounting, and the laundry list together with the current systems capabilities and completely rewrote the system under the guise of patching and maintaining it. This proved to be much less costly than "maintenance." What is more, it was more rewarding professionally and almost completely avoided the inevitable side effects from modifying an existing system that has not been designed to be easily changed and most likely contains many "accidents of history" for which there is no current rhyme nor reason.

After his initial euphoria, Johnson had second thoughts about what he had done. "I have misled my client. Is what I have done right? Or wrong?

Assignment Questions

1. Once the cost system was operating "satisfactorily" it failed to meet the "perceived" needs of the cost accountants. How could this have been so?
2. Johnson's unauthorized rewrite was in direct violation of his client's wishes. Was it, however, in his client's best interests?
3. If Johnson had just worked on the laundry list as instructed do you think he would have ever really finished?

Chapter 7

Review

The review stage of the SDLC evaluates the information system and the project, and produces a report that may contain recommendations for improving the information system.

POSTIMPLEMENTATION REVIEW

Not too long after the implementation of the new information system a postimplementation review should be conducted on both the new information system and the project.

Information System Review

This review determines how well the new information system is working and what adjustments may be needed. Once the user has had an initial period of exposure to the information system, this experience may lead to the identification of information system changes to improve functionality. Aspects to be investigated could include timeliness of information presentation, appropriateness of information format, and ease of use. A general assessment of overall user confidence in the information system would also be valuable input to this review. Usually data are gathered here by interviewing those individuals directly involved with the daily operation of the information system.

Project Review

This review determines if the project team followed the standard system development, SDLC, approach adopted by the company. First, the company should have a standard SDLC. Second, it is usual that each project follows this standard. However, in some cases, there may be valid reasons for deviating from this standard. These reasons should be documented for future reference either by other project teams or by those responsible for evaluating the established SDLC standard.

PERIODIC REVIEW

On a regular basis, as determined by the company, a review of the information system should be conducted. This review will determine whether requirements in a changing environment are continuing to be met. Areas to be investigated could include system response time, error levels, and equipment utilization. Significant variation in any of these areas may lead to the necessity to conduct some form of maintenance or could lead to the establishment of a new SDLC project.

THE CASES

SAGA: The System for Andre's Great Advantage

William K. McHenry

Between 1991 and 1993 a system was developed and refined to attempt to help Andre Agassi improve his tennis. The major decision to be made now is whether to continue the project or not. Although the system has yet to prove itself, there have been some successes and there seems to be a potential for large payoffs. The case illustrates several pitfalls of systems development, including use of prototyping without sufficient involvement of the main end user and the use of hardware, software, and consultants because they are convenient, available, or known, not because they are necessarily right for the job.

InterTech Refocusing

Nancy J. Johnson

Restructuring a large IS department is challenging even under the best of circumstances. Trying to accomplish it with the additional factors of civil service and four collective bargaining units added even more complexity. Under the leadership of Bernie Conlin, the central IS service unit of the government of the State of Minnesota was recently reorganized to provide closer alignment with the needs of their customers—the 128 state agencies. Two consultants' reports cited the growing dissatisfaction of the agencies in terms of the responsiveness and service levels provided. The restructuring was in response to the criticism. Almost 300 positions were redefined and restructured in a period of less than 18 months, without a single grievance by a collective bargaining unit or the civil service. Only five individuals were laid off in the process. User agencies were surveyed for satisfaction, and significant improvements were noted after the restructuring process. The case cites reasons the manager, participants, and author believe were critical for success.

Federal Government Internet Applications: Effectiveness Review

Rick Gibson

In 1993 Congress developed the National Information Infrastructure, a legislative policy to guide attempts to distribute electronic government information, with an emphasis on public access through the Internet. Currently the federal government uses 750 Internet sites to provide information, products, services, and training to its business clients and customers. This case presents the results of an effective review of current federal government Internet applications.

SAGA: THE SYSTEM FOR ANDRE'S GREAT ADVANTAGE

William K. McHenry

On a warm summer night in July 1993, Perry Rogers sat with his best friend, Andre Agassi, near the pool behind Agassi's modest Las Vegas home. As Rogers sipped a cool ice tea and the mist machine around the pool lowered the temperature to a pleasant 75°, Rogers pondered the future of the computer application he pioneered—SAGA: The System for Andre's Great Advantage. Was it worth the $100,000 of Andre's money he had spent on it since the work began in May 1991? Could it still prove to be the key to Andre's future success? Perry had a lot to

consider as the moon gently rose behind the Vegas mountainscape and strains of Kenny G ethereally wafted from the hidden poolside speakers.

The Beginnings of SAGA

In May 1991 Perry Rogers graduated from the Georgetown University School of Business. Ever since he had taken a course on management information systems with Visiting Professor Cameron Welles, he had been thinking that there must be some way to use the computer to help his childhood friend, Andre Agassi, become the number one men's tennis player in the world. Just before he left for Vegas and then law school at the University of Arizona in Tucson, Rogers gave Professor Welles a call. He described in general what he wanted to do. Welles got

---

This case was prepared by William K. McHenry, Georgetown University, as the basis for class presentation and discussion rather than to illustrate either effective or ineffective handling of an administrative situation.

TABLE 7–1

Position shot Hit from	Stroke	Outcome

FIGURE 7–1

Baseline

Service Line

Add side   Deuce side

Net

excited and told Rogers that he would put together a very small demonstration.

On the next day, Welles showed Rogers a prototype of a data entry module. He divided the court into several sectors, assigning a name with a unique first letter to each one. He also created a set of codes for each kind of stroke, for example, forehand, backhand, serve, and overhead. Each event in the match was then modeled as a record consisting of three fields. It would take three keystrokes to record each event in a match (see Table 7–1). Welles reasoned that if students could play Nintendo and Sega video games at lightning speeds, a properly trained data entry person should be able to capture all aspects of a tennis match in real time. Once this basic data were recorded, every conceivable statistic could be derived. Rogers was impressed. He spoke to Agassi, who gave approval for the development of an initial prototype. Welles and Rogers signed a preliminary agreement which stated that they were the joint owners of whatever was developed, and that if a viable product were developed, a corporation might be founded.

The Game of Tennis

According to Grolier's *American Academic Encyclopedia*,[1] the precursor to the modern game of tennis apparently originated in France at the end of the 13th century and was called *tenetz*. At first, the ball was struck by the palm of the hand; only later

were racquets introduced. The aristocracy in Britain started to play the game about 100 years later, and this version came to be known as "real tennis" in Britain or "court tennis" in the United States. "Lawn tennis," the modern version of the game, was invented by Major Walter Clopton Wingfield in 1873. The game soon spread to the United States, and the first U.S. championship (now the U.S. Open) was held in 1881. Three other international tennis tournaments are considered "majors": the French Open (1891), Wimbledon (1877), and the Australian Open (1905). Country-based teams have competed for the Davis Cup since 1900, and recently tennis was made an Olympic sport.

Grolier's reports, "The basic object of the game is to use a racquet to hit the ball over a net but within the boundaries of the opposite half of the court [see Figure 7–1]. Serve is determined by flipping a coin. Players serve for one complete game. The serve . . . is accomplished by tossing the ball into the air and, with a throwing motion of the racquet hand, hitting the ball with the face of the racquet. The server must stand behind the baseline and on the first serve of the game must stay to the right of the center of the court (the 'Add' side). A proper serve will pass over the net into the service court

---

[1]1994 edition, as published on CompuServe.

diagonally opposite. On each serve the server has two opportunities to make a legal serve. Missing both serves results in a 'double fault' and the loss of a point. After the scoring of the first point in any individual game, the server moves to the left of the center (the 'deuce' side) of the court and serves to the other service area."

Grolier's continues, "After the serve the players attempt to hit the ball back and forth over the net until one player fails to hit the ball before the second bounce, hits the ball into the net, hits the ball out of bounds, touches the net with the racquet or with the body, hits the ball twice, is hit by the ball, or hits the ball before it crosses the net." When a player fails to return the ball because of his own mistake, it is called an *unforced error*. When, however, the player manages to touch the ball with his racquet but still cannot return it, it is called a *forced error*. When the player had no chance to return the ball, i.e., the other player hit a really good shot, the shot is called a *winner*. When the server loses a game, he is said to have been *broken,* and it is called a *break* of serve.

Explains Grolier's, "Tennis uses a unique scoring system. Each four-point game is scored as follows: 'love' indicates no score, '15' indicates a point scored, '30' indicates two points, '40' indicates three points, and 'game' indicates four points. If a tie of 40-all occurs, the situation is called deuce, and one player must score two points more than the opponents to win that game. Tennis matches are usually won by winning the best out of three or the best out of five 'sets.' In most cases, a set is awarded to the player who wins six games before the opponent has won more than four." A score of 6–2, 2–6, 6–4 means that the first player won the first and last sets by winning six games; his opponent won just two and four respectively. The opponent won the second set. A score of 7–6 means that the set was tied at 6–6 so that a tiebreaker had to be played.

The Meteoric Rise of Andre Agassi

In the early 1980s, the U.S. men's professional tennis circuit was dominated by Jimmy Connors and John McEnroe. Connors combined tremendously hard groundstrokes with a wily intelligence and great tenaciousness in battle, while McEnroe was endowed with an almost superhuman talent and a temper that could explode at any moment. But Connors began to age and McEnroe went through sabbaticals and Hamlet-like reexaminations of his game. The new generation of U.S. men's tennis stars, including Aaron Krickstein and Jimmy Arias, did not live up to expectations. By the end of the decade, foreign stars were dominating the game, which led to lower television ratings and advertising revenues in the crucial American market. Ivan Lendl, the tennis equivalent to RoboCop, dominated a game that seemed to become more boring with every match he won.

Into this vacuum came Andre Agassi. Like many of the up and coming tennis stars, Andre left high school early, finishing by correspondence, and attended Nick Bolletteri's tennis academy. Among his contemporaries were Jim Courier and Pete Sampras, but no one was considered as promising as Agassi. Agassi, after all, had been recognized as a tennis child prodigy at age 4, when his father arranged for public practice sessions with Connors and Bjorn Borg. Agassi had one of Borg's wooden racquets in his bedroom. As a 15-year-old amateur in 1985, Agassi was tied at a ranking of 618th. He turned pro in 1986, rising to 91st. In 1987 he reached 25th. And then as an 18-year-old in 1988, Agassi won six tournaments and reached the final ranking of number three. Connors, already well past his prime, would never again make it that high. McEnroe had long before begun his descent.

When Agassi rudely dispatched Connors in the quarterfinals of the 1988 U.S. Open, a new American star was born. All Agassi had to do was win the requisite matches, and his place in tennis history would be secure. He would be the savior of the American game.

Unfortunately, Agassi failed to live up to these expectations in the subsequent years. He lost one French Open final to the aging Andres Gomez and another to Jim Courier. He lost the U.S. Open final match to Pete Sampras, and observers started to think his number three ranking at the end of 1988 was as high as he would ever get. He angered the tennis establishment by skipping Wimbledon and the Australian Open, while drawing more attention to his clothes and his endorsements than to his tennis. In short, he was in danger of becoming a "has been" before his time. Those who focused only on these externals, however, failed to recognize that the innovations in the game brought in by Agassi had now come to haunt him. Agassi took the ball earlier and hit it harder than anyone had ever done before. For a while this was enough to beat many, many players. But Agassi himself was not particularly tall (only about 5′11″). As bigger and stronger players also learned to wield these weapons, Agassi found himself being beaten at his own game. He would then resort to more and more risky shots and his game would often go astray. In May 1991 Agassi's ranking had already started to fluctuate and to drop. If it fell too far, he would not be seeded in major tournaments and his endorsement income would dry up. Endorsement deals, which could bring in millions more than the tournaments themselves, would be renegotiated on a fairly frequent basis. By mid-1992 he had won $4,480,129 at tournaments, but his annual income as reported by *Forbes* in 1992 was $11 million. Something had to be done.

Computers, Tennis, and the Competition

When Rogers and Welles started developing SAGA in May 1991, there was just one other similar product on the market. CompuTennis was developed by computer systems engineer Bill Jacobson, 47, a former South African amateur. He founded Sports Software in Palo Alto, California. *Sports Illustrated* reported in 1984 that, "Late in 1982 he started charting tennis matches for his son Mark, a ranked junior in northern California. At first he fed hand-collected data into a microcomputer. He soon designed a four-pound portable computer with which a single observer could directly record 10 times as much data. CompuTennis was on its way when several top junior coaches and the Stanford men's team bought computers on which to produce their own match reports. [In June, 1984, Jacobson] was given a contract by the United States Tennis Association to chart matches for all four national junior teams."[2]

SI continued: "Jacobson's computer program [didn't] cover every shot in a match. Because players [could] rally for minutes at a time, only the end of the points were recorded. The observer [could] describe the shots (i.e., half volley, passing shot) and note whether [they were] forehand or backhand, the zones of the court they [went] between and the result (i.e., forcing shot, error). There [were] console keys on which to record 10 other statistics, such as the number of times a player [ran] around his backhand. . . . The analyst could also note the surface and weather conditions. . . . Since printouts [could] be produced as the match [progressed], television broadcasters [could] display and discuss constantly updated

---

[2]Arnold Schechter, "A Computer Service Scores Points with a Good Many Tennis Players," *Sports Illustrated,* September 17, 1984, p. 6.

statistics. A complete match report provided a blizzard of statistics. Among its choicest categories were ratios of winners to errors for different strokes, tendencies to rely on certain strokes and success rates at the net and from the backcourt."[3]

By 1985 the CompuTennis staff had compiled data on more than 1,000 players and 2,100 matches. By 1986, UPI reported (8/11/1986), Sports Software had 150 part-time operators throughout the United States who would go to matches and enter the data into the computer for anyone who wanted to pay $75 and expenses. Sports Software was offering special scoresheets for $40, the *New York Times* reported in 1989 (10/23/1989). Users could then send in the manually filled-in sheets for analysis. At this time the court-side computers cost around $2,000. Just the software could be purchased for $195 for use on a laptop computer. By 1993, according to the *Chicago Sun-Times,* the price had risen to about $5,000 for the computer and all accessories (2/12/1993).

Welles and Rogers did not particularly research CompuTennis when SAGA was started. Rogers wanted something different and better, and Welles wanted to avoid any possible charges that they had used any of CompuTennis's intellectual property. In any case, SAGA tried to store every match in a database in a portable computer that would be available throughout tournaments on sight and have interactive analysis capabilities built in.

Professor Cameron Welles

Cameron Welles was a tenured associate professor in the Department of Systems Sciences and Management Information Systems at a midwestern state university. Welles had

---

[3]Ibid.

rather varied research interests. He received a technical MIS degree from the Massachusetts Institute of Technology, but recently had been doing research on the interaction of computers and politics. His paper "The Management of Open-Ended Exit Poll Interview Information" had received critical acclaim, and he kept up an active research profile in this field. In graduate school he had designed and helped implement a database system to manage chunks of texts associated with politics, both from published sources and interviews. This system was programmed partially in FORTRAN, a third-generation procedural computer language dating back to the late 1950s. Welles taught a standard load of two courses each semester.

The First Prototype

In the early summer months of 1991, Welles programmed the first iteration of SAGA using the tools that were available to him. Virtually the entire system was created in Dataease. Dataease was a very useful tool because it was possible to define a field in such a way that pressing one key would enter the data into the field. For example, for the field that recorded the outcome of the point, the following coding could be used: **U**—unforced error, **F**—forced error, **W**—winner, **L**—loser. By pressing just one key, the data entry person could record the outcome of the point. As the work progressed Welles frequently called Rogers and discussed little problems he was having in adapting the Dataease program to the given requirements. Often they would brainstorm together, and sometimes the program would change on an hourly basis. Finally Rogers offered to fund a trip for Welles to Las Vegas on the 4th of July weekend, 1991. Agassi had won an IBM PC at one tournament. Set up in his bedroom at his parents' house, this computer would serve as the workstation for putting the finishing touches on the proto- type. It did not have all the same software tools, however, that were available on the home computer of Welles.

When Welles arrived in Vegas, the atmos- phere was electric. Andre had made it to the quarterfinals of Wimbledon, where he would play another upcoming young American, David Wheaton. All of the Agassis treated Welles with great deference. As Welles worked in Andre's bedroom, his father would come in to give Welles periodic updates on Andre's progress. Mr. Agassi hoped the SAGA project would persuade Andre to work on his serve, which Mr. Agassi felt was weak at that time. Unfortunately for Andre, but fortunately for the SAGA project, Andre lost. This meant that he was coming home, and would arrive in time to see the demo.

In the meantime Rogers and Welles sat in front of one of the many TV sets in the Agassi home to try out SAGA on a real match. With Welles at the computer and Rogers running the VCR, they managed to log the first set of the Agassi–Wheaton match. This experience showed that the idea of using three key- strokes to represent each event (stroke) in the match was too much. It would be necessary to get this down to one. By combining court posi- tion and stroke into one description and elim- inating the field that said what happened after each stroke, they were able to define a keyboard that used almost all 26 keys (A–Z) to record the events in the match (see Figure 7–2). Welles worked furiously to incorporate this change by the time Andre arrived from Wimbledon. There was no time for such niceties as documentation or a users manual.

When Agassi returned from Wimbledon he was in excellent spirits. Not liking to be pinned down to meeting times that had been defined in advance, he preferred to go with the flow. Agassi, Rogers, and Welles went gambling at several Vegas clubs and played golf. Finally the next day Agassi consented to

FIGURE 7–2

Baseline	
Service Line	
Add side	Deuce side
	Net

Front left	Front right	S D
		A i
		G v
		A i
Mid left	Mid right	s
		i
Back left	Back right	o
		n

view the program. After a few minutes he seemed to like what he saw, although he made few concrete suggestions about what kind of statistics he wanted to see coming out of the program. Nevertheless the next phase of development was approved. Before he left Vegas, Welles sketched out a wide-ranging development plan that included eventually adding graphic representations of the data and perhaps even using the data to create a realistic Agassi tennis video game. Welles went ahead and created a number of reports which are shown on subsequent pages as Exhibits 7–1, 7–2, 7–3, 7–4, 7–6, and 7–9. These basic reports covered all aspects of ten- nis, providing a multitude of statistics.

At this time some principles of compensa- tion were also negotiated. Rogers and Welles would own the package under development. Agassi would have exclusive rights to use it for as long as he wished, but when he was finished, it could be marketed to other tennis players. In the meantime Welles would be paid retainers for doing certain chunks of the development work and for being available for maintenance and consultations. Rogers, as Agassi's best friend, declined to take any compensation up front. It was also decided that the data entry person would be a close friend of Rogers from college, Jennifer Stone, who had excellent computer and typing skills, but little knowledge of tennis. Stone was already known to Agassi through her close friendship with Rogers. The computer she would use would be a Dell laptop using a 386 chip which Rogers had purchased for Agassi sometime earlier. In this way development expenses could be kept down.

The First Davis Cup Success

Development continued through the summer of 1991. Among the many problems that had to be solved were how to distribute the new versions of the package to Stone; it was decided to send her diskettes. At first the program fit on one diskette, then two. As the database started to grow it was necessary for Welles to keep a fully updated copy on his computer and then send out new versions of the program and data to Stone. Thus there were some times when she had to stop working because he was making modifications.

Rogers decided that the first real tests of SAGA would come at the Davis Cup semifinal matches in Kansas City. Stone was prepared with a bogus story about doing research on tennis for her "dissertation" in case anyone wanted to know what she was doing with a computer in the stands. The matches were indoors, an important consideration since it turned out that the Dell computer screen started to malfunction in the hot sun of outdoor matches in August and September.

In the first round of the Davis Cup "tie" (round), Agassi beat Michael Stich and Jim Courier beat Carl Uwe-Steeb. Stone logged both of these matches without a hitch. But on Saturday disaster struck. The team of Scott Davis and David Pate lost to Michael

Stich and Eric Jelen of Germany to reduce the U.S. lead to 2–1, after which Jim Courier fell to Stich in singles. It was left to Andre Agassi to pull out the weekend and save the U.S.'s Davis Cup chances. On Friday night and Saturday Stone was on the phone several times to Welles to understand how to get the reports printed from the computer. Her training to this point had largely focused on putting the data in, not getting it out. When the reports finally did come out, she needed help analyzing them. Welles was able to spot that Steeb was serving almost exclusively to the outside on his second serves from the add side of the court. Armed with this knowledge, Andre was able to break Steeb's serve twice in the first set. When the dust settled, he had routed Steeb 6–2, 6–2, 6–3 with a performance that erased the stain of his recent first round loss in the U.S. Open. It was a victory that Agassi desperately needed. Having dropped to number eight in the world from a high of number 3 in November 1988, he was already being written off by many critics and fans.

On the strength of this performance, Rogers decided to go ahead with further development of SAGA. He and Welles mapped out a plan for its further development, and the decision was made to concentrate on entering a large amount of data in the early months of 1992 leading up to the French Open and the U.S. Open. It was hoped that by that time there would be sufficient data in the computer to begin to take advantage of all of the capabilities that were being put into SAGA. Agassi provided a salary for Stone and a travel schedule that brought her to many of the tournaments in the spring. Everything was in place for a major push forward.

Dataease

Dataease was first marketed in about 1983; by 1992 the renamed company Dataease

EXHIBIT 7–1   SAGA (Early Report, Generated June 7, 1992)

Server Stats for the Most Recent Query Set

Generated using the following criteria:
These data have been tabulated using the following conditions:
All the statistics reported here refer to the game of Becker.

	Number	Percent
Total number of points	371	
Total number of serves	536	
First serve percentage		55.53
Second serve percentage		95.03
Number of aces, first, second serve	63, 4	
Number of points won, first serve	173	83.98
Number of points lost, first serve	33	16.02
Number of points won, second serve	103	62.42
Number of points lost, second serve	62	37.58
Points lost off double faults	8	

	Attempted (%)	In %	Percentage of which Lead to Pt. Won	Aces (%)
1st ser. wide	176 (47.4)	92 (52.3)	84.8	21 (33.3)
1st ser. jam	28 (7.5)	19 (67.9)	63.2	0 (0.0)
1st ser. middle	167 (45.0)	95 (56.9)	87.4	42 (66.7)
2d ser. wide	75 (45.5)	72 (96.0)	63.9	0 (0.0)
2d ser. jam	34 (20.6)	33 (97.1)	66.7	0 (0.0)
2d ser. middle	56 (33.9)	52 (92.9)	67.3	4 (100.0)
Tot ser. wide	251 (46.8)	164 (65.3)	75.6	21 (31.3)
Tot ser. jam	62 (11.6)	52 (83.9)	65.4	0 (0.0)
Tot ser. middle	223 (41.6)	147 (65.9)	80.3	46 (68.7)

	In net (%)	Long (%)	Wide (%)	Foot Fault (%)
First	39 (10.5)	86 (23.2)	40 (10.8)	0 (0.0)
Second	2 (1.2)	5 (3.1)	1 (0.6)	0 (0.0)
Third	41 (7.7)	91 (17.1)	41 (7.7)	0 (0.0)

International was a $33 million privately held company. A DOS-based package, Dataease was easy to use, yet sufficiently powerful to allow users to create complete systems. By 1993 Dataease had a total of about 1 million users worldwide, relatively few in comparison to the number of users of rival products dBase and Paradox. It had 44 percent of the PC DBMS market in the United Kingdom and a 65 percent market share in Denmark. It was

EXHIBIT 7–2   SAGA (Early Report, Generated January 9, 1992)

Return Percentages for Return of Serve

For the following query parameter(s):
These data have been tabulated using the following conditions:
All the statistics reported here refer to the game of Todd Martin.

First Serves

	Wide (%)	Jam (%)	Center (%)	All (%)
Tot. to return	251 (49.0)	71 (13.9)	190 (37.1)	512
Tot. in play	163 (64.9)	53 (74.6)	128 (67.4)	344 (67.2)
Tot. winner	11 (4.4)	4 (5.6)	2 (1.1)	17 (3.3)
Tot. unforced	19 (7.6)	6 (8.5)	14 (7.4)	39 (7.6)
Tot. forced	38 (15.1)	8 (11.3)	32 (16.8)	78 (15.2)
Tot. aces	20 (8.0)	0 (0.0)	14 (7.4)	34 (6.6)

Second Serves

	Wide (%)	Jam (%)	Center (%)	All (%)
Tot. to return	123 (39.5)	81 (26.0)	107 (34.4)	311
Tot. in play	86 (69.9)	60 (74.1)	77 (72.0)	223 (71.7)
Tot. winner	11 (8.9)	3 (3.7)	6 (5.6)	20 (6.4)
Tot. unforced	20 (16.3)	16 (19.8)	21 (19.6)	57 (18.3)
Tot. forced	6 (4.9)	2 (2.5)	3 (2.8)	11 (3.5)
Tot. aces	0 (0.0)	0 (0.0)	0 (0.0)	0 (0.0)

the number two PC database throughout Europe, but had only an 11 percent market share in the United States. In 1992 a portion of the sales force was laid off to make it look better for acquisition by Lotus or another major firm, and a 1993 reorganization brought the head of the European sales group to become Dataease CEO. In early 1993 Dataease announced a new version for Windows which did not include its query language. SAGA relied heavily on the query language and could not use the Windows version. While Dataease International was desperately trying to get its Windows product to market, it neglected the core DOS product. By 1993 Dataease was getting consistently lower scores in the software reviews. A *PC* magazine (May 1993, p. 108) review noted that "Dataease adeptly combines a powerful application builder with ease of use, but . . . at the expense of speed." A promised improved DOS version remained on hold.

On to Wimbledon

During the spring of 1992, Welles and Rogers were quite hopeful that SAGA would lead to a big breakthrough in Andre's game. His ranking continued to fall. It seemed that he needed some kind of injection of intelli-

FIGURE 7–3 Basic Structure of SAGA Tables

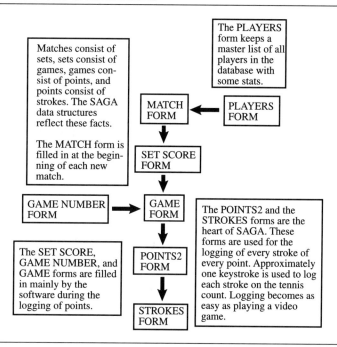

gence into his game. This was a time when the fundamental modules of SAGA were really completed. As the database structure evolved, there were seven basic tables (called forms in Dataease) in which the data were stored (see Figure 7–3).

The data logging procedure was quite simple. A match would be initialized by filling in data on the match form. Then as the match proceeded each point would be logged on the points2 form. The computer would keep track of the score on the basis of the logged data, relieving the data entry person from having to worry about this. Occasionally if a mistake were entered the score could be adjusted manually. The computer would also figure out when a game had been won, who won the game, when a set was over, etc.

Once the match was over, it was necessary to "log the statistics" from the match. Essen-

tially this consisted of doing some of the processing of the raw data right away, and storing a second set of semiprocessed data on which the queries could be processed. The advantage to this method was that this first processing was done only once, regardless of how many queries were then executed using this data. Welles also found this conceptually easier to deal with. However, this took up about the same amount of space as the match itself, almost doubling the size of the database. Each match could use as much as 300,000 bytes if it went five sets. Queries could not be made before the extra "logging" was done.

At first all the statistical processing was done within Dataease itself. This required writing Dataease procedures, some of which had 500 lines or more of code. As Stone continued to log matches and the number of matches in the computer grew from 10 to 20 and then to 30, it became apparent that Dataease was very slow. Welles responded by rewriting some of the key routines in FORTRAN IV. The raw data would be downloaded from Dataease into an ASCII file, processed by the FORTRAN routine in a matter of seconds, and the resulting data uploaded back into Dataease, which was then used to display and print the results.

Some of these FORTRAN routines were quite complex. Fortunately Welles used Microsoft FORTRAN V4.10, which included a debugger that Welles used (although he did not use a MAKE utility). A package called Dataease Developer 4.2, which allowed Welles to access a partial data dictionary of the database, also helped, although again, Welles did not use the tools in this package for making distribution versions of the database on multiple diskettes. And Welles rarely kept any notes or documentation on this code, let alone gave documentation about it to Rogers or Agassi. If he were to be hit by a truck, all would be lost. He consulted with no one about the design of the program. In addition, when a modification was requested, it would take Welles some time to get back into the code in order to change it. In one case he worked all night on one routine, and inserted some bugs in the statistics that were not discovered until a year later. Whenever new versions of the Dataease/FORTRAN code were created, they would be tested by Welles. When he felt there were no more errors, they would be sent to Stone and installed on her computer. It was up to her to test the database from that point. If a function went unused, it also went untested.

The basic design of SAGA incorporated a huge amount of data about the players and the matches. For example, the PLAYERS form stored data about which hand he used, how tall he was, and how much he weighed. The MATCH form kept data about the sur-

face, the tournament and round of the tournament, and the players' rankings as of that date. It was therefore possible to do a query such as show the return of serve performance of all left-handed players with rank greater than 20 and height greater than 5'10" against right-handed players with rank greater than 20. There were a total of 41 separate fields that could be filled in for queries (see Figure 7–4). This meant that the number of combinations was astronomical. Every time a constraint was added by filling in another field, the amount of time it took to process the query would increase. Once the query fields were filled in, Dataease would be used to select a subset of the data corresponding to those conditions. Usually that data would then be downloaded and processed by a FORTRAN program. It could take 15–20 minutes to select and download the data and 30 seconds or a minute to process it using the FORTRAN program. By the summer of 1992, there were five statistics modules completed. These comprised: (1) Stats About the Serve, (2) Stats About Ground Strokes, (3) Stats About Return of Serve, (4) View Individual Pts, and (5) String Analysis.

As the spring progressed, the SAGA team ran into a few hitches. During one of the matches the Dell laptop computer started to smoke. It had to be replaced. From that point on the machines that Dell sent all failed in one way or another. At one point Dell apparently became confused, and sent two complete computers to Stone. During the tournaments Stone would try to generate the statistics she thought that Andre might want, and would slip them under his door the night before or morning of a match. Rogers would tell her which matches to log. Sometimes she was included in the Agassi entourage, but often she was not. Sometimes she would get frustrated, not knowing how the results of her work were being used. The

FIGURE 7–4 Entry Screen for Query Parameters

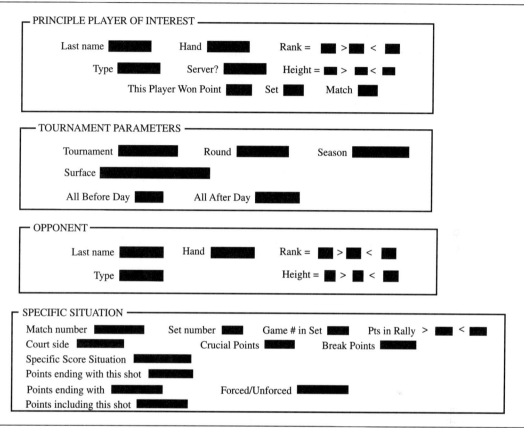

---

decision was made to not bring Stone to the French Open, where Andre's performance was below par. It seemed impossible at the time, but he went on to win Wimbledon in a spectacular display of tennis and a mutual love affair with the British fans. But because he had played few matches on grass up until that point, and Wimbledon tickets are hard to come by, even for players, Stone did not go to that tournament. Riding high on victory at Wimbledon, Agassi came into the U.S. Open. His performance here was again poor, however. Afterward he went into yet another reexamination of himself and tennis. Stone could no longer be away from her boyfriend

in San Diego and suddenly quit. It seemed like SAGA might die a premature death.

Tami to the Rescue

The fall of 1992 was a dormant period for the SAGA team. There was no one to put data in the computer and Andre was not playing much tennis. Welles was busy teaching and Rogers was in law school. Nevertheless, Rogers and Welles felt that they had created the foundation for some truly innovative analysis. It would be a shame to let it die.

At this point, Tami Agassi came into the picture. One of Andre's sisters, Tami had lived and breathed tennis just like the rest of the Agassi clan. When she expressed an interest in being the data entry person, SAGA was back in business.

The contrasts between Stone and Tami could not have been more dramatic. Whereas Stone loved to be on her own and study the SAGA package, Tami liked to be with people and hated computers. Stone would take the initiative to make a backup of the database after each week, whereas Tami never once made a backup. If something went wrong with the computer, it was unlikely Tami would come up with a solution

---

EXHIBIT 7–3 SAGA (Early Report, Generated January 9, 1993)

Ground Stroke Report for Selected Query Set

These data have been tabulated using the following conditions:
All the statistics reported here refer to the game of Chang.
Number of points: 968
Won: 451 (46.59%). Lost: 517 (53.41%)

Total ground strokes:	3,495
Total unforced errors:	247, which is 7.07% of all ground strokes
Total forced errors:	172, which is 4.92% of all ground strokes
Total winners:	180, which is 5.15 % of all ground strokes
Total errors Chang forced opponent to make:	139, which is 3.98% of all ground strokes

Most Productive Shots

	Rank	Total Hit	Unforced Errors	Winners	Forced Winners
Lob	.29025	23	2	10	2
Forehand volley	.19763	57	10	16	7
Inside out mid forehand	.15561	79	14	15	11
Backhand volley	.14649	68	5	13	5
Center forehand	.13762	921	54	10	26

Most Frequent Shots

	Rank	Total Hit	Unforced Errors	Winners	Forced Winners
Center forehand	.13762	921	54	10	26
Center backhand	.13026	867	46	15	17
Wide backhand	.08116	408	9	15	5
Wide forehand	.06047	351	18	8	7
Center mid backhand	.08254	229	24	10	21

Average rank for backhand shots: .0674
Average rank for forehand shots: .1021
Average rank for other shots: .2556

EXHIBIT 7–4   SAGA (Early Report, Generated January 9, 1992)

String Report for Selected Query Set

These data have been tabulated using the following conditions:
All the statistics reported here refer to the game of Chang.
String analysis size increment is 3
Minimum number of repeat patterns is 3
Cutoff ratio for won points to total, lost to tot. is .70

Players hits: wide backhand	Total times hit: 6
Chang hits: center mid-forehand	Times point won: 6
Players hits: wide forehand	Times point lost: 0
	Rating: .6004

Won pt. ended: k (long, center)	Forced 3 times
Won pt. ended: s (wide right)	Forced
Won pt. ended: w (net, center)	Forced 2 times

Players hits: wide backhand	Total times hit: 5
Chang hits: center forehand	Times point won: 5
Players hits: wide forehand	Times point lost: 0
	Rating: .6004

Won pt. ended: e (net, right)	Forced
Won pt. ended: j (long, left)	Forced
Won pt. ended: m (mishit)	Forced
Won pt. ended: q (net, left)	Forced 2 times

Chang hits: wide backhand	Total times hit: 7
Players hits: wide backhand	Times point won: 0
Chang hits: wide forehand	Times point lost: 7
	Rating: −.5005

Lost pt. ended: a (wide left)	Forced
Lost pt. ended: e (net, right)	Forced 2 times
Lost pt. ended: j (long, left)	Forced
Lost pt. ended: s (side right)	Forced
Lost pt. ended: s (wide right)	Unforced
Lost pt. ended: w (net, center)	Unforced

Analysis (not part of the report): In the above report, the first set of data indicates that when Chang
   is standing in midcenter and his (right-handed) opponent first has to hit a backhand from the far
   left and then run over to hit a forehand on the far right, Chang *always* won the point—all six
   times he made his opponents hit forced errors. The next data set shows that Chang was able to
   do the same thing from behind the baseline. On the other hand, the next set of data shows
   that when Chang was forced into the far left to hit a backhand, and he came cross court to his
   opponent's backhand, and his opponent could put it down the opposite line, Chang lost the point
   every time.

on her own. At this time Welles finally created a users manual.

Tami was easygoing and extremely sharp when it came to tennis. She immediately pointed out some ways in which the terminology in the package could be cleaned up, and with her help some problems with certain statistics were resolved. It was also clear that Tami was not going to read the reports that Stone was, at least in theory, reading. It was time for a higher level of user friendliness in SAGA. And Tami had little confidence in the statistics entered by Stone. More than 40 matches were discarded and the database was started anew. This was a boon to Welles who now had more breathing space to figure out ways to make things run faster.

Artificial Intelligence Anyone?

Rogers and Welles were convinced that there was enough innovative elements in SAGA to make a big difference for Agassi. One of the most interesting reports in the package was called the "String Analysis." It viewed each rally as a sequence of strokes that could be represented as a string of characters. The computer then tried to find string patterns which commonly occurred, and then correlate them with winning or losing the point. In theory this would permit Andre to figure out how to play a certain opponent, for example, by knowing that he always hit the ball out when forced to hit three left rear backhands in a row. As initially written, the algorithm tried to examine all strings of arbitrary length, regardless of where they occurred in the point. However, it became apparent that the strokes leading up to the end of the point were most important, so SAGA was changed to work from the back of the point backward. Also it was very rare to find more than one or two occurrences of any strings longer than three exchanges.

In the Spring of 1993, Andre parted ways with long-time coach Nick Bolletteri. He had already received some coaching from John McEnroe, and now sought others who could help him. Once on an airplane Bolletteri had listened to an explanation of SAGA from Rogers. Although he showed some interest, he felt that the court should be divided into even more zones. Therefore he was never involved in using the data. The new coach, who was a lower-ranked player on the tournament and known for good teaching skills, had some particular ideas about tennis. He felt that it was very important to reach the score of 30 first. He also felt that forcing the opponent to sprint during points was a key to winning. On the basis of these insights, Welles created new SAGA reports to investigate the value of getting to 30 first and the impact of forcing the opponent to sprint. The "To 30 First Report" shows the new trend in SAGA of writing the results in English sentences (see Exhibit 7–5). This was possible because Welles had now switched to doing almost all calculations in FORTRAN. This was faster and more flexible than using Dataease itself.

In addition to these new reports, Welles also added a bunch of information reports and reports that aggregated some statistics. In some cases Welles simply decided to put these in on his own initiative. The information reports included: (1) Show How Many Matches Logged for Each Player, (2) Show

---

EXHIBIT 7–5   SAGA to 30 First Report (Generated July 9, 1992)

Player of interest is Agassi. Total number of games: 780. Agassi got to 30 first 435 times. He won 83.22% of these games. Opponent(s) got to 30 first 435 times. He/they won 69.57% of these games. When Agassi broke serve, he got to 30 first 115 times, or 70.55% of the time.

EXHIBIT 7–6   SAGA (Generated April 19, 1993)

Movement Analysis

These data have been tabulated using the following conditions:
All the statistics reported here refer to the game of Chang.
Total points: 1,474. Percentage won: 48.98%.

Distribution of Sprints Chang Forced to Make by Opponent

Number of Sprints	Times Occurred	Win Percentage
0	1,098	50.82
1	247	42.91
2	87	43.68
3	33	45.45
4	6	83.33
5	3	.00

Chang had to sprint on 25.51% of the points.

Distribution of Sprints Chang Forced Opponent to Make

Number of Sprints	Times Occurred	Win Percentage
0	1,085	47.00
1	252	53.17
2	84	57.14
3	39	53.85
4	7	57.14
5	7	71.43

Chang forced opponent to sprint on 26.39% of the points.

Analysis (not part of report): The more sprints Chang had to make during a point, the more likely he was to lose it, except when he had to make four—then he would win a remarkable percentage. This could mean that four sprints in a point would "set him on fire" and make him more dangerous. The more sprints Chang forced his opponents to make, the more likely he was to win.

---

the Matches that Have Been Logged, (3) Show Database Status: No. of Matches, etc., (4) Show the Players in the Database Now, and (5) Show Overall Tour Stats. The aggregation reports ranked who had the best serve on the tour by several measures, showed who had the best of each type of groundstroke, and attempted to correlate the average length of rallies with whether or not the player won the match. If the average length of rallies in a match was closer to the overall average for the player that won, it was likely that he was controlling (dictating) the points. A report was created to compare stats for the players from one match. Finally, a short player profile was added.

Despite the new coach, Andre's performance continued to slide. By the end of May 1993, his ranking dropped to 12th. The new coach wanted Andre to do a lot of drills, which was not his style. Soon he too got the axe, and Poncho Seguro, a tennis legend, was retained. Poncho was quite impressed with SAGA, but took no role in using it.

At this point the biggest final push for SAGA began. It was decided to create a single unified strategy report that would report, in English sentences, the most important information about a player. Unlike most of the rest of the reports, this report would find exceptional pieces of information. But how to decide if a statistic was exceptional or not? Two approaches were used. First, Rogers simply dictated to Welles what was exceptional and what was not. Second, Welles derived statistics for the whole tour and then did comparisons with them. It was hoped that Andre or Poncho would read these reports and be able to take a few salient tips into the matches. The routines were again written in FORTRAN. Dataease had an interface for the language C that would have speeded things up, but Welles said he couldn't take the time to learn it.

All efforts were now directed toward the U.S. Open. A good warm-up tournament for this had been the Washington, D.C., tennis tournament, which Andre won in 1991. Welles was flown in to be close to the action. By now there were more than 75 matches in the computer, taking up abut 30 Mbytes of space. Fortunately yet another laptop sent by Dell—because of a problem with one of the two previously sent—had a larger hard drive in it.

Everything went fine during the opening round, but during the second round Tami had to replace the laptop battery during the match. She turned off the computer, and when she got it running again, could not figure out how to resume logging the match. She started a new match, adjusted the score, and kept going. Now Welles had to figure out a way to integrate the data. By the time it was all tabulated it was 4 P.M. on the day of Andre's match. Welles called the hotel to talk to Rogers, who would relay the information. He was excited because the data again showed a very distinct pattern of how Carlsson served, especially on the second serve (see

EXHIBIT 7–7   Carlsson Serve Pattern

	Deuce	*Add*
Wide (1st)		61.4%
Wide (2d)		95.8%
Jam (1st)		
Jam (2d)		
Middle (1st)	45.6%	
Middle (2d)	69.6%	

Exhibit 7–7). To his great surprise, Welles got Andre, who was hanging out in Rogers' room. Welles was reluctant to bother Andre with information he might not want, so he just asked for Rogers to call back. When, 45 minutes later, Rogers had not called, Welles called again. He got Andre again, and had Andre get Rogers, who was negotiating a deal on a cellular phone. Finally the data were relayed. Andre smashed Carlsson that night, partly because he knew about the serving patterns. He broke him five times in the match; Carlsson held serve just three times. The data circled on the side-by-side player comparison report show how much better Andre did at returning first serves than he had been doing at that time (see Exhibit 7–8).

In the third round Andre played Aaron Krickstein, the same player who had caused a first round loss two years earlier in the U.S. Open. The unified strategy report had shown that forcing him to hit a backhand in the center behind the baseline followed by a backhand wide to the left and a forehand wide to the right was a good way to win points (see Exhibit 7–9). Welles and Rogers sat in the stands. When the first instance of this sequence arose and Krickstein hit it into the net, they exchanged knowing glances. When it happened again, they were on their feet cheering. SAGA had finally proven itself under match conditions! Andre

EXHIBIT 7–8 SAGA (Generated July 24, 1993)

Side-by-Side Player Comparison for a Match

Three-set match between Andre Agassi and Johan Carlsson on July 21, 1993
Tournament: Washington, D.C.; round: second.
Played on hard court, normal
Agassi: ATP rank at time of match: 21
Match winner: Agassi. Sets played: 2.
Score: 6–3, 6–2

Agassi		Carlsson
63.83	First serve percentage this match	66.67
62.87	Average first serve percentage	58.77
70.00	Percent points won off first serve	50.00
11	Number of unforced errors	15
23.4	Avg. unforced errors in two set matches	26.0
12	Number of winners	7
14.9	Avg. winners in two set matches	16.5
11/9	Times to net/number of points won	9/3
80.77	Return of first serve percent this match	56.67
60.32	Avg. first serve return percent	51.95
17	Total number of games in match	17
11/11	Games player reached 30 first/number won	5/5

won the first set convincingly, but failed to hold on for victory. Nevertheless, they were riding high going into the U.S. Open.

Time for a Decision

As Rogers and Agassi faced the upcoming U.S. Open, they had to decide. Was it worth

EXHIBIT 7–9 SAGA (Generated July 23, 1993)

Unified Strategy Report

These data have been tabulated using the following conditions:
All the statistics reported here refer to the game of Krickstein.

Movement Analysis

Krickstein uses his *right* hand. Forehand side is right. Krickstein does not move as well to the forehand side. His largest problem moving to the forehand side is he will tend to make forced errors. He is moved to the backhand side by opponents 2.7 times as often as to the forehand side. This means players have not figured out his weaker side concerning movement. Krickstein hits 2.86 percent winners on forehand side. Krickstein hits a lot of inside-out forehands.

Game Start Analysis

Krickstein starts games average, getting to 30 first 42.67 percent of the time. You get to 30 first 55.77 percent of the time.

Shot Sequences

Some good ways to play Krickstein are to make him hit one or more of these shot sequences in order: center backhand, wide backhand, wide forehand. On points when he was made to hit this sequence, he won .00 percent, and he made .00 percent unforced errors and 66.67 percent forced errors.

Serve Analysis

Krickstein's serve is below average. Krickstein has first serve percent 53.45. Krickstein will hit a first serve *ace* 10.48 percent of the time. The *tour* percentage of first serve *aces* is 12.39 percent. Krickstein hits same number of deuce-side first serves: to wide and middle. Krickstein rarely serves and volleys on first serve; expect it few or no times per match.

it to keep sending Tami to log the tournaments? What was the real result that could be expected from SAGA? What was the future of SAGA? As Rogers got up to put on the latest CD by the artist formerly known as Prince, he knew they had a difficult decision ahead.

Assignment Questions

1. Describe and categorize SAGA. What kind of user interface did it use, and on what kind of technology was it based? What CASE tools were in use?
2. What went wrong with the systems development process, if anything? Was Welles qualified to do the job he was supposed to do?
3. What is the potential payoff from SAGA? Is there a relationship between the database and the desired outcome, i.e., winning tennis matches?

INTERTECH REFOCUSING

Nancy J. Johnson

Background

The State of Minnesota had been served by the centralized data processing service organization, InterTech, since computers were introduced in the sixties. The organization is part of the Department of Administration and reports directly to the commissioner of administration. It serves the data processing and telecommunications needs of many of the 128 state agencies, the largest of which have developed their own internal IS staffs. InterTech is funded by a revolving fund, which means it does not receive direct appropriations from the legislature. Instead, individual agencies include a budget item in their appropriation requests for services that will be provided by InterTech. InterTech then in turn charges the agencies for actual

---

This case was prepared by Nancy J. Johnson, Metropolitan State University, as the basis for class presentation and discussion rather than to illustrate either effective or ineffective handling of an administrative situation.

services provided, although the rates are established on projected transaction and usage volumes from the individual agencies. Cost and quality of services are critical success factors in order to attract, retain, and increase business from the state agencies.

InterTech has had several managers (assistant commissioners) over the past 10 years who brought in a variety of managerial styles and delivery strategies. The organization had grown to almost 300 positions, but studies done in 1990 by IBM and 1991 by KPMG Peat Marwick cited increasing dissatisfaction from some of the state agencies using InterTech's services. Focus groups were conducted for InterTech employees and other state agencies using the services of InterTech. KPMG and IBM had also conducted evaluations of the services provided. The InterTech users in the state agencies indicated in surveys and interviews that they did not feel that they were getting the level of service for which they were charged. They also questioned the strategies of InterTech and the focus for the future. The studies showed that InterTech charged more for its services than comparable centralized service groups in peer organizations in similar industries. The feelings of animosity between the agencies and InterTech was tangible and detrimental to success. Some of the agency CIOs were seriously considering soliciting outsourcing bids to replace the services from InterTech, and one of the external studies suggested outsourcing as a strategy.

Bernie Conlin was brought in to lead the InterTech group in June 1991, after a long and successful career in private industry. The commissioner of administration told him to figure out what to do with InterTech and then get it done. Bernie immediately began personally meeting with the IS representatives of the agencies to assess their concerns and the roots of their animosity toward InterTech. It was apparent that the services provided by InterTech did not meet all the perceived needs of the state agencies, and that the internal perceptions varied drastically from external perceptions. Basic functions such as business resumption planning and telecommunications were seriously understaffed. The mission of InterTech was unclear, as were its performance measurements and goals, and there was a long history of estrangement between InterTech management and its key customers.

Conlin termed the InterTech employees' attitude one of "complacency"—the belief that the state agencies were captive customers and InterTech would continue on in situ, unchanged by the evolution of customer needs or advances in technology. Employees did not perceive the need to upgrade their technical skill sets to serve the demands of new technology utilization, despite protests from their "customers." The previous management team was reluctant to listen to their customers, identify their needs, and create an organization that responded to those needs.

The Refocusing Project

In response to pressures to provide better service and a focus on the "right" activities, Conlin designed and launched a major initiative to refocus the resources of InterTech in September of 1991. The goals of the project were to construct an organization that would concentrate its resources on serving the needs of the state agencies and create a culture of partnership with the agencies. The refocusing project was not specifically intended to downsize, but rather to redirect InterTech's existing resources on the needs of the agencies served and to create an environment that would allow InterTech to respond to new initiatives and incorporate emerging technologies. The organization chart at the time of the start of the refocusing effort is included in Appendix A.

Not only was the goal of redirecting the efforts of the entire department a very ambitious one, the project included the additional dimension of working within a civil service environment with four different employee collective bargaining units (unions) in InterTech. The goal of designing the right organization to serve the customers included designing jobs that involved the appropriate knowledge and skills to meet the challenge of new technologies, particularly telecommunications.

Conlin's private industry experience with very large operational and back room consolidations and major organizational redirection projects convinced him that this refocusing project had to embrace the following four principles in order to be successful.

1. Clearly state the goal of the project and the end result, so all employees know why the effort is being undertaken.
2. It is not possible to communicate too much to all employees. Honesty, openness, and frequent communications are critical to common understanding.

(Disagreeing with an answer doesn't make it the wrong answer.)

3. Establish the operating ground rules and follow them. Work with the collective bargaining units up front and work within their contract stipulations.

4. Use a bottom-up, broadly based inclusionary mode of involving as many employees as possible in the project to increase understanding of the goals and process itself. Broaden the employees' views of the whole of InterTech so they better understand the contribution that they can make to its success.

Rejecting the option of bringing in external consultants, Conlin assembled a project team of State of Minnesota employees to design and lead the refocusing project. The team included the five directors of InterTech, staff from the Department of Administration's Management Analysis and Human Resources Divisions. After all the new position descriptions were completed, the Department of Employee Relations (DOER) was brought in for the evaluation and classification process. The management analysis team members were credited with keeping the process moving by facilitating meetings, and synthesizing ideas. They also guided the planning activity, evaluated the interviews and focus group input, produced reports, and led the director planning meetings.

The first three months of the project were spent creating the strategic plan based on focus group meetings with customers, staff, and other stakeholders. Benchmarking interviews with private sector organizations were also used in the development of the mission, vision, and strategies. The plan was distributed to all the employees.

The business planning stage, over the next three months, included identification of strategic business units (SBU) within InterTech and assessments of competition and demand. A strategy for each SBU was developed: growth, maintenance, reduction, or divestment. A functional organization chart was constructed from this analysis. See Appendix B for the charts.

The organization design phase was done over the next three months, and included work unit functional definitional analysis with number of and attributes of positions. The rewriting of the job descriptions was conducted over five months and included development of accountability statements for supervisory and managerial positions. A number of current staff position anomalies, outdated descriptions, and inappropriate position classifications were also resolved in the process. The implementation phase started in October of 1992 with the filling of key director positions. The majority of positions in the new organization were filled by January of 1993: 77 jobs and 8 supervisor positions were eliminated and 79 new positions were created. Some employees opted for retirement or moving to positions in other state agencies, but the majority filled InterTech positions (often with additional training to obtain new skills). Only five individuals were "laid off" in the refocusing process.

Two significant positions at the director level were filled from outside the organization due to lack of appropriate skills in InterTech. One individual came from a major customer agency and one came from the private sector. Conlin intentionally did not bring in any former private sector coworkers to fill key positions. In his experience, it was more important to design the right organization and utilize existing personnel to the extent possible to execute the plan under strong leadership, than to bring in an "insider group" with allegiance to the senior manager, thus creating a "us versus them" environment.

Results

The refocusing project was completed in less than 18 months without an employee grievance. There are very few other organizational redirection efforts that can cite these measures of success in either private or public sectors. InterTech now administers an annual survey to measure customers' perceptions of satisfaction and service quality. The responses indicate a high degree of satisfaction with InterTech's service. However, since this data is unavailable for the period prior to the refocusing effort, no measurable comparisons can be made. A more concrete measure of organizational success can be seen from InterTech's annual charge-back rate structure. Average rates charged to customer agencies have been reduced in each of the fiscal years following the refocusing:

FY 92—36%	FY 95—13%
FY 93—13%	FY 96—13%
FY 94—9%	FY 97—7%

The data center baseline study that precipitated refocusing is being repeated in FY 97. InterTech believes that the organization will compare favorably with other data centers.

Since refocusing, InterTech had taken deliberate steps to develop closer working relationships with customer agencies. Regular meetings are now held with the MIS directors and the CIOs of the major customer agencies. A "customer liaison" program assigns InterTech's managers and directors to particular agencies, and provides a key contact in both organizations. While progress may be called slow, there have been no defections to outsourcers by the customer agencies, and recently InterTech and its customers have entered into several collaborative projects in which they share the risks, the work, and the rewards.

While some agency CIOs hoped for a massive InterTech retrenchment, downsizing, and wholesale replacement of all employees in a very short amount of time, the ability to use such draconian methods within a civil service and union environment are not realistic nor do they take advantage of existing employee knowledge bases. Long held attitudes of user agency animosity do not evaporate easily and a trusting relationship with InterTech is still evolving. One agency CIO was frustrated because his agency had open positions into which InterTech employees were qualified to post, and he didn't want to hire them or have them work at InterTech. (Yet interestingly, the agency IT managers interviewed all cited their general concern about ethics of any layoffs from state jobs and resulting stress for employees—a diametrically opposed view when they were forced to hire the displaced employees themselves due to civil service seniority placement rules for displaced workers. Apparently they hoped the employees would disappear into another agency and not be as visible.)

The agency CIOs face challenges similar to those of InterTech within their own IS organizations: focusing energies on the appropriate goals, ensuring that employee skills are current with new technologies, establishing an awareness of need for continuing change, and maintaining or improving service delivery with reduced costs. Performance measurement is a critical area in all public service agencies in order to assure the funders that the best possible job is being performed.

Most InterTech employees had worked within the state for many years (some since the 1960s) and had not taken the two previous negative external consultant evaluation reports seriously. The threat of outsourcing didn't appear to be real since the agencies were considered a captive customer base and the user hostility was returned by the InterTech employees. Many employees believed that the managerial priorities would shift again when the governor's administration changed (and the commissioner), and that they could ignore the growing frustration from the agencies using InterTech's services. Their isolationist attitudes led to complacency.

A sense of partnering with the user agencies was lacking, and the interagency relationships were often adversarial. Some InterTech employees felt entitled to a job that they wanted to do or knew how to do, instead of what the user agencies needed which often did not fit the existing skill sets. Many InterTech employees feared losing their jobs within the state because they didn't think they could find a job in private industry with their outdated skill sets, yet they had done little to improve their marketability through personal initiative.

Analysis

What made this project successful in a relatively short amount of time? The leadership, the team members, and the techniques. The Human Resources Division director, Karen Hanson, provided a critical success component by creating a memo of understanding (MOU) at the start of the refocusing. An addendum to the then-current union contracts, the MOU addressed any unique employment issues likely to arrive as a result of refocusing. This MOU device was used continually to ensure that any proposed organizational changes were within the rules and procedures of the unions, to protect the employees' union rights. The MOU was the key to avoiding any situations which would have resulted in employee grievances, thus extending the implementation of the refocusing effort. Negotiating an MOU with four unions simultaneously was

a first for the State of Minnesota, and it ensured that all employee collective bargaining units were treated equally.

Linda Diedrich-Arvey, HR–Department of Administration, replaced the original HR team member on the refocusing team after the basic functional areas were defined. Arvey's responsibilities included writing formal response communications to questions related to human resource issues (with Deb Erdman from InterTech), doing individual employee counseling, doing informal communications with employees, and reviewing every one of the 260 job descriptions in InterTech. Managers wrote the position descriptions, in consultation with Diedrich-Arvey, to accurately reflect the knowledge, skills and abilities required of the jobs as well as addressing the evaluative components of the Hay system (i.e., know how, problem solving, and accountability). The position descriptions also needed to include all the information for DOER classification. Conlin cited Diedrich-Arvey's in-depth knowledge of all personnel systems and contractual rules within the State of Minnesota as being the key factor in successfully rewriting so many position descriptions, without employee grievance or union protest, in such a short amount of time.

Diedrich-Arvey described the strength of the team unity as being the critical component to successfully navigating through the extraordinary stresses of the project. Everyone involved struggled with the unknown impacts of the changes in both their personal and professional lives. The InterTech directors did not even have a guarantee of a continued job after the implementation of the redesign, yet they participated fully and enthusiastically.

Arvey said that consistent, frequent, and repetitive communications were the most important technique to demonstrate the shared vision, goals, and activities of the team. Disgruntled employees "shopped" the team members with questions in hopes of receiving the answer they wanted instead of the right answer. If the team members had not been working in unison and documenting all actions and decisions, they would not have been able to provide the right answers consistently. Arvey and other team members credit the leadership of Conlin for ensuring that the team did not fall apart under the stress of the implementation.

The team utilized written and verbal communication techniques to disseminate information to a wide group of employees simultaneously. Deb Erdman managed the "rumor central hot line," chaired the ad hoc communication group and wrote the weekly newsletter. E-mail was a good tool for communications. Team members often responded to inquiries at night and on weekends to provide factual feedback as quickly as possible. New positions were also available electronically on the LAN. The team members also used calendaring/scheduling on the e-mail system to allow employees to schedule meetings.

As a representative from the project's management team, Deb Erdman chaired an ad hoc employee group that met biweekly to discuss issues and concerns that employees directed to the group members. Rumors, dissatisfaction, speculation, and factoids were all included in the discussions. Erdman provided information to resolve issues and answer questions, and documented it in weekly newsletters and via e-mail. Response to rumors was immediate and assertive. When questions were asked repeatedly in hopes that the answers had changed, Erdman was able to refer to previously published answers. The weekly forum established a vehicle for employees to receive consistent and open information and to know that their voices were heard.

Future Efforts for InterTech

With the refocusing project completed, the managers of InterTech continue to improve the service provided to agencies. An InterTech manager has been assigned as the key liaison for each of the major agencies to facilitate communication and proactive planning. Internal newsletters are still used to celebrate achievements of employees as well as to share information about projects and other initiatives. Improved help desk services, back-up depth, and faster problem resolution for all agencies are high priorities for InterTech. A fully supportive technical service environment for a 7 by 24 operating environment is being designed to serve the needs of the citizens of the state. Developing a reliable information highway for citizen access to public information is also critical.

Culturally within InterTech, the managers are working to instill an attitude of accountability by implementing work plans for all positions. On-site visits by InterTech employees to the agencies create an enhanced perception of teamwork. Developing partnership relations between InterTech employees and the agencies is part of building the sense of accountability.

While consistently providing the best quality computer operations, data services, and telecommunications network service to agencies within the framework of a declining revenue base InterTech management is also working on planning for new technology uses. Providing leadership in technology utilization, along with proven business capability is the three-year vision of InterTech.

Follow-up Since the Refocusing Effort

Refocusing effectively established an expectation of change in InterTech's culture. It emphasized the need for flexibility in order to continue to meet customer needs. For example, although the applications development unit was formed as a result of the refocusing, drawing together programming staff who had been scattered throughout the organization, it was disbanded in 1994. The agency customers had found other sources of programming skills, and the InterTech unit lost money each year due to lack of demand. In another department, when automation was introduced into the mainframe console operations unit, the need for the number of operators was reduced. These smaller changes were handled as necessary business adjustments in response to demands. As in the major refocusing effort, the needs of all stakeholders were taken into consideration.

In addition to fostering redeployment of technical resources to better meet the needs of customers, refocusing positioned InterTech to move forward aggressively with projects that fit its mission. The prime example is the implementation of a statewide router-based network for voice, data, and video services. Statutory authority to build the network was received by the Minnesota legislature in 1989. The network currently consists of 12 hub sites and leased communication lines which provide network connections throughout the state for public sector operations. The potential growth of the network is exponential. InterTech has added a network operations center of trained staff who monitor the network, detect and diagnose malfunctions, and dispatch personnel. During the same time InterTech's central processing ability capacity grew by 450 percent, tape storage by 45 percent, and disk storage by 400 percent.

Even with this increase in capacity and throughput, InterTech's total employee complement has remained stable from 1992 to 1996.

For questions, contact Deb Erdman at deb.erdman@state.mn.us, or visit the InterTech home page on the North Star network for the State of Minnesota, under the Department of Administration home page.

Assignment Questions

1. How did the different stakeholders view the situation for InterTech prior to the refocusing effort?
2. What were the tools and techniques used to change the culture of InterTech from within and without the agency?
3. Would outsourcing the IT function have been a better solution for the State of Minnesota?
4. What challenges does InterTech face going forward?
5. What is the appropriate role for a centralized IT organization in terms of charging for its services, setting standards for other agencies, and providing services?
6. What are reasonable measures of success for the refocusing project from these different perspectives: an individual IT practitioner, InterTech management, the state agencies using the services of InterTech, the commissioner of the Department of Administration, the taxpayers of the state?

Appendix A

Organization Charts September 1991

FIGURE A–1 InterTechnologies Group of the Department of Administration

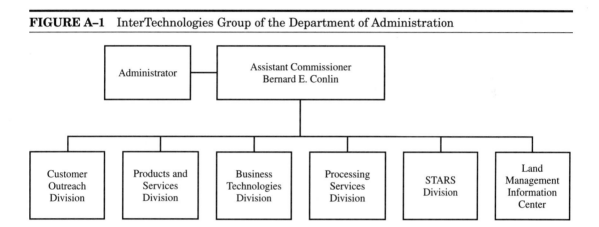

FIGURE A–2 Customer Outreach Division

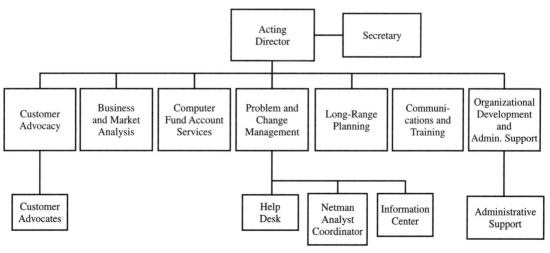

FIGURE A–3   Customer Outreach Division: Long-Range Planning

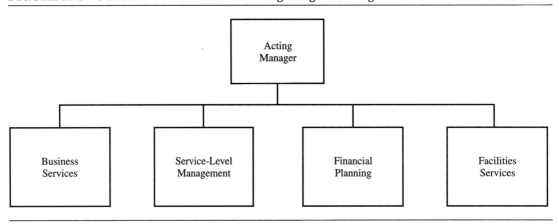

FIGURE A–4   Customer Outreach Division: Communications and Training

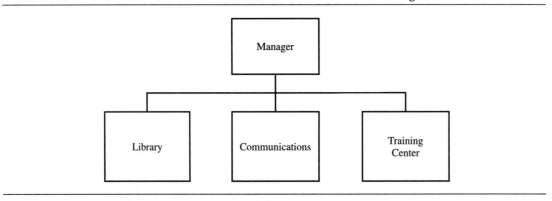

FIGURE A–5   Products and Services Division

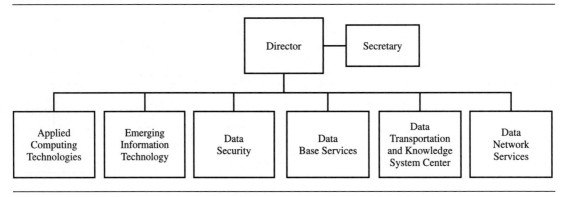

FIGURE A–6   Products and Services Division: Data Transformation and Knowledge
Systems Center

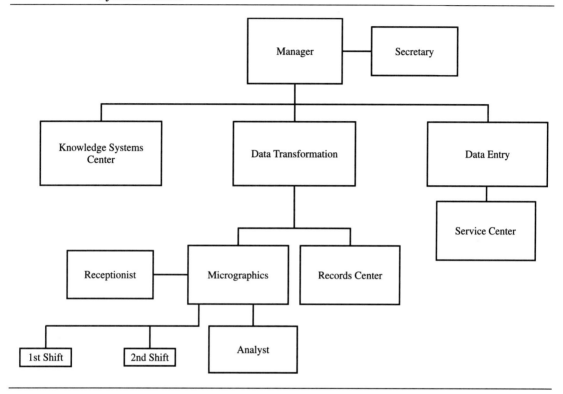

FIGURE A–7   Products and Services Division: Database Services

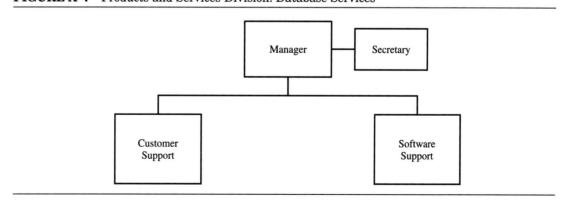

FIGURE A–8   Business Technologies Division

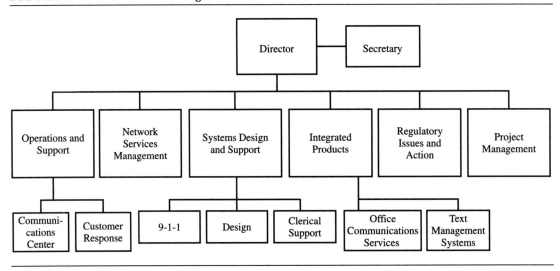

FIGURE A–9   Processing Services Division

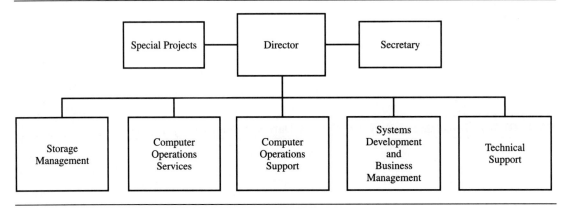

FIGURE A–10   Processing Services Division: Computer Operations Services

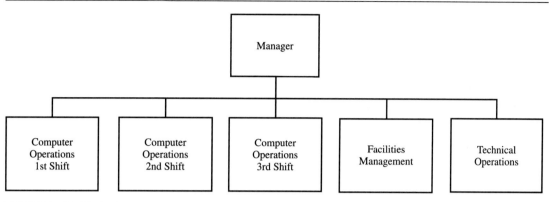

FIGURE A–11   Processing Services Division: Computer Operations Support

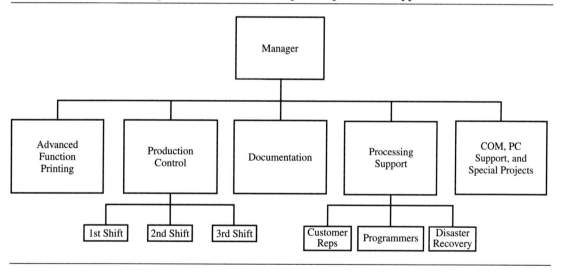

FIGURE A–12   STARS Division

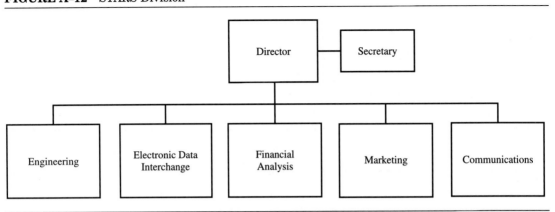

FIGURE A–13   Land Management Information Center

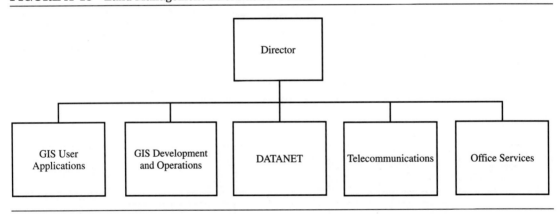

Appendix B

Organization Charts March 1992

FIGURE B–1 Functional Organizational Design Chart Draft, March 4, 1992

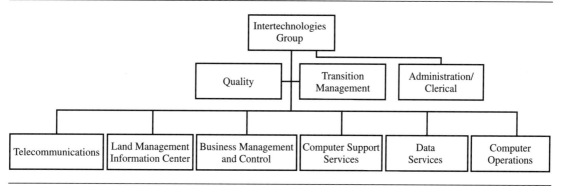

FIGURE B–2 Functional Organizational Design Chart Draft, March 4, 1992

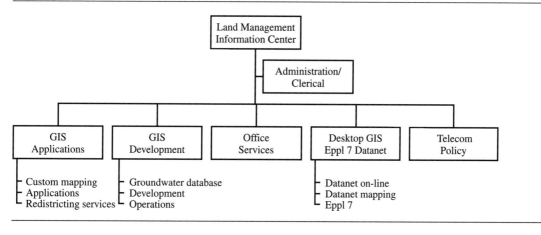

FIGURE B–3 Functional Organizational Design Chart Draft, March 4, 1992

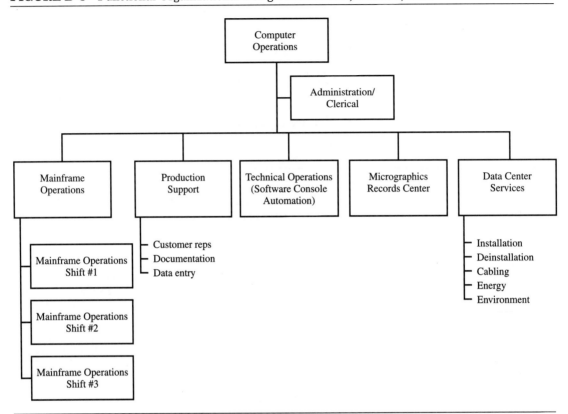

FIGURE B–4 Functional Organizational Design Chart Draft, March 4, 1992

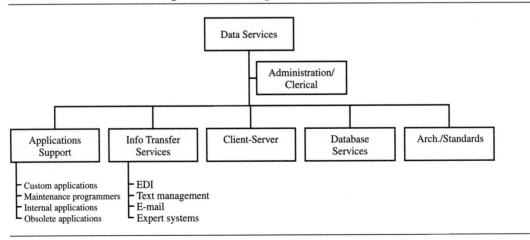

FIGURE B-5 Functional Organizational Design Chart Draft, March 4, 1992

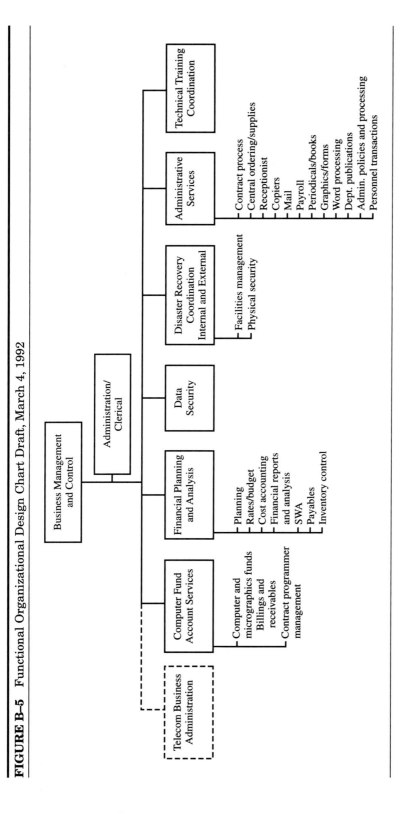

FIGURE B–6   Functional Organizational Design Chart Draft, March 4, 1992

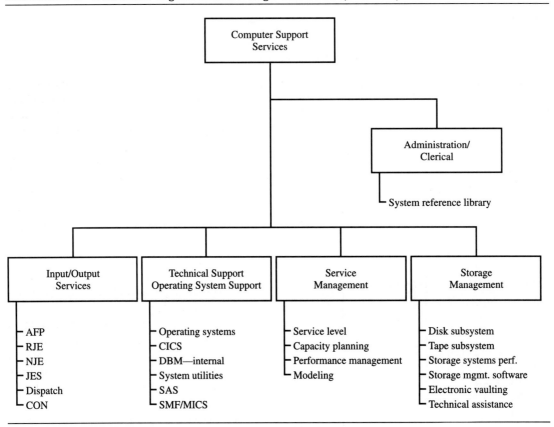

FEDERAL GOVERNMENT INTERNET APPLICATIONS: EFFECTIVENESS REVIEW

Rick Gibson

Introduction

In 1993 Congress developed the National Information Infrastructure, a legislative policy to guide attempts to distribute electronic government information, with an emphasis on public access via the Internet. Currently, the federal government uses 750 Internet sites to provide information, products, services, and training to its business clients and customers. The Internet evolved in 1969, by the U.S. Defense Department, as the Advance Research Projects Agency Network (ARPANET). This experimental network was built as a military research project for building reliable communication networks during time of war. In 1986 the National Science Foundation (NSF) developed the NSFNET, which consisted of six nationally funded supercomputer centers. As a result, advance network technology was available to individuals outside the military area, such as researchers, educational institutions, and private firms. The first collaborative Internet business partnership was developed, in 1987, with NSF, MCI, IBM, and Michigan State for the purpose of managing and upgrading the NSFNET.

Advantages of Internet

Currently, businesses have developed Internet systems to enhance communication and business processes internally within an organization, and externally with its clients, to provide better products in the marketplace. The use of Internet for electronic meeting forums is a significant advantage for enhancing communications. Business colleagues across the country can establish discussion sessions or formal meetings to exchange information on the network. Many companies use the Internet as a mechanism to distribute or demonstrate marketing products to clients. Hence companies can solicit immediate feedback from specific clients through the Internet. Some organizations are using the Internet in daily business activities. For example, in order to expedite the emergency response activities of hazardous chemical accidents, the U.S. Environment Protection Agency's (EPA) Hazdat database, is accessible in full text search and retrieval format on the Internet at the host name *http://atsdr1.atsdr. cdc.gov:8080/atsdrhome.html*. This database contains health assessments and profiles on hazardous substances. The EPA also provides press releases on-line through a computer server. A business customer can subscribe or send a message to a listserver and press releases will be sent directly to an individual via e-mail on the Internet by the agency.

Most consumers are not interested in reading long full-text records. The new congressional World Wide Web site, THOMAS, at the Library of Congress (*http://www.thomas.loc.gov*) provides direct access to thousands of congressional and executive branch documents. Users can access depository libraries of public laws,

---

This case was prepared by Rick Gibson, American University, as the basis for class presentation and discussion rather than to illustrate either effective or ineffective handling of an administrative situation.

the *Congressional Record,* and GAO reports, because of the Electronic Information Enhancement Act of 1993. The federal government has created open access informational forums with the public, yet, it would be more advantageous to the public to read a short abstract with a reference to the source document, instead of the full text document version. Therefore, several private firms are competing with the government. Firms are providing information by adding value to the governmental data and repackaging the information for an on-line fee to the consumer. Other vendors, such as America Online, CompuServe, and Prodigy are providing access via graphical interfaces to Internet using high-speed gateway connections. Many professionals have debated the best method to supply appropriate network capabilities and devices to the public.

According to Maxwell, those agencies committed to providing various access methods were the most highly ranked (see Table 7–2). The St. Olaf College Server Internet site provided five access methods—World Wide Web, Gopher, FTP, Usenet news group, and dial-in. Access to FedWorld site, included the World Wide Web, telnet, FTP, and dial-in methods. The providers of these sites considered the broad scope of users and did not limit access to only users with high technological capabilities.

The one-stop shopping directory format of the LC Marvel and FedWorld sites was a useful feature. The LC Marvel site links to other sites operated by federal agencies, state governments, city governments, foreign governments, and international organizations, such as the United Nations. The FedWorld site provided additional links to more than 100 federal bulletin boards, Internal Revenue Service's tax forms and publications, and federal employment opportunities. Sites were ranked high also, if search strategy software was provided on the Internet home page. A large segment of users may have limited access to search browsers, such as Netscape, Deckscape, or Yahoo. Sites such as LC Marvel, and University of Missouri–St. Louis Gopher provided a search software program, called Jughead. Jughead provides the capability to search by directory title, search by an abbreviation, or customize a search retrieval

TABLE 7–2 10 Best Federal Internet Sites

Internet Site	Address
LC Marvel	marvel.loc.gov
Library of Congress Information System (LOCIS)	locis.loc.gov
FedWorld	http://www.fedworld.gov
University of Michigan	una.hh.lib.umich.edu
University of Missouri	umslvma.umsl.edu
Columbia Online Information Network (COIN)	128.206.1.3
U.S. House of Representatives	http://www.house.gov
Cornell Law School	http://www.law.cornell.edu
Internet Town Hall	http://town.hall.org
St. Olaf College Servers	http://www.stolaf.edu/network/traveladvisories.html

From B. Maxwell, "The 10 Best Federal Government Internet Sites," *Database* 18, 1995, pp. 42–47.

strategy. For example, if one needed to find the Internet site address of the Federal Deposit Insurance Corporation, by typing in *fdic,* the home page would transfer to the FDIC's gopher site.

The user's capability to retrieve and download information from data banks was another important factor. The Library of Congress Information System (LOCIS) site provided access to several card catalog databases. It also indexed English and foreign books by title, author, subject, or call number. Federal legislative databases that provided summary information on bills can be accessed via LOCIS, Cornell Law School Servers, and Columbia Online Information Network sites. Download capabilities are features on the University of Michigan's Gopher site.

Several sites provided daily updates to information on the home pages. LOCIS, University of Michigan's Gopher, and Columbia Online Information Network sites provided daily updated status of Congressional legislation. The graphical interfaces of the FedWorld, U.S. House of Representatives, and COIN sites were far better than most sites. A detailed analysis of interfaces is discussed later in the research paper.

All the federal Internet sites provided cost savings. Information from the Internet is retrieved at no cost. However, manual documents must be ordered for a charge. The University of Michigan's Gopher site provided free download capabilities of the Commerce's Economic Bulletin Board that would cost a user $3–$24 per hour on a commercial database, such as CompuServe. The Columbia Online Information Network Internet site provides free access to databases containing full-text Congressional information.

Further analyses of Maxwell's best Internet sites were conducted using the hypermedia design analysis, an evaluation tool (see Table 7–3). The criteria included an analysis of the Internet sites' content, struc-

ture, presentation, dynamics, and interaction. A review of content determined if the Internet site is static (passive) media, such as formatted data, text, images, or active (dynamic) media, such as video clips, sound tracks, animation. The structure analysis included the organization and entity relationship of the components of the home pages. The number of page levels included in the Internet site was reviewed. The application content and presentation to the users were either text or graphic visual cues. Dynamics and interaction analysis looks at how users interact with individual home pages and move or navigate among them. Search software and movement factors, such as Next Page, Go Back, Backward Scan, and Direct Jump were analyzed.

The organizational structure of most of the home pages included an overall description of the Internet site, the most frequently requested information, or news. As one moved through the various levels of home page, more detailed information was provided. The FedWorld site consisted of 14 pages and over 55 hyperlinks to other federal Internet sites. The U.S. House of Representatives site included over 65 pages.

Five sites had advanced features such as direct jump to a specific topic. The FedWorld site provided an alphabetic index of government topics and a direct jump capability to other government Internet sites associated with the topics. The St. Olaf College site had a direct jump feature to the State Department's list of foreign travel advisories and detail maps of listed countries. The retrieval time was very slow during the retrieval of these graphical maps. Two different view options were provided in the Cornell Law School site. One home page view consisted of detailed information for the new Internet user. The other home page view provided summary information of the most frequently requested information for the expert user.

TABLE 7–3   Hypermedia Design Model Evaluation of the 10 Best Federal Internet Sites

Internet Sites	Content	Structure	Presentation		Dynamics / Interaction
		Number of page levels	Text	Graphic	N = Next Page GB = Go Back FS = Forward Scan BS = Back Scan DJ = Direct Jump GS = Guided Prompt
L C Marvel	Static	1 page	Text		N, GB
LOCIS	Static	11 pages	Text		GB
FedWorld	Static	14 pages/ 55 hyperlinks	Text		N, GB, DJ
University of Michigan	Static	1 page	Text		N, GB
University of Missouri	Static	1 page	Text		N, GB
COIN	Static	1 page	Text		N, GB
U.S. House of Representatives	Static	65 pages	Text		N, GB, DJ, / search software
Cornell Law School	Static	58 pages	Text		N, GB, DJ, / search software
Internet Town Hall	Static	6 pages/ 36 hyperlinks	Text		N, GB, DJ, / audio
St. Olaf College Servers	Static	10 pages/ 25 hyperlinks	Text		N, GB, DJ

The U.S. House of Representative site provided retrieval software features for searching the U.S. Code. The Cornell Law School site provided the best navigational feature. This site had a directory of various search tools, such as Yahoo, Lyco, Infoseek, and Webcrawler. The Internet Town Hall site provided a direct jump feature to corporate sites such as IBM and MCI Internet sites. It was the only site that included an audio sound device feature for one to listen to various audio tapes of different cultural music.

The graphical interfaces options of the HUD sites were far better than most sites. The scope of the content of the FedWorld and St. Olaf College home pages lead individuals to other sites that were relevant to either a broader or a specific topic.

Some Internet sites—Cornell Law School, LC Marvel, U.S. House of Representatives—provided direct search software capabilities. The FedWorld site, for example, provided an index of topics such as housing. The housing topic would allow one to directly link to the HUD home page and Veterans' home page. Thus, the one-stop shopping directory system is very beneficial to users. Since the clientele of the government varies from the user at home to foreign governments, various access methods must be developed to access federal information. Some sites, such as LC Marvel and LOCIS, were not available after government hours. Therefore, information retrieval was limited. GPO, St. Olaf College, and FedWorld provided the most access methods.

Assignment Question

1. Given the vast amount of information involved—both manual and automated—how can the federal government effectively disseminate the most relevant information to service its customers?